# Let's Celebrate!

# Let's Celebrate!

*Written by*
Caroline Parry

*Many happy celebrations!*

*Caroline Parry*
*11 May 1990*

**Kids Can Press Ltd.**
**Toronto**

Kids Can Press Ltd. gratefully acknowledges the assistance of the Canada Council, the Ontario Arts Council and Multiculturalism Canada in the production of this book.

**Canadian Cataloguing in Publication Data**

Parry, Caroline.
  Let's celebrate!

Includes index.
ISBN 0-921103-38-7 (bound) ISBN 0-921103-40-9 (pbk.)

1. Holidays – Canada – Juvenile literature
2. Fasts and feasts – Canada – Juvenile literature.
3. Creative activities and seat work. I. Title.

GT4813.A2P37 1987   j394.2'6971   C87-093179-2

Book design by Michael Solomon
Edited by Valerie Wyatt
Copy edited by Barbara Czarnecki
Typeset by Spencer Brennan
Printed in Canada

87 0 9 8 7 6 5 4 3 2

# Contents

Grateful acknowledgement is made to the following publishers, authors and other copyright holders for permission to reprint copyrighted material.

*Page 25:* "Frozen Words" from "Tall Tales and Other Yarns from Calgary, Alberta," *California Folklore Quarterly* (now *Western Folklore*) Vol. 4, No. 1, January 1945, pp.24-49. Used by permission of the University of California Press.

*Page 62:* "The Ballad of Blasphemous Bill" ©1909 Dodd Mead & Co. Used by permission, estate of Robert Service.

*Page 92:* "Ouch" from *Folklore of Canada* by Edith Fowke. Used by permission of the Canadian Publishers, McClelland and Stewart, Toronto.

*Page 92:* "Skipping rhyme" from *Sally Go Round the Sun* by Edith Fowke. Used by permission of the Canadian Publishers, McClelland and Stewart, Toronto.

*Page 140:* "Ball bouncing game" from *Sally Go Round the Sun* by Edith Fowke. Used by permission of the Canadian Publishers, McClelland and Stewart, Toronto.

*Page 149:* "Summer Doings" by William Cole. Used by permission of the author.

To all my women friends and relations
who give me such good support in every season,
especially the three Elizabeths
and two Evalyns in my family.

## Illustrations

**Paul Barker:** 13, 16, 17, 21, 27, 34, 59, 63, 68, 70, 71, 80, 84, 87, 89, 98 left, 102, 103 bottom, 104, 107, 108, 112 left, 118-119, 127, 133, 137, 141 top, 145, 150, 153 top, 157, 159, 164, 166, 174, 181, 185, 201, 206, 212, 216, 217 left, 223 top, 226 top, 230, 233, 236-237, 244, 249

**Chris Hayes:** 15 right, 26, 28, 37, 41 left, 43 right, 45 right, 46, right, 49, 54, 58, 67, 74, 75, 82, 86, 97, 100, 112 right, 122, 126, 129, 140, 155 top, 161, 162-163 centre, 169, 172, 176, 186-187, 192 bottom, 197, 198-199, 215, 222, 226 left, 243

**Linda Hendry:** 10 bottom, 22, 31, 39, 43 left, 51, 55, 65 top, 66, 72, 79, 83, 85, 90, 101 top, 110, 115, 116, 117, 134, 139, 146, 152, 160, 167, 177, 182, 184, 192 top, 196, 202, 207, 208, 213, 219, 221 right, 225, 238, 239, 240, 246, 248, 250

**Sharon Matthews:** 10 top, 18, 30, 33, 36, 38, 45 left, 47, 60, 61, 64, 65 right, 69, 81, 95, 98-99, 105, 109, 111, 114, 119 right, 120, 124, 125, 128, 131, 132, 138, 142, 151, 153 bottom, 156, 165, 178, 179, 183, 194, 209, 210, 217 right, 218, 221 top, 229, 234, 241

**Roslyn Schwartz:** 14, 15 left, 24, 25, 29, 32, 35, 41 right, 46 left, 48, 50, 52, 53, 57, 62, 73, 76, 77, 78, 92, 93, 101 right, 103 top, 113, 123, 136, 143, 148-149, 155 bottom, 158, 162 left, 163 right, 168, 170-171, 180, 188, 190-191, 193, 195, 204-205, 214, 223 bottom, 224, 231, 232

## Acknowledgements

I would like to thank the scores of people in dozens of organizations who took time to help me with my research. Without them, and their customs, this book could not have been created. There are far too many people and institutions to list here, but a few deserve extra appreciation for their extensive help and interest: Professor Stanley Fefferman and John Negru of the Buddhist Council of Canada; Dr. Mahmoud M. Ayoub, research associate of the Centre for Religious Studies, University of Toronto; Sitansu S. Chakravarti of the Bharat Sevashram Sangha Temple, Toronto; Alok Mukherjee, adviser, race relations, and Olivia Chow, trustee, both of the Toronto Board of Education; Valerie Mah; Iris Harvey, librarian at King Edward Public School, Toronto; Sussan Ekrami of the New Day Cultural Foundation, Toronto; Father John Iverinci of St. Andrew's Church, Rexdale; Alita Limberti of the Community Folk Art Council of Metropolitan Toronto; the Woodland Indian Cultural Educational Centre, Brantford, Ontario; the Multicultural History Society of Ontario; the Cross Cultural Communication Centre, Toronto; the Ontario Black History Society; the Canadian Museum of Civilization (formerly the National Museum of Man), Ottawa; Slava Sylvia Pastyr; Jim Nicoloff; Reena Singha; Joseph O'Connell; David Mandel; Andrea Haddad; Jacqueline Gelineau; and the librarians of the Language Centre at the Metropolitan Toronto Reference Library.

Finally, I am deeply grateful to my neighbours, Anne and Michael Anderson and their sons David and Craig, for their wonderful generosity and computer expertise; to my editor, Val Wyatt, for her unfailing enthusiasm and good sense; and to my husband, David Parry, for his great love and patience.

## Foreword

This is a book about Canada's special days and ways to celebrate them. *Let's Celebrate!* begins with an explanation of seasons, calendars and why people celebrate particular days. **Winter**, beginning in December and including Canada's official New Year on January 1, is the first season you will come to. **Fall**, the last, is followed by a section explaining the Muslim festivals, which have no fixed date. You needn't read from start to finish, though — skip through, sampling wherever you wish. There's no real beginning or end to the book (or to the year), and the last page takes you back to the first.

*Let's Celebrate!* is also about remembering and renewing our roots — about the customs people keep or change or create in Canada. Space does not permit the mention of every Canadian group, whether cultural, social or religious, nor of every celebration held here. If you notice something that should be changed or added, please write to me, in care of Kids Can Press. I have attempted to make this book both as fascinating and as factually accurate as possible. Any mistakes are my own, and I hope your enjoyment far outweighs them. May the joy of each season be yours!

# Let's Celebrate...

## Chinese birthdays

*The Chinese say that babies have their first birthday on the next New Year's Day after they are born. Even if a baby's real age is only a few weeks, it will be considered a year old at the New Year.*

*Chinese people once celebrated their birthdays only at the New Year. Today Chinese-Canadians celebrate both dates. Every 12 years, when your animal sign comes around again, there is an extra big birthday bash.*

What is your favourite day of the year? Chances are it's your birthday. And chances are you celebrate when that special day comes around!

For Chinese-Canadians, the *year* you were born is almost as important as the day. Each year has an animal sign. So you might be a tiger, a monkey or one of ten other animals, depending on your birth year. The Chinese believe your animal sign affects your character. For instance, if you are a monkey, they say you are likely to be curious and highly observant. Suppose you were curious about birthdays — there are lots of things to find out about them.

To begin with, what day of the week were you born? Some people say the day determines what kind of child you are. Find out what day you were born, then check this poem:

> Monday's child is fair of face,
> Tuesday's child is full of grace,
> Wednesday's child is full of woe,
> Thursday's child has far to go,
> Friday's child is loving and giving,
> Saturday's child works hard for a living,
> But the child that is born on the Sabbath day
> Is bonny and blithe and good and gay.

Some people believe the day of the month on which you were born also determines your future. They divide the year

into 12 periods, and they believe the astrological signs for each period affect a person's character. So rather than considering yourself a curious monkey or a talkative rooster as the Chinese do, you might say, "Because I'm a Taurus, I'm stubborn, like a bull."

Even if you don't believe any of these birthday predictions, you probably think of birthdays as a great time to celebrate. But don't stop celebrating when your birthday's over. In Canada there are more than 250 other special days to celebrate. Many of these are also birthdays, perhaps of a province or a famous person. Others are anniversaries of special events. Still other celebrations are directly related to the seasons. For instance, the Persian/Iranian New Year festival, called Now Ruz, is held on the first day of spring. This is when a "new year" of plants is beginning to grow and young animals are being born.

Many of the festivals and special days we celebrate are hundreds of years old. Some, like Now Ruz, are thousands of years old! Long ago survival was the most important part of people's lives. Getting enough food to eat was a constant problem. People tried to ensure their food supply by holding ceremonies or festivals. For example, they might hold a ceremony to shorten the winter storms and bring the spring. They believed that ceremonies and rituals, prayers or magic helped bring about changes.

Our earliest ancestors knew that the sun helped things grow somehow, so many early rituals were held to strengthen the sun. The sun's strongest and weakest periods — as well as the mid-points of its cycle — were key times for ceremonies. Fire usually symbolizes the sun. Can you think of celebrations today that include fire ceremonies? The candles on your birthday cake might be related!

Our ancestors also knew that, along with the life-giving rays of the sun, water helped things grow. That is why rain

## Sonday?

*Q. Why is there a Mother's Day, a Father's Day, but not a Son's Day?*

*A. But there is — there's a Sunday every week.*

## What's a holiday?

*The old English word for a special religious day was "hallowed" day, or "halliday." That sounded like holy day — it means the same thing — and eventually turned into holiday.*

## Name-days

*A name-day is a day named after a saint. For example, March 17 is St. Patrick's Day because St. Patrick died on that date hundreds of years ago. Some boys who are born on March 17 are named after St. Patrick. Of course others born on other days are also named Patrick. All Patricks have St. Patrick's Day as their name-day. They may celebrate both their birthday and their name-day. What luck — two celebrations instead of just one!*

prayers — either to make it fall, or in thanks for it — and other water rituals were a big part of early festivals. As you explore the different festivals in these pages, watch for ceremonies that have to do with water as well as fire. See if you can figure out which season they occur in most often.

The first religions grew out of seasonal festivals and the beliefs that surrounded them. Gradually new religions added new celebrations or changed existing ones. Nations and groups added still more. In Canada we're especially lucky. When the first Europeans came to Canada, they brought with them the special customs and holidays of their home countries. They also learned about various festivals of the native people and even created new ones. More recent immigrants to Canada have added their holidays. In many countries there's only one set of special days to celebrate because everyone comes from the same background. But here, there are many ethnic and religious groups, each with its own customs and celebrations. They add up to more than 250 ways to celebrate.

However, it may not be as easy to observe the old festivals here in Canada as it was in the home country. Often customs are modified or adapted, for a number of reasons. For one thing, the Canadian climate affects holidays. For example, a festival that's held outdoors in India may take place in the dead of the Canadian winter, so the celebration must be changed. For another, the Canadian work week interferes with some holidays. Often long holidays are moved to the closest weekend. And holidays change because people sometimes lose their sense of community and pride in their heritage when they leave their old homes.

Although some celebrations are lost, others have grown in new ways in the New World or have been proudly remembered and revived. Often new situations in Canada have led to new festivities. If you too want to adopt or revive or create a special day, use *Let's Celebrate!* as your guide.

## What's a zodiac?

The term ''zodiac cycle'' comes from the Greek words zodiakos kyklos, which means a circle of animals. In astronomy, the zodiac is the zone or belt of constellations in the sky along which the sun, moon and major planets move during the year. Ancient sky-gazers divided this great heavenly circle into 12 sections, each the same size and each with its own astrological sign, taken from the constellations.

## Chinese animal signs

Find the year you were born to see what animal governs your character. The Chinese New Year starts in late January or February. If you were born between January 1 and the Chinese New Year, you should look for your animal sign in the year before you were born.

# Calendars

A calendar is a way of keeping track of birthdays and other special days. It is also a way of organizing time. You can think of a calendar as a kind of clock for the year. Just like clocks, there are different kinds of calendars — not everyone uses the same one.

Long ago, people used the sun, moon or stars as calendars. Sun-watchers figured out that a year was the number of days it took for the sun to move — or so it seemed — from one position in the heavens back to the same place again. We now know that a year is the amount of time it takes the earth to make a complete circle around the sun. A year lasts a bit more than 365 days — in fact, about six hours more. A year based on this cycle of the sun is called a "solar" year, from the Latin word for sun, *sol*. Canada's official calendar is based on the solar year.

Moon-watchers saw that the moon also follows a predictable pattern: it waxes (grows bigger) and then wanes (grows smaller). The days in one complete cycle of waxing and waning almost make up a month. They also figured out that the cycle of the four seasons was about 12½ of these moon months. In fact, a year based on 12 moon months, called a "lunar" year (*luna* is Latin for moon), is about 12½ days shorter than the solar year.

Muslims, or members of the Islamic religion, use a strictly lunar calendar. Each year their holidays occur at a slightly different time. (For more information on these holidays that move with the moon, see the final section of this book.) The Iroquois used a lunar calendar too, as did other North American native people. The Iroquois often added a 13th month during winter to make the days add up properly. They also watched the stars to make three major divisions in their year, in mid-January, in late April and in August.

If you find all this confusing, you are not alone; the difference between the solar year and the lunar year has caused

## *Time-line*

*Instead of marking special dates on a calendar, try marking them on a time-line. To make a time-line, cut sheets of paper into narrow strips about 5 cm (2 inches) wide. Glue the strips end to end. Stop adding strips when it's long enough to go all the way around your bedroom walls. The middle of this strip is July 1. Divide each half into six equal sections, one for each month. Now that you've got the months, start marking your own special days on this time-line. Feeling ambitious? Why not make a time-line representing your whole life!*

# When in Rome...

The Romans invented the calendar (with a little help from the Greeks) around the 8th century B.C. Their calendar had 10 months (they ignored the 60 days in the middle of winter), and their year started with March. They named the first four months Martius, Aprilis, Maius and Junius after gods and goddesses. The other six months had numerical names: Quintilis meant the fifth month, Sextilis meant the sixth, September the seventh, October the eighth, November the ninth, and December the tenth. A later Roman ruler added January (named for Janus, the two-headed god) and February (the word refers to an ancient purification feast).

By the 1st century B.C. the mistakes in the Roman Calendar made it about three months ahead of the seasons. So, in 46 B.C., Julius Caesar corrected it. That year had 445 days. No wonder the Romans called it "the year of confusion"! Caesar was honoured by having the former fifth month named after him — July. The Romans named the sixth month August, after his nephew, Caesar Augustus. All the months in Caesar's new year had 30 or 31 days except for February, which had 29. It's said that Augustus was jealous because July was one day longer than August, so he took a day for his month from February, leaving the 28 days it has today!

## New moon superstitions

Some people say that you will be rich if you always turn over the silver change in your pockets when you first see a new moon. The first new moon in the year is especially lucky — you should bow or curtsy to it at least three times, or nine times if you are very serious, before you make a wish.

## The sun's four special days

*If you think of the year like a circular clock, the four seasons are like the four quarters of an hour. Each quarter begins with a special sun day. On the "spring equinox" (March 20 or 21) and "autumn equinox" (September 22 or 23), the day is divided equally into 12 hours of daylight and 12 hours of darkness. At the "winter solstice" (December 21 or 22) there are fewer than nine hours of daylight in southern Canada and more than 15 hours of night. At the "summer solstice" (June 20 or 21) that situation is reversed — there are more than 15 hours of daylight and fewer than nine of night. The farther north you go, the greater the split becomes. For example, in Tuktoyaktuk, the sun doesn't even rise for the three weeks before and after the winter solstice. It's dark the whole time!*

*The word solstice comes from the Latin words meaning "sun standing still," and equinox means "equal night."*

## How's the weather?

*Spring: flowery, showery, bowery.*
*Summer: hoppy, croppy, poppy.*
*Autumn: slippy, drippy, nippy.*
*Winter: freezy, breezy, sneezy.*

mix-ups about calendars for thousands of years! The calendars we use now have long histories, and people are still trying to make a world calendar that will improve them.

The standard (solar) calendar on our walls and desks today is the Gregorian Calendar. It is named for Pope Gregory XIII, who adjusted the calendar in the 16th century. He corrected the Julian Calendar, which had been in use throughout Europe since the time of Julius Caesar. This Julian Calendar, sometimes called the Old Calendar, had been behind for hundreds of years — like a watch that runs slow. Most of western Europe agreed to Pope Gregory's improvements to the Julian Calendar in the year 1582 and skipped ten days in their datebooks. The days in between were "lost." Many people were upset.

The British Isles did not change over until 1752, almost two hundred years later. By that time, they had to skip over eleven days rather than ten, to be correct. Because Canada was part of a group of British colonies, we also did not change our calendars until 1752. Romania did not change calendars until 1924, and some groups of people never corrected their calendars at all. These were mostly members of the Orthodox Eastern churches, which are Christian and similar to the Catholic church but do not acknowledge the Pope as their head. This is why some Greek or Russian Orthodox people celebrate church holidays such as Christmas after the usual date.

To make things even more confusing, there are "lunisolar" calendars — that is, calendars partly based on the moon and partly on the sun. In lunisolar calendars, the months are determined by the moon and the years by the sun. These calendars need frequent adjustments — not only are there leap year days, but whole leap months! The Jewish calendar is lunisolar. Jewish special days are not fixed in the way that Christmas is, for example (it always falls on December 25), but they do come in the same season every year. That's why the exact dates of Chanukah change, yet it always comes in December, so we think of it as a winter festival.

The Hindu calendar is different in still another way: it is based on a solar year, which always begins at Baisakhi, April 13. The Hindu year is divided into 12 months, which also begin on fixed dates. But the actual dates of the religious holidays depend on the moon's cycle, and so they change from year to year. Perhaps this should be called a "solilunar" calendar!

## The medicine wheel

*Native people don't use a linear calendar (one that starts in January and ends in December) for their own customs and ceremonies. They see the passage of time as circular. Here's a simplified sacred medicine wheel that shows not only the cycle of the seasons but also the cycle of life. This medicine wheel is lined up with the four directions — north, east, south and west — and each of these directions also has a colour and an animal. Can you think of other colours or animals that would be appropriate?*

*Circles of one sort or another play an important part in native religious celebrations. They use a circular drum to accompany ritual songs and dances. They also sit and dance in circles.*

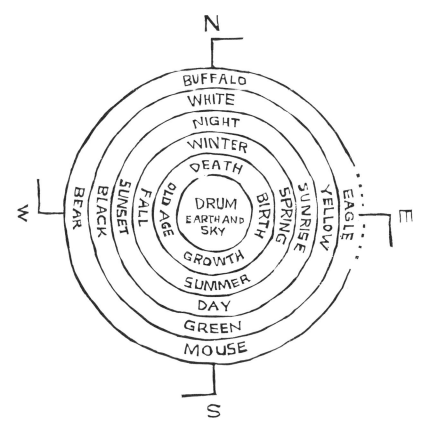

## Two-season calendars

The Celts were ancient Europeans who divided their year into two seasons instead of our four. One Celtic season was summer — the sun's strength; the other was winter — its weakness. In summer, which began on May 1, the Celts kept their flocks and herds of animals out in the pastures; in winter, which began on October 31, they kept their animals under shelter.

Native peoples such as the Kwakiutl on the northwest coast of North America have traditionally had two main seasons too. They think of the winter as the time when supernatural powers have the most influence, and that is when they hold most of their religious ceremonies. The Mistassini Cree, in central Quebec, still organize their year around two major seasons — the period of frozen lakes and rivers (pipun) and the period of open water (niipin). In pipun they travel by snowshoe and toboggan, rather than canoe, and live by hunting and trapping. In niipin they live in larger, changeable groups in settlements and do more work for wages and buy more store food.

## "Come day, go day God send Sunday"

When does your family try to relax and do no work? Sunday is a holiday for many people. However, Jewish families and some Christians keep Saturday rather than Sunday as their day of rest. The idea of a Sabbath (or Shabbat in Hebrew) as the day of rest following six days of work comes to us from the ancient Hebrews. Today in Jewish homes the Shabbat is celebrated with a ceremony of welcoming every Friday evening. A ritual to say farewell to the Shabbat is held 24 hours later, one hour after sundown. In its way, Shabbat is a weekly festival, celebrating the Creator's rest from his labours. Early Christians chose the first, rather than last, day of the week for the Sabbath because Jesus came back to life on Sunday. Some Christians simply call Sunday "First Day" because they do not like to honour the sun on that day.

Then there are weekly calendars — lots of people use weekly calendars nowadays to plan their work schedules. The word "week" comes from words that mean sequence and change, and probably our seven-day week is related to the changes of the moon: new moon, half moon, full moon, old half moon and back to a dark sky. Each phase lasts just over one week. The seven-day week we use today in Canada and most of the world is also related to the ancient Hebrew or Jewish calendar. The Jews adopted the seven-day idea from Babylon, an older Middle Eastern culture where the number seven was very important and magical. For the Babylonians, the number seven signified the seven most prominent heavenly bodies: the sun, the moon and the five planets that seem to be the brightest stars in the night sky and that are visible to the naked eye. For many people, seven is a magical number — watch for it as you read further in this book.

Weekly, yearly, solar, lunar, lunisolar, "solilunar," Gregorian, Julian — in Canada we have people who use all these different calendars. That makes a calendar of Canada's special days awfully complicated — but also very full and interesting.

## How do you measure time?

*The word "month" comes from an Indo-European root meaning "to measure." The native people in North America measured time in terms of moon months, which are shorter than today's calendar months. They spoke of "many moons" when they referred to the past. Can you invent a different way of marking time periods — something other than weeks, months or years? Here are a few others:*

- *Buddhists in some parts of the world use a nine-day week.*
- *Some African people count periods of time from one market day to another.*
- *Baha'is have 19-day months. Each of their 19 months begins with a special day for their religious observances, called the 19-Day Feast.*
- *In England, the term "fortnight," for a 14-night period, is as common as "week."*

# WINTER

In Canada, winter weather begins long before the official first day of winter on December 21 or 22 and may last well beyond the official first day of spring. The temperatures drop and drop, the wind blows and blows, and ice and snow are part of the lives of most Canadians for many months. Birds, animals and humans all keep to their shelters.

"Winter" is an old English word that comes from even older words for "water" and "wet." In Europe winter is wet and cold. Here, water freezes! The Inuit people in the North have the coldest and longest winter weather conditions in Canada. In their language there are almost a hundred words to describe different kinds of ice and *more* than a hundred terms for various types of snow and snowstorms!

Winter is not only a cold time; it is dark too. Evening comes early after school, and in the morning many of us get up before the sun does. No wonder some native people called early winter the Long Night Moon.

Indoors it feels good to be snug and warm, to see a fire flickering or candles glowing. Think how much darker and colder winter must have seemed before there were electric lights and central heating.

Long ago, people could not be so sure of light and warmth in the winter months. Perhaps that is why people in many parts of the world have held festivals of fire or light at the beginning of winter, just at the time when the sun is at its weakest. People probably hoped that by lighting fires for the dying sun they could actually help to strengthen it.

Many ceremonies were held around December 21 or 22 — the time of the winter solstice. For example, thousands of years ago the Persians worshipped a sun god named Mithras. The Romans "adopted" him about 75 B.C. They celebrated the Birthday of the Unconquered Sun in honour of Mithras at the solstice. Early Christians realized that if they called Jesus Christ "the light of the world" and put his birthday at the same time as this older, more popular festival, it would help attract followers to their new religion. Today Christmas is not the only festival of light observed in Canada. Other religions and groups also use rituals of light at this time of year. Chanukah, the Jewish festival in December, and Divali, the Hindu festival in late autumn, are two examples.

Christmas is also a time of feasting, with many special foods for the season. Long ago many early winter celebrations took place after the harvest and the slaughter of animals that could not be fed over the winter. Therefore early winter was a time of abundance — a good time to share foods in the community. As you learn more about different winter holidays, notice how many of them include sharing food with family, friends and neighbours.

House-visiting is another traditional part of winter celebrations. Sometimes visitors played pranks and made fun of one another, often in costume. Perhaps these customs sprang up because winter can be a hard, grim time, and people need a chance to be wild or silly. In return for their "performances," visitors were "paid" with drinks or even small gifts.

Today visitors often sing carols or good luck songs. In some cultures they may also dance or perform a play. Whatever your visitors sing or do, they will also wish you good fortune and health in the months to come. You may need it — those months will be cold!

## Where does the snow come from?

People everywhere in the world have stories and legends to explain the weather. These were made up long before scientists knew what was really happening. People also have special sayings to "make" weather happen, change or stop.

Here's a chant to say when the snow begins to fall and you want it to keep falling:

Snow, snow, faster!
Ally, ally-blaster!
The old woman's plucking her geese,
Selling the feathers a penny apiece.

Have you ever looked closely at goose feathers or down? They look like snowflakes, so it's not suprising someone thought of feathers when it snowed.

You can also say this at the first snowfall:

Snow, snow, faster
The cow's in the pasture.

And when you are tired of it falling, try:

Snow, snow, give over,
The cow's in clover!

### What is it?

Lives in winter,
Dies in summer,
And grows with its roots upwards?

*An icicle*

### Knock-knock!

Who's there?
Snow.
Snow who?
Snow idea, have you?

### Whoops!

There once was a charming young
    miss
Who considered ice-skating bliss;
But one day, alack
Her skates they were slack
*And she ended up something like this.*

### Frozen words

This is a tall tale from Alberta told by
Charles K. Underwood.
*The foreman came out to give orders
on the ranch — it was at the Bar U.
It was 75° below zero. It was so cold,*
*d'you see, that the words froze in his
mouth — and so he broke them off
and handed them around so the men
could get their orders for the day.*

*An old Acadian belief in eastern
Canada is that Advent is a good time
to predict the weather. A cold Advent,
they say, means a mild winter. But if
the weather is still mild during
Advent, watch out! We'll have a
hard, long winter.*

*Stir-up
Sunday*

*The last Sunday before Advent is
called Stir-up Sunday by many
people of British descent. This is the
traditional day to stir up the
Christmas plum pudding and cook it.
Some families stir a coin or a ring
into the pudding mixture. Whoever
finds this surprise is supposed to have
good fortune or be the next to marry.
The name Stir-up Sunday comes from
a Bible reading for that day in the
old Anglican prayer book that begins,
"Stir up, we beseech thee O Lord, the
hearts of thy faithful people."
Perhaps these words reminded
everyone of how soon those puddings
would be needed, and they rushed
home to stir them up after church!*

# Advent

*Begins the fourth Sunday before Christmas*

Advent means "arrival," and it is the name Christians give to
the four weeks leading up to Christmas. In homes and
churches, people set out special candleholders or Advent
wreaths. These hold four candles. One candle is lit the fourth
Sunday before Christmas, two the next Sunday and so on until all of the candles are lit. Some families sing Advent carols
and eat Advent treats while the candles burn. Many churches
hold special candlelit Advent carol processions.

The German custom of giving children Advent calendars
helps the days pass until Christmas. The calendars have 24
little doors. One is opened each day from December 1 until
Christmas Eve. In Canada, Advent calendars with a chocolate
behind each door are especially popular, but sometimes it's
hard to resist opening all those doors at once!

# Chanukah

*Some time in December*

The Jewish festival Chanukah, which comes around the time
of the winter solstice, is often called the Festival of Lights
because it is celebrated by lighting special candles each day at
sundown. Chanukah also involves attending family or community parties, playing special games and eating holiday
foods.

Chanukah commemorates a victory that took place more
than 2000 years ago. In 164 B.C. a band of Hebrews, led by
Judah Maccabee, recaptured their temple in Jerusalem from
the ruling Syrians. They set to work to clean and purify the
temple and to re-light the holy temple lamp, called a
*menorah*. The word Chanukah means "dedication," and in
re-lighting the holy oil lamp, the Maccabees were re-dedi-

cating the temple to God. There is a story that they found only one jar of sacred oil left, barely enough for one day, but it burned for eight days, until more was prepared. This became the miracle of Chanukah.

Today a special candleholder called a *chanukkiyah* is used in Chanukah celebrations. It has places for eight candles, and a ninth place, a little above all the others, is kept for the *shammus* (worker) candle. Each day the *shammus* is lit before sundown and then used to light the correct number of candles for the day of the festival: three candles on the third night, four on the fourth and so on. During the time the candles burn, no one is supposed to do any work of any kind.

Chanukah candles are brightly coloured like fat birthday cake candles, and they burn for about half an hour. As they burn, many Jewish children play betting games with coins they have been given as presents on the first night of the holiday. (Sometimes this money, known as Chanukah *gelt*, is chocolate, wrapped in gold foil and packaged in little net bags.) Children bet on a special top called a *dreydel*. The four sides of the *dreydel* have Hebrew letters on them, which are the initials of the Hebrew words meaning "a great miracle happened there" and refer to the story of the miraculous oil in the temple lamp. If the *dreydel* lands on *nun* in your turn, you get "nothing"; *gimmel* means you get "all"; *hay* — "half"; and *shin* — spin again.

In addition to gifts of money at Chanukah, some Jewish children receive a present for each of the eight nights. This is not a traditional custom, but one that has begun in recent years. Perhaps it has to do with TV commercials and other advertisements for Christmas presents at this season.

The special Jewish foods for this festival are things like potato pancakes, called *latkes*, which are fried in oil. Latkes are often served with applesauce and sour cream at Canadian Chanukah parties.

*A dreydel*

## Mitten Tree Day

*The people of Lord's Cove Church of Christ in Deer Island, in southwestern New Brunswick, are famous for making hundreds of pairs of mittens to give away to those in need on the first Sunday in December. Over the years this has come to be called Mitten Tree Day, because all the bright pairs of mittens are hung on a tree in the church as they are donated.*

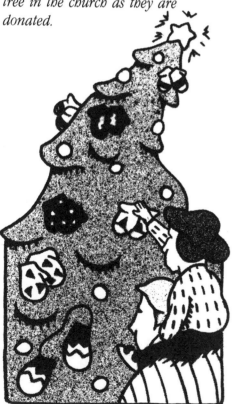

# St. Nicholas Day

*December 6*

St. Nicholas was a very generous bishop in fourth-century Turkey. He is now considered to be the patron saint, or protector, of children. His day is celebrated in Canada by the Dutch and German communities and also by many Eastern European families.

The Dutch say that Sint Nikolaas (or Sinterklaas) and his dark-skinned clowning helper Zwarte Piet (or Black Pete) travel by horse. Their tradition is that children must put out a pair of shoes, filled with hay and carrots for the horse, on the eve of St. Nicholas Day. If the children have been good, they find gifts and sweets in the morning. Otherwise, Black Peter may leave a piece of coal or a birch switch to give them a beating!

Dutch children also get other "surprises," wrapped in unusual ways. For instance, a present might come in a hollowed out cabbage and include a funny or teasing poem. The poems are homemade and connect the present and container to the person. So the cabbage present might go to a child who hates cabbages, and the poem might remind him or her to eat more vegetables! These surprises are either brought by St. Nicholas or left on the doorstep. A loud knock at the door after dark on St. Nicholas Eve lets children know the presents have arrived. Every family member helps to make these surprises, but they are always given "from St. Nicholas."

In Nova Scotia children in German families are given figures of Sankt Nikolaus made from bread dough. German children put out either a stocking *or* a shoe for their gifts — nuts, apples and chocolates are favourites.

## Christmas stockings

The stockings were hung by the
   chimney with care,
In hopes that St. Nicholas soon would
   be there....

When Clement C. Moore wrote the
now-famous Christmas poem "The
Night Before Christmas" for his
children in 1822, the family in the
poem hung up stockings, instead of
putting out their shoes as Dutch children do. This is probably because of
another legend about St. Nicholas. It
is said that he knew of three poor
girls who could not marry without
some dowry money. Secretly, Nicholas
threw three bags of gold down their
chimney for them. The story says that
the money happened to fall into their
stockings, hung by the chimney to
dry!

   Instead of hanging up a stocking
at Christmas, some English-Canadian
children leave an empty pillowcase
tied to the ends of their beds. Imagine
all the room for goodies! Cree
children in the James Bay area are
even luckier. On Christmas Eve, they
visit relatives' homes and, at each
house, are given a cloth bag (the kind
used to store sugar and tea) to hang
up with their name on. Then on
Christmas Day they go visiting again
to collect their bags full of presents
— usually clothes, toys and candies.

   Have you ever been threatened
with getting no stocking presents, or
bad ones like a potato or a piece of
coal, if you don't behave well before
Christmas? That's the old Québécois
custom. You might even be given soap
if you don't like to wash!

## St. Lucia sprouts

*Some Croatian families in Canada believe that if wheat seeds planted on St. Lucia Day sprout by Christmas, it means they will have good luck in the next year's harvest. You could try to foretell your luck by using wheat kernels you buy in a health food store. Place the seeds between two layers of damp paper towels. Make sure you keep the towels moist. Then watch for them to sprout. Good luck!*

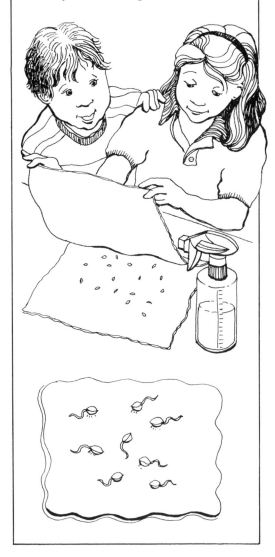

# St. Lucia Day

*December 13*

Imagine wearing a crown of flickering candles! That's what the oldest daughter in many Scandinavian families does on St. Lucia Day. St. Lucia Day is a festival of light that marks the beginning of the Christmas season for people who come from the Scandinavian countries of Sweden, Norway and Denmark. They say St. Lucia comes to make the darkness disappear. Her name means "light," and her day used to fall on the solstice. Perhaps that explains this old rhyme: "Lucia-light, Lucia-light, shortest day and longest night."

On December 13, the girl who plays the part of St. Lucia in a Scandinavian family wears a white dress with a red sash and a crown of candles. She and her sisters wake the family at dawn, serve them a breakfast of sun-coloured saffron buns and sing the old song "Santa Lucia." This is an Italian song, because the original Lucia was from Sicily, which is a part of Italy. She was supposed to have been killed in 304 A.D. because of her faith. Legend has it that she sailed from Italy to Sweden on the shortest day of the year.

In Nova Scotia, the Scandinavian Society pays tribute to St. Lucia as a part of their annual Julbord feast. This is a big buffet dinner, like a smorgasbord, served for the Yuletide season. Swedish meatballs and a huge Christmas ham are favourite dishes.

In Ontario, the Scandinavian community chooses a Queen of Light. She gives a speech from the steps of the Legislative Buildings in Toronto. All across the Prairie provinces, where the majority of Swedes in Canada live, Swedish Vasa Lodges organize similar St. Lucia pageants.

Another Swedish custom is for boys to carry star-shaped lanterns on long poles and go carolling from door to door. These "Star Boys" used to go out after St. Lucia Day. In

Q. *Which burns longer, a blue candle or a red one?*

A. *Neither — candles burn shorter.*

Q. *How many times can you light a new candle?*

A. *Only once — after that it isn't new.*

Q. *What's the best place to light a candle?*

A. *On the wick.*

Q. *What's long and thin and has teeth?*

A. *A candle — I made up the part about the teeth.*

Toronto you can see them at Harbourfront at the Swedish Christmas Fair on the first weekend in December. A Lucia reigns over the fair with a court of Lucia Maidens and Star Boys. They sing Swedish carols that they have practised for weeks. There are also Swedish folk dancers, demonstrations of Swedish crafts, Christmas items and food for sale.

St. Lucia is, naturally enough, the patron saint of the Caribbean island of the same name. Canadians from St. Lucia gather every year in Toronto to have a "Feast for St. Lucy" — usually a dinner-dance with entertainment.

## Feast of Sedna

*Long ago, before the coming of Christian missionaries, the Inuit observed a midwinter ceremony about the time of the winter solstice. The ceremony was called the Feast of Sedna, after Sedna, the evil mistress of the underworld. She was defeated in a special ritual held each year at this time. People also played a kind of tug-of-war in which "ptarmigans" (people born in winter) pulled against "ducks" (people born in the summer). If the ducks won, it was said that there would be fewer storms throughout the winter.*

## St. Thomas Day

*On the Catholic and Anglican church calendars, the day of the solstice was named St. Thomas Day until quite recently. An old English rhyme goes:*

*St. Thomas Grey, St. Thomas Grey, The longest night and the shortest day.*

*At one time this was the day for widows and poor women to go out "a-Thomassing" — collecting money or gifts of food and clothes from their neighbours to help them through the hard winter to come. These days the whole holiday season is a time to give.*

# Mexican Posadas

*December 16 - 24*

The traditional Mexican way to prepare for Christmas is to hold processions called Posadas, which represent a pilgrimage, on the nine nights before Jesus' birthday. People dress as Mary and Joseph or carry little figures of the holy couple and go from house to house seeking shelter. Just as it was so long ago in Bethlehem, they are told over and over that there is no room. Each night, however, a home has been chosen as the place for a party, and when Joseph and Mary ask at that door, they are welcomed in. Then the party begins, with guitar music, dancing and good food. The party ends each evening with a piñata for all the children. The final Posada is on Christmas Eve, or Noche Buena (the Good Night), when the pilgrimage ends up at church for midnight mass. In Vancouver the Mexican community organizes Posadas around the homes of its members.

# The Winter Solstice

*December 21*

Winter officially begins on the shortest day of the year. This is December 21 (or December 22 in some years), the date of the solstice. Solstice means "the sun stands still." The winter solstice is the day when the midday sun is at its lowest point above the horizon in its journey across the sky. Wherever you live in Canada, this day will have fewer hours and minutes of daylight than any other. If you live far enough north, in fact, you'll have none at all, and it may have been dark for some days already!

Today the winter solstice goes by almost unnoticed in Canada, except in a few traditional Chinese families. They

## Make a piñata

When Spanish-speaking communities hold a special event for children, there's almost always a piñata-bashing. Piñatas are large hollow containers, often shaped like animals, filled with small treats — candies, toys, coins and so forth. At a piñata party, the piñata is hung high above everyone's heads. Then one by one the guests are blindfolded and each tries to bash the hanging piñata with a long stick. When it finally breaks, the treats shower down on the players and everyone scrambles to gather a share of them.

To make a piñata, start at least one week before your party, to give the papier-mâché time to dry. You'll need:

a round balloon
newspaper
paste made from equal parts
    of flour and water
glue
poster paint and other decor-
    ations (streamers, cotton
    batting, netting, etc.)
string
lots of wrapped candies, nuts, small
    toys, coins and other goodies

1. Blow up the balloon and put it on a work area covered with newspapers.
2. Tear other newspapers into strips about 5 cm (2 inches) wide. Dip each strip into the flour-and-water paste, then wipe off excess paste and smooth the strip around the balloon. Continue this process until the whole surface has been covered twice.
3. Allow the papier-mâché to dry, then repeat the whole process two more times. This will give you a strong piñata that won't crack too easily.
4. Burst the balloon and remove it. Cut a round hole about 13 cm (5 inches) across in the top of the piñata. Fasten string to opposite sides of this hole to make a handle.
5. Paint and decorate as you wish, then fill with goodies.

## Chinese ancestor worship and religion

*Although many Chinese-Canadian people today are Christians, their older religious heritage is a complex mixture of three religions: Buddhism, Confucianism and Taoism. These were built on the even more ancient foundations of nature worship and ancestor worship.*

*For centuries, farming was very important in China. Because their survival depended on the weather, people were very aware of the changing seasons. People and nature were thought to be so strongly connected that bad behaviour could upset heaven and cause earthly events to go wrong.*

*The Chinese also believe that each person is a link in an endless, all-important chain of family. Traditionally, Chinese families include not only the living, but the honoured dead too. Family life begins with respect for parents and ancestors, for members of the older generation and older brothers and sisters. This is the basis for each child's relationship to the rest of the world.*

may still observe the old Chinese Festival of the Winter Solstice with prayers and offerings to their ancestors. However, some people from other backgrounds are trying to revive old winter solstice celebrations or create new ones. In Victoria, B.C., for example, a local artist holds a private "bring back the light" party on December 21, which has become a community tradition. As you read about different winter customs, think of activities *you* could do at a winter solstice party. To get you thinking, here's what they do in Victoria:

- the party is an afternoon-to-night open house;
- it starts with decorating an evergreen Christmas tree and continues with a potluck supper;
- after supper there are Balkan folk dances;
- at 9 p.m., everyone is given a candle and the lights are turned out. The hostess shouts, "The days are getting longer!" and everyone cheers;
- the candles on the Christmas tree are lit, then a flame is passed around until everyone's candle is burning softly;
- people sing carols together.

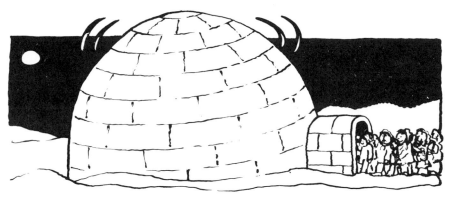

# Christmas Eve

*December 24*

In many families, Christmas Eve is celebrated with big dinners, visiting and carol-singing, often followed by midnight church services. Norwegians say that the "Christmas peace" descends at 4 o'clock in the afternoon, and they all try to be at home by that time.

In Polish-Canadian families, Christmas Eve celebrations start when the first evening star is sighted — it symbolizes the Star of Bethlehem. The Polish Wigilia celebration is the most solemn event in the year, marked by a special 12-course, meatless meal. The table is spread with the finest cloth (a few wisps of hay are put underneath to represent the manger where Jesus was born) and set with the best china and silver. An extra place is always set for any lonely stranger who might happen by (he might be Jesus himself!) and in memory of relatives who died during the last year.

Italian-Canadians often gather in large family groups on Christmas Eve. After a fast that began 24 hours earlier, they too eat a meatless meal. Italians from the Abruzzi region serve three sets of three special dishes: three kinds of beans, three kinds of pasta with meatless sauce and three kinds of fish. Southern Italians eat plenty of fish: fish soup, grilled fish, salt cod, octopus, eel, squid and shrimp. Children sometimes leave a special thank-you letter under their parents' plates on Christmas Eve. Or they may make a short speech of their love and appreciation for their parents, recite a poem or sing a song after the meal.

At home and both inside and outside Italian churches there are often splendid scenes of the stable in Bethlehem, called the *presepio*. Some even have life-sized figures of Mary and Joseph and the animals. Apparently Nativity scenes such as these were begun by St. Francis of Assisi, who used live

## Hungarian Bethlehem players

*Some Hungarian groups perform Nativity plays, called* betlehemezes, *on or before Christmas Eve. Long ago in Hungary, a group of actors would go from house to house, carrying a model of the stable where Jesus was born, called "the Bethlehem." This portable crèche at one time had puppets inside it, as well as candles. A messenger went to each house to ask if the Bethlehem players might enter. If so, the Bethlehem was set down and the story of Jesus' birth was acted out in front of it. When the drama finished, the actors blessed the household that had welcomed them and were given some money or small gifts in return. In Canada,* betlehemezes *take place in Hungarian-Canadian schools, scout troops or folk-dance groups.*

## Christmas logs

*When homes were heated by open fires, many areas of Europe had customs to do with burning a special Yule log during the Christmas season. These fires were probably a reminder of solstice fires lit to encourage the sun to shine more.*

*In the 19th century, the Québécois custom was to burn a special birch Christmas log on the hearth after returning from midnight mass. Later, when fireplaces were no longer the sole source of heat, people still kept a symbolic log on the table for this special night. At first it was probably a real piece of wood. Nowadays it is a chocolate cake, shaped like a log and covered with white icing to look like snow. This* Bûche de Noël *is delicious — but it doesn't burn very well!*

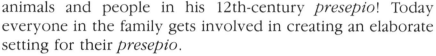

animals and people in his 12th-century *presepio*! Today everyone in the family gets involved in creating an elaborate setting for their *presepio*.

German-Canadians call the night before Christmas Heilig Abend, which means holy evening. Many believe that the Christ child himself brings gifts for everyone, and they wait for him after a family supper that features such traditional foods as roast goose, dumplings and red cabbage. One child in each family may be the Christ child's helper and hand out the presents. Once the presents are opened, many families gather around a candlelit tree to sing carols and then go to church together. Some Germans still keep the custom of blessing every room of the house (and barn, if there is one) with holy water and a small branch from the Christmas tree.

In Nova Scotia people of German descent have revived the old custom of "belsnicking" on Christmas Eve. Belsnickers are groups of rather rowdy carollers who wear rough disguises (a fisherman's scallop bag over the head, a silly hat and old clothes are typical). The idea is to sing and dance until your neighbours guess who you are, and then off comes your headgear and out come the drinks to share. The belsnickers often carry rope "tails" and threaten to thrash any children who are naughty!

As midnight approaches on Christmas Eve, many people make their way to church to celebrate midnight mass and rejoice in the story of the birth of Jesus. In many churches, bells are rung to announce services. Most of these bells are actually tape-recordings. But at Holy Rosary Cathedral in Vancouver and in a few other communities across Canada, real bells are rung by specially trained volunteer bell-ringers.

All over Quebec, and wherever French-Canadians have settled, families reunite for Christmas. For many families, the most important part of this is midnight mass, or the *minuitte*, when the priest and the children from the choir walk around

the church carrying a statue of the baby Jesus. Most families return from midnight church for the *réveillon*. These are huge feasts for families and friends, followed by singing and dancing. The children get to open their presents after mass and can stay up until dawn, if they can stay awake. *Tourtière* is the traditional Québécois meat pie to eat on this night, either hot or cold.

A favourite Polish dish to eat after midnight mass is hunter's stew, made of cabbage, sauerkraut, onions, mushrooms, kielbasa sausage, beef ribs and other meat. The stew keeps well and is added to throughout the holidays.

The Portuguese call their midnight mass the Missa do Galo, which means a mass "for the rooster." It probably got this name because people used to stay up so late on Christmas Eve they would hear the rooster crow in the morning. Nowadays in Canada, the mass still has the same name but is held as early as 9 p.m., so that families are not too tired by the end of the long service.

## Christmas by radio

*CBC Radio has its own special Christmas Eve observance on "As It Happens" every year. Soldiers at Canadian Armed Forces bases around the world are put in touch with their families and friends at home — over the radio! The program finishes with a "round robin" Christmas carol — each base sings one verse.*

## Carols

*The earliest carols were sung to fast, cheery tunes, for the word comes from the French* carole, *which means a song that people danced to. The tune of "Good King Wenceslas" (if not sung too solemnly) is a good example. Some of our present-day carols were simple house-visiting songs ("We Wish You a Merry Christmas"); others came from pre-Christian customs ("Here we come a-wassailing"). Can you find out the history of some more recently composed carols, such as "Silent Night" or "O Little Town of Bethlehem"?*

# The Huron Carol

Often known as the Canadian Carol, "The Huron Carol" was composed by Father Jean de Brébeuf about 1641 to tell the familiar Christmas story in a way that the Huron Indians could understand. The words were in the Huron language, and the tune was that of an earlier French carol. Father Brébeuf was the most famous of the Jesuit priests who worked as missionaries among the Huron people at Fort Ste. Marie, near what is now Midland, Ontario. In 1648 an Iroquois war party killed or drove out the Hurons, and Father Brébeuf was burned at the stake. Some of the Hurons escaped to the Quebec City area, where a hundred years later another Jesuit priest heard the carol and wrote it down. It was translated into French under the title "Jésus est né," and in 1926 Canadian poet J.E. Middleton wrote the English words that are widely known today.

1. 'Twas in the moon of winter time
   When all the birds had fled
   That mighty Gitchi Manitou
   Sent angel choirs instead
   Before their light the stars grew
     dim
   And wandering hunters heard
     the hymn:
   "Jesus your King is born
   Jesus is born: In excelsis gloria!"

2. Within a lodge of broken bark
   The tender babe was found,
   A ragged robe of rabbit skin
   Enwrapped his beauty 'round;
   And as the hunter braves drew
     nigh
   The angel song rang loud and
     high:
   "Jesus your King is born,
   Jesus is born: In excelsis gloria!"

3. The earliest moon of winter time
   Is not so round and fair
   As was the ring of glory on
   The helpless infant there.
   The chiefs from far before him
     knelt
   With gifts of fox and beaver pelt.
   "Jesus your King is born,
   Jesus is born: In excelsis gloria!"

4. O children of the forest free,
   O sons of Manitou,
   The holy child of earth and heaven
   Is born today for you.
   Come kneel before the radiant boy
   Who brings you beauty, peace, and
     joy.
   "Jesus your King is born,
   Jesus is born: In excelsis gloria!"

## Tracking down Santa

Santa wasn't always fat and didn't always wear red. At Doon Pioneer Village in Waterloo County, Ontario, there are photographs of an old, thin German-style Green Santa, dressed in a fur-trimmed green coat. There are also several carved figures of a *Weihnachtsmann,* or Christmas Man, wearing brown and blue robes, with white or brown fur trim. These Christmas Men carry evergreen trees and represent the old idea of the spirit of the woods or of midwinter.

Did you know that Santa isn't always called Santa? Bulgarian children may call him Grandpa Koleda, and the Danes call him Julemanden. Both these names refer to the time of year: Koleda is related to the Calends, or beginning of January; Jule indicates the Yule or Christmas season. In some places, Santa isn't even a man — the Russian gift-bringer is Grandmother Babushka, and the Italians have Befana.

## Christmas greetings — in any language

*Can you match up the greetings below with the correct language? (Answers below.)*

1. Portuguese
2. German
3. Danish
4. Dutch
5. French
6. Swedish
7. Italian
8. Spanish


a. Fröhliche Weihnachten
b. Hartelijke Kerstgroeten
c. God Jul
d. Feliz Natal, Boas Festas
e. Buon Natale
f. Joyeux Noël
g. Feliz Navidad
h. Glaedelig Jul

Answers: 1d, 2a, 3h, 4b, 5f, 6c, 7e, 8g

## Door decor

*St. Andrews, New Brunswick, has an annual door-decorating contest at Christmas. Some doors feature traditional Christmas materials such as evergreen boughs and holly; others look like enormous gift boxes. This Christmas try decorating the door of your home or classroom. Or, to get into the spirit of giving, decorate a neighbour's door!*

# Christmas Day

*December 25*

Christmas is the most widely observed Christian festival of the year. It celebrates Jesus Christ's birth almost 2000 years ago. No one knows the real historical date of the birth of Jesus, but in 336 A.D. the church declared that his birthday mass (or Christ's Mass, which was gradually shortened to our modern word "Christmas") would be celebrated thereafter on December 25. At that time, astronomers thought December 25 was the shortest day of the year. Over the centuries since then, the holiday has absorbed many customs that came from earlier solstice celebrations. Customs having to do with lighting special fires and candles and all the evergreen decorations are good examples.

### Christmas lights

If you lived in Tuktoyaktuk, 320 km (200 miles) inside the Arctic Circle, you'd be glad to see the Christmas lights turn on! In Tuk, as the locals call it, the sun doesn't shine for the three weeks before and after the winter solstice. Christmas lights all across Canada brighten the dark Christmas season:

- In Esquimalt, B.C., Canadian navy ships are strung with coloured lights, and a Christmas tree is attached to the top of every mast.
- Vancouverite Ed Stevens makes the front of his house into an enormous Christmas wonderland of sparkling lights and props. Donations from visiting sightseers are passed on to his favourite cause, the burns unit at Vancouver General Hospital.
- In Calgary, strings of orange and amber lights turn a 122-m (400-foot) radio tower into the world's tallest Christmas tree.

- Cape Bretoners flock to visit Sydney's Wentworth Park to see an illuminated Nativity scene that is more than 25 years old.
- In the east end of Saskatoon, two neighbourhoods have gone Christmas-light crazy. On McDermid and nearby Bell Crescent, all the homeowners decorate with a common theme, such as 2-m (6-foot) candy canes. When one of these houses is sold, the street decorations go with the house, not with the family that moves out!

Lights are used indoors too. In Ukrainian homes, a candle is set on the table on Christmas Eve to symbolize the star of Bethlehem. It is placed in the centre of three special loaves of rich bread, which symbolize the Holy Trinity (God the Father, the Son and the Holy Ghost).

Many families use lights on their Christmas trees. Some Swiss- and German-Canadians even use real candles, lighting them carefully for a short while each evening and keeping the fire extinguisher handy.

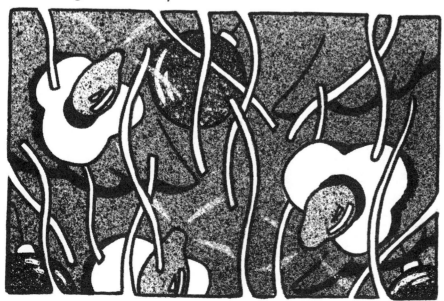

## Under the mistletoe

Many people of British descent hang a bunch of mistletoe over a doorway or under a hall lamp for the Christmas season. If you are caught under it, anyone may claim a kiss. If you don't like kisses, pinch off a berry for each kiss taken — eventually you'll be safe!

Mistletoe has been considered special for centuries. Thousands of years ago, the Celtic priests (called Druids) had a sacred ritual of cutting mistletoe on the shortest day of the year. Mistletoe was perhaps the most magical-seeming of all the evergreens, because it is a parasite, a plant that grows on another plant called a "host." Its usual host plant is an oak tree, which looks dead in winter. So it seems as if the host tree dies and the mistletoe comes to life.

At one time, mistletoe was thought to protect homes from fire or lightning and to cure sores and toothaches. The French call mistletoe "the herb of the Cross" because of an old legend that mistletoe wood was used to build Jesus' cross. They say that is why it is no longer a strong tree.

## Children's Day

*Tibetan Buddhists in Canada have begun to observe December 25 as Children's Day, a time to appreciate children. A special home shrine is set up and covered in silk. All the children in the family collect the objects that mean the most to them and arrange them on this shrine. They are given presents of dolls or figures of inspiring people to place on the shrine. Parents and other adults all celebrate the children in their lives on this day.*

## Season's greeting cards

*The first printed Christmas card was probably designed in 1846 for Sir Henry Cole, an Englishman who was the first director of the London museum now world famous as the Victoria and Albert Museum. His idea of sending Christmas cards didn't really catch on for another 20 years, until many more people had learned to read and write, thanks to the growth of public education in the late 19th century.*

*The idea of Christmas seals began in Denmark in 1904. A postal clerk thought up the idea of selling special stamps to show you had made a donation to a worthy cause.*

## Evergreens

Imagine how magical evergreens such as cedar, pine and holly must have seemed to early humans! These plants stay green and healthy through cold winds, ice and snow while others die. Holly plants, which bear red fruit during the cold months, must have seemed especially powerful. The magical "strength" of these evergreens was invoked in ancient winter solstice celebrations.

Gradually early Christians "borrowed" evergreens for *their* celebrations, and the evergreens took on Christian meanings. For instance, the holly berries are called "Christ's blood" in some carols. Sometimes Jesus' crown of thorns is said to have been made of holly leaves. And our circular door wreaths are said to imitate the prickly crown he wore.

The custom of decorating evergreen trees at Christmas comes from Germany, where the first mention of a fir tree in a parlour, hung with paper roses, gold foil and apples, was in 1605. There is a legend that Martin Luther (the famous German churchman who protested against Roman Catholicism) got the idea of a candlelit tree from walking in the woods and seeing all the starry skies above the winter trees. That made him think of an ornamental tree, symbolizing the heavens from which Christ came. Another early legend says that St. Boniface (an 8th-century English monk) decorated the first pine tree. Whichever of these stories is true, the use of such special trees took root most firmly in Protestant countries.

Christmas trees reached North America in the late 1700s. At first they were put on public exhibit, and the public had to pay a hefty admission fee of 6¼ cents. The first *family* Christmas tree was probably erected in Canada by Lady Friederike von Riedesel. Homesick for her native Germany, she insisted on having a candle-laden tree in Sorel, Quebec, in 1781.

## Christmas treats

No Christmas treat would be complete without a family feast. Visit an Inuit family at Christmas and you might be served reindeer (not Rudolph!) or caribou meat. Other ethnic groups and cultures have their own special Christmas foods.

People from El Salvador make and exchange *tamales*, meat or egg and vegetable filling covered with a bread-like layer made from corn flour and wrapped in corn husks. "Feliz Navidad" is the greeting that goes with the *tamale*.

French-Canadians often make special gingerbread, and Germans, gingerbread men and hearts. Scandinavians eat *stollen*, and Italians eat *panettone*, both rich Christmas breads; the Scots love shortbread.

Candies are often around at Christmas too — remember "visions of sugar plums"? Italians like *torrone*, a honey-nut candy. Maritimers enjoy two special kinds of locally made candies: barley candy (shaped like Santas, dogs, cats and rabbits) from the Yarmouth Candy Company in Nova Scotia, and "chicken bones," hand-made skinny sticks with chocolate fillings, from St. Stephen, New Brunswick. And everywhere, everyone eats peppermint candy canes. Why we eat sweets over the holidays may go back to ancient times. Long ago people thought that by eating sweet things at the turn of the year they could bring on sweetness for the coming year.

## Community Christmas trees

- The City of Toronto lights a huge tree in front of City Hall on the last Friday evening in November.

- A Tree of Love is erected annually on December 1 in the Parkway Mall, Saint John, New Brunswick. The Red Cross does this to encourage blood donations during the busy holiday month. December donors are honoured with an ornament on the Tree of Love.
- Lunenberg County, Nova Scotia, the "Christmas tree capital of Canada," accounts for more than a third of all Canadian Christmas tree exports. Since 1973, Nova Scotia has made an annual gift of the year's best tree to Boston, Massachusetts, where it is installed in front of the Prudential Centre, the city's tallest building.

---

*Ho ho ho...*

Q. What do you get when you cross Dracula and Santa Claus?

A. Something that comes down chimneys and sucks the sap of Christmas trees.

---

## Long-lived trees

*To keep your Christmas tree healthy, saw off at least 2 cm (1 inch) of the trunk diagonally and put the trunk in a hot solution made of 4 L (1 gallon) water, 500 mL (2 cups) corn syrup and 20 mL (4 tsp) bleach. In Lunenburg County a man named Murray Fraser has kept a Christmas tree up and decorated in his living room for more than 17 years! He says it is still pretty, and none of the needles have fallen off, but it's rather brown.*

## Gift-giving

*Christmas wouldn't be Christmas without exchanging presents! The custom of gift-giving has its roots in the old Roman festival of Saturnalia. During that early winter festival, Roman citizens used to give each other good luck gifts (called* strenae) *of wax candles and small clay figurines, gold coins or food such as fruits and pastries. The Christmas story about shepherds bringing gifts to the newborn baby Jesus added new meaning to the old Roman custom, and it allowed people to continue a custom they enjoyed. Later on in Christian history, St. Nicholas became the gift-bringer. (See page 28 for more information on this jolly old chap.) St. Nicholas gradually evolved into our modern Santa.*

## A family day

Christmas Day today is almost always a quiet family day. Portuguese-Canadians, in fact, often call it Dia da Familiã (Family Day). For many Canadians it is a day of church services, joyfully remembering the story of the Nativity. Macedonian churchgoers in Canada often dance as well as sing on Christmas Day. For others it is simply a peaceful time to enjoy the love being shared between family members and close friends.

Christmas can also be a lonesome time for people without families or friends nearby or for newly arrived immigrants from countries where Christmas is not a festival they observe. And so there are special Christmas parties wherever thoughtful Canadians try to share their enjoyment of the season.

- In 1979, a priest at Calgary's St. Elizabeth of Hungary Church started a Christmas Day event for newcomers. Now called the Stray Cats Party, it includes many new immigrants, refugees and unemployed people. The all-day festivities finish with everyone singing "Silent Night" together, but each sings in his or her own language!
- In Winnipeg, the International Centre has hosted a huge multicultural party on the Sunday before Christmas since 1969. The invitation is printed in Polish, Spanish, Laotian, Chinese and Arabic and reads: "In Canada, Christmas is not only a religious holiday for those of the Christian faith. It is also a time we pause to remember the ties of humanity that bind us all. Please join us at the International Centre for a celebration of the season."

## Kissing boughs

Before Christmas trees became popular, the British settlers in Canada sometimes decorated a ''kissing bough'' as the centre of their Christmas festivities. These are globe- or crown-shaped frames, covered with greenery and hung with apples, candles and other pretty things. They always include a central bunch of mistletoe. To make a kissing bough of your own:

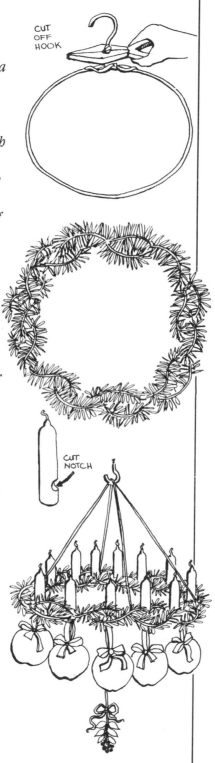

1. Bend coat-hanger wire (you need sharp-nosed pliers and patience) into a globe or crown. (If you're lazy, buy a wire lampshade frame or find an old one.)
2. Cover the ribs with evergreen boughs gathered from the woods or scavenged from a Christmas tree lot. You can also buy ropes of cedar already tied together for decorating windows and doors — try your local florist. Lots of green twist-ties are helpful in this process.
3. Attach to this green frame any of the following: 12 candles (use wire to hold them or buy German Christmas-tree candleholders); 12 red apples hung from ribbons; paper rosettes or other ornaments.
4. Fasten a bunch of mistletoe in the centre of the globe.
5. Light all the candles each night of the Twelve Days of Christmas (see page 50.)

## Kado Matsu

An old Japanese tradition is for families to go to the woods and cut down a pine tree to place near their front door during the week before New Year's Day. To the Japanese, the pine tree symbolizes strength and long life, because it is strong and always green.

## Dear Santa

If you've got a request for Santa, here's where to write:

Santa Claus,
North Pole,
Canada HOH OHO

P.S. If you live in the Brandon, Manitoba, area, your letter may be answered by Gisele Solon. A secretary at that post office, she not only helps Santa with all his letters, but also puts ads in the newspapers to make sure children know where to write.

P.P.S. If you live down east, the St. John's Evening Telegram may print your letter to Santa. They publish about a third of the letters received every year and give prizes to the ten best.

## Rudolph

Although the Dutch Sint Nikolaas travels by horse and the old Father Christmas was often seen on a goat in 19th-century pictures, nowadays Santa almost always arrives in a reindeer-pulled sleigh, with Rudolph in the lead.

Rudolph was the invention of an American employee of Montgomery Ward, the mail-order store based in Chicago. In 1938 Mr. May wrote a poem beginning, "'Twas the day before Christmas/ When all through the hills/ The reindeer were playing/ Enjoying the spills...." The "star" of his poem was a reindeer named Rudolph. Eventually Rudolph was immortalized in song by composer Johnny Marks. Gene Autry recorded the song in 1949, and there have been more than 350 different recordings of it since then! The version you know may begin like this:

Rudolph, the red-nosed reindeer (reindeer)
Had a very shiny nose (like a light bulb)
And if you ever saw it (saw it)
You would even say it glows.
All of the other reindeer (reindeer)
Used to laugh and call him names (like "stupid");
They never let poor Rudolph (Rudolph)
Join in any reindeer games (like poker).

In Wolfville, Nova Scotia, Rudolph is not quite so important. In the Santa Claus parade there, Santa arrives by horse-drawn hay wagon, and children get to ride along with him!

# Tree decorations

Many ethnic groups have traditional decorations to hang on their Christmas trees. Because Christmas trees themselves are a relatively new part of Christmas, some decorations have been adapted from other holiday customs. Ukrainians, for instance, make "Baba dolls" to hang on their trees. These have a pine cone body, an acorn head and a cloth apron and head scarf. Baba dolls are modelled after the Russian gift-bearer, Babushka. Armenian-Canadians sometimes hang their decorations on a large oak branch that has kept its dry, brown leaves.

Here's how to make Danish heart-shaped baskets, traditionally woven of red and white paper strips. When you finish them — they are easier than they may look — stick handles on the baskets, fill them with Christmas candies and hang them on your tree.

1. Cut two pieces of different coloured paper 7 cm by 22 cm (2 ½ inches by 8 ½ inches) each. Fold them in half (try to work with them together so they are exactly the same). Origami paper is a good type of paper to use because it doesn't tear easily, but you can experiment with different papers and colours.

2. Round off the open end as shown. Make two cuts in the folded edge. These cuts should end where the unfolded edges start to curve. Now you have two folded papers, each with three strips or loops (the strips are actually double). After you learn the basics, try making more strips or varying the width of the cuts in the square part to produce different designs.

3. Now you are ready to weave the two folded pieces together to form a heart. The trick is to weave the loops around and through each other, not just over and under. To do this, hold the two pieces as shown in 3A, and poke loop 1 in between the top and bottom layers of loop A. Then open up loop 1 and slide sloop B through the gap. Finally, poke the end of loop 1 inside loop C. Continue weaving your heart until it looks like 3B. Then add a handle.

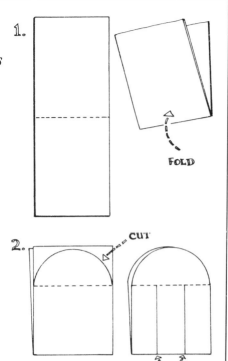

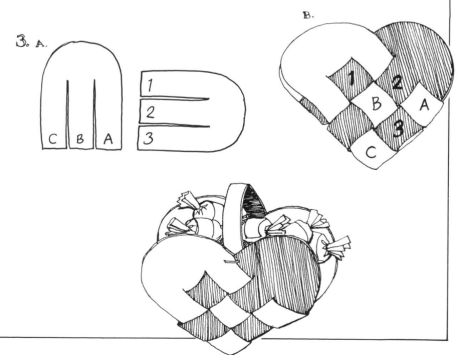

## *Brrrr*

*In Nanaimo, B.C., on the eastern shore of Vancouver Island, Boxing Day is the date for an annual Polar Bear Swim. From the sound of it, this custom seems to need no further explanation!*

# Boxing Day

*December 26*

In Canada, Boxing Day is usually a day of relaxing after Christmas. Lots of people either go to department-store sales or get ready to go to them the next day.

The day gets its name from the 19th-century English custom of giving Christmas boxes containing food or money or both to family servants and suppliers on December 26. Long before then, it was common to give food, money or clothing to poor people on Boxing Day, or St. Stephen's Day as it was then called. You may be familiar with St. Stephen's Day from this carol:

> Good King Wenceslas looked out,
> On the feast of Stephen,
> When the snow lay round about,
> Deep and crisp and even.

St. Stephen's Day is a special day for Austrian-Canadians — is it for your church or community?

# Mummering

*December 26 - January 6*

Starting on Boxing Day and all through the holiday period, homes in northern Newfoundland are visited by neighbours in disguise. Known as "mummers" (or janneys, johnnies, maskers or mumpers), they sing, dance or play music, but try to disguise their voices.

Mummering, or going from house to house in disguise, is not as widespread as it once was throughout the province, although it is being revived in some areas. The old traditions included parades of mummers in costumes, masks or blackened faces. Sometimes they wore or carried an animal head symbolizing the vital need for healthy animals and good

crops. And sometimes the mummers performed silly plays on Boxing Day before beginning the regular visiting-mummering the next day.

A mummers' play always features a fight in which a "good guy" is killed by a "bad guy" and revived by a doctor. There is an ancient connection between the death and rebirth of the year at the solstice and the death and revival of the hero of the play. The actors used to learn these folk plays from one another, never from a book, so the words had an easy-to-speak rhyming rhythm but didn't always make sense. The plays also poked fun at local people or events.

# Kwanza

*December 26*

A professor who wanted to encourage blacks to celebrate their heritage started Kwanza (pronounced "kuh-wan-sa") in California in 1966. In Canada, Kwanza is a new holiday, and Kwanza customs are still developing.

Beginning December 26, black families exchange gifts and have African-style feasts, visiting one another's homes in turn. There are seven principles underlying the seven-day holiday: unity, self-determination, working together, sharing, purpose, creativity and faith. Many families try to have an activity related to the principle being observed for the day. It is also a time for sharing family history and pride in black history.

There are special seven-pronged candleholders for Kwanza; one candle is lit for the first night, two for the second and so forth. A Kwanza table in many homes holds the candles, any special family mementoes and a unity cup. Every guest who visits during the seven days of Kwanza takes a sip of water from the unity cup. Some blacks send Kwanza cards, in which the usual greeting is "Let the seven principles of Kwanza be your guiding light."

## Playful plays

*Here's a snippet from a mummers' play to give you an idea of the silly, singsong words. Why not try making up a mummers' play of your own.*

Doctor: *Three drops to his temple and one to his heart,*
*Rise up, brother, and play your part.*
The dead Turk is brought to life by the Doctor's medicine and cries out:
*Terrible! Terrible! The like was never seen,*
*A man knocked out of seven senses into a hundred and nineteen;*
*Not by bucks nor yet by bears, one of the divil's whirligigs blowed me up in the air.*
*If you don't believe what I do say, step in Turkish Knight and clear the way!*

Four Beavers Building

# The Twelve Days of Christmas

*December 26 - January 6*

Everyone sings the old carol about the partridge in the pear tree and the Twelve Days of Christmas, but what does it mean? The days from Boxing Day to Epiphany (December 26 to January 6) are those famous 12 days. (In Canada, we only celebrate six of the 12 days: Boxing Day, Holy Innocents' Day, New Year's Eve, New Year's Day, Twelfth Night and Epiphany.)

Long ago the 12 days were considered an out-of-the-ordinary time when strange things could take place. The idea of 12 "odd" days came about because people measured time by watching the sun *and* the moon. Sun-watching gave them a year of 365¼ days. Moon-watching gave them a year of only 354. The difference between the two was 11¼ days. (For convenience they called it 12 days.) In Europe the 12 days were celebrated just after the winter solstice.

Sometimes people's behaviour during this period was allowed to be out of the ordinary too. It was a rowdy, wild time when lords waited upon servants, slaves were temporary masters and so forth. Later, the ancient Roman Saturnalia festival, held at the dark of the year, was characterized by lots of reversed roles like these. When Christianity began, some of the customs associated with the Saturnalia were adopted into Christmas practices. During the Middle Ages, for example, a Lord of Misrule was appointed to reign during the Twelve Days of Christmas.

In Canada we have our very own out-of-the-ordinary events during the 12 days. Belsnickers in Nova Scotia and mummers in Newfoundland visit homes, playing tricks and games. On Her Majesty's ships stationed in Esquimalt, B.C., the officers serve dinner to the rest of the sailors, and the youngest able seaman is made captain on Christmas Day.

# Day of the Holy Innocents

*December 28*

The name of this Catholic holy day refers to the biblical event when Herod tried to kill the baby Jesus by ordering all babies under age two in Bethlehem to be killed. Because he didn't succeed — do you know why? — many traditions developed around this day of bad luck. In many Spanish-speaking countries, no one works on this day, and pranks and tricks are played: things like doughnuts with mustard-flavoured fillings and false newspaper headlines are common. Sounds like April Fool's, doesn't it? In Canada some people from countries like El Salvador still play tricks on this day. So watch out!

In other Christian groups, the holiday has no tomfoolery attached to it. It is simply a time for the children to be especially blessed in church.

# New Year's Eve

*December 31*

Since the early days of Canada, New Year's Eve has been a more important time than Christmas for French–Canadians to socialize. Their old house-visiting custom (now being revived in St. Boniface, Manitoba, and other places) is called the *guignolée*. Bell-ringers called Ignoleux announce that visitors have arrived, then an old song (*la guignolée*) is sung about house-visiting and gifts of mistletoe (or *gui* in French). After singing, the visitors collect money, food (especially pork, the traditional meat prized by the Ignoleux) and clothes for needy people. The visitors say silly things to get donations — they might threaten to carry off the eldest daughter, even picking her up and pretending to do so!

The Scots call New Year's Eve Hogmanay. (Both the words Hogmanay and *guignolée* come from a French phrase mean-

## Gaelic house-visiting

*On Cape Breton the Gaelic name for New Year's Eve, Oidhche Challuinn, is still used. Scots on Cape Breton have an old house-visiting custom for Oidhche Challuinn that was once meant to be for the benefit of the poorest families. People would go from door to door at New Year, reciting a kind of poem called* duan, *and asking for gifts of potatoes and onions. In turn they would give these to the most needy people in the community.*

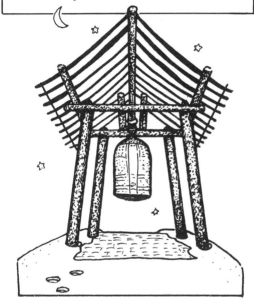

## 108 bells

*The Japanese Buddhist community in Toronto tolls a bell 108 times at midnight on New Year's Eve at Ontario Place. The number 108 is sacred for Buddhists: there are 108 beads on every Buddhist rosary, and Buddhists often walk around a sacred building 108 times.*

## New Year's Eve two weeks later

*Ukrainian-Canadians don't hold their New Year's celebrations until January 13, because they use a different calendar. Around their New Year's Eve, Ukrainians go to a supper dance or costume ball, called a* malanka. *The word refers to an old legend about winter being captured and spring released. At one time the* malanka *was a man dressed as a woman who, with a party of supporting actors, went house-visiting, just like mummers.*

ing "to the mistletoe, the New Year.") Welcoming in the New Year was more of a party than Christmas to the Scots at one time too, and many of their customs are still with us today. The best known is probably the Scottish New Year song, "Auld Lang Syne," written by Robert Burns.

Before a Hogmanay celebration, Scottish families used to clean their homes, pay all debts, mend clothes, tune instruments and return anything borrowed to its owner. Some said that visitors at the New Year should bring bread, salt and coal to their hosts — symbolizing life, hospitality and warmth. Others said an uncut cake should be served as a symbol of hospitality: the oldest person present should pour the drinks, the second oldest should cut the cake and the youngest should pass around the slices.

Today, at midnight on Hogmanay, pots and pans might be banged together as noise-makers, and often there's a round of kissing. The first person to come in the front door (or across the threshold) after midnight is called "the first-footer." He or she is supposed to be a token of the kind of luck that household will have in the new year. Male, black-haired first-footers carrying a sprig of mistletoe (there's that magical plant again!) are especially good omens.

Early Scottish settlers influenced the Cree nation with their New Year's Eve customs, although the Cree now celebrate a day later. On New Year's night, in the James Bay region, the Cree fire shotguns into the sky in front of the homes of people they want to greet or honour. During the day the Cree chief or another elder kisses everyone in the community — kissing was unknown among the Cree before the Scots came.

Lots of other people celebrate in different ways on New Year's Eve. Chileans sing their national anthem. Austrians eat marzipan candy pigs — because pigs (who dig forward with their snouts) stand for good luck and a fat future! The Portuguese have parties to mark the Passagem do Ano (Passage of

the Year). Just at midnight they eat 12 raisins, one for each stroke of the clock, and all for good luck.

Korean-Canadians may stay awake all night to greet the Honourable New Year. Adults may give "forgetting-the-year" parties, at which they have a ceremony to forget any past disappointments. The Japanese eat *soba*, or buckwheat noodles, for their New Year's Eve meal — noodles symbolize a long life. Then they must eat *ozoni* (a soup with pounded sweet rice cake as its main ingredient) for their first meal the next day. Each of the vegetables in *ozoni* has a meaning related to luck for the New Year. For example, *kobu* seaweed is included because its name forms part of the word *yorokobu*, which means "to be glad."

Syrian families in Canada gather together on New Year's Eve and greet one another at the stroke of midnight with the Arabic words "Sana Mubaraka," meaning "Blessed New Year." The proper response is "Kul sana wa antum bikhair," or "May you be well and happy."

Not everyone goes to a party or a noisy celebration, however. Many people treat New Year's Eve as a religious time to pray and meditate in preparation for the New Year. For the Portuguese, the Te Deum service on New Year's Eve, giving thanks for the year that has passed, is one of the most important times to go to church all year. Some Korean churchgoers attend a "sending-off-the-year" service. Other people simply go to bed! What happens in your family?

## New Year's Day

*January 1*

The Greeks call New Year's Day St. Basil's Day. They exchange gifts with family members and friends, and every household makes a special round sponge cake called a *basilopita* (named for the saint but the first letter is pronounced as a "v"). It is orange-flavoured and baked with a

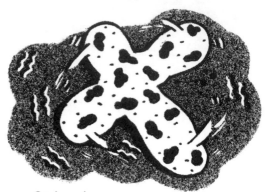

## Spinning cross

*During the holiday season many Greek-Canadians make* lalangita, *a deep-fried bread something like a doughnut. The dough is simple, with raisins in it. The first* lalangita *is shaped like a cross, and everyone watches as it cooks. If it spins in the hot fat and turns over to the right, everything in the new year will be "right" too.*

coin inside it. If you are named after St. Basil, then it is your name-day and you must bake the cake! The person who gets the slice with the coin will have good luck throughout the new year. Greeks also eat sweet cookies called *tsourekia* all during the Twelve Days of Christmas.

The Macedonians eat a special yeast pastry called *maznik*. It has a coin in it too. They turn the cake three times and then cut it into the correct number of pieces for the family members and pets, including one for the family farm or business! They say, "Za mnogu godini!" to wish one another many more years.

Are you given any gifts for New Year's Day? On the Six Nations Reserve in Ontario, children visit from house to house on the morning of New Year's Day, collecting gifts of home-made cookies, doughnuts, candies and other treats.

Père Noël used to visit French-Canadian children on this day as well, but he seems to have switched to Christmas Eve during the 1950s. Some French children still get gifts from their godparents on New Year's Day.

On New Year's morning it is also the Québécois custom for the eldest son to ask his father for his blessing. Later in the day, French-Canadian families try to gather together under the roof of the oldest member for a special dinner. Dried apple pie is a traditional specialty. After dinner families attend mass together.

Around Victoria, B.C., many places hold New Year's Day levees at midday. "Levee" is an old-fashioned word that means a special reception, and these levees are another way for the blessings of the New Year to be shared — officially! In Victoria itself, anyone can visit Government House to meet the Lieutenant-Governor and his or her spouse, and other local dignitaries. Guests may look through the historic building and sample sherry and Christmas cake. If you go to the levees at Victoria's City Hall or at the municipalities of Oak

Bay or Saanich, you will meet the mayors. Or you can attend an open house at the officers' mess in the naval dockyard. Be prepared to shake lots of hands!

# Sŏlnal

*January 1*

Korean New Year's Day is the biggest festive event of the year for that community. Usually Sŏlnal is celebrated on the first of January, but some Koreans celebrate it at the lunar New Year, later in the winter, like the Chinese. Most Korean children enjoy Sŏlnal, for they get to wear new clothes and their many-coloured traditional costumes, called *han pok*. Koreans say, "Sae hae e pok manhi paduseyo," or "Please receive many happinesses in the New Year."

Christian Koreans go to church on Sŏlnal, while Buddhists make offerings to their ancestors at their temples. Everyone visits friends and relatives for three or four days. When

## Koleda bonfires

*Macedonian-Canadians using the Julian Calendar light a huge bonfire on January 5, which is their December 23. The old custom still practised at St. Clement's Church in Toronto is for the men to sit around the fire until early the next morning, called Koleda. Then they go house-visiting in costume, singing wishes for good health and long life. Special kolachinja rolls are baked for them.*

## Wassail punch

*This hot fruit juice punch makes 16 servings.*

| | |
|---|---|
| a whole lemon or orange | |
| a handful of cloves | |
| 2 L apple cider | ½ gal |
| 2 L cranberry juice | ½ gal |
| 125 mL brown sugar | ½ cup |
| 2 mL cinnamon | ½ tsp |
| 5 mL ground ginger | 1 tsp |
| 2 mL ground allspice | ½ tsp |
| 5 mL ground cloves | 1 tsp |
| whole cinnamon sticks (optional) | |

1. *Punch holes all over the lemon or orange and put a clove into each hole.*
2. *Put all of the ingredients, including the clove-studded fruit, into a large pot. Heat on stove at medium. Bring the punch almost to the boil, then simmer for about 30 minutes.*
3. *Ladle the warm punch directly into cups or mugs. Add a whole cinnamon stick to each if you wish. Or pour it into a punch bowl and let people help themselves. Delicious!*

*People once believed that wassail punch could be used to foretell the future. To try it yourself, drop a ring or a piece of fruit that won't float (try a fig or prune) into the wassail bowl or the large pot you used to heat the punch. Whoever gets this token in his or her punch is supposed to marry during the coming year.*

Koreans call on their elders for the New Year, they give a deep bow called *sebae*, and the elders give them fruit, gifts and money in return. *Ttukgook* is the name of the special rice soup cooked for Sŏlnal.

Fifteen days after Sŏlnal, on the first full moon day (called Porum), Koreans celebrate the end of the New Year period by eating a five-grain meal and praying for a bountiful harvest. They crack nuts and light firecrackers to frighten away evil.

# Twelfth Night

*January 5*

If you count the night of December 25 as the first night of Christmas, then January 5 is the Twelfth Night. At one time people had a "king of the bean," and sometimes a queen, on Twelfth Night to preside over the revelries for the end of the season. The king and queen were the pair who found a bean and a dried pea in their slices of a special cake. (French-Canadians still make this cake, called a *galette* or *gateau des rois*, on this night.)

In Quebec, the king and queen were responsible for organizing activities for the evening. Card games were special favourites. Often they were played each Sunday evening from Twelfth Night until Easter. Today, Québécois children still get to choose a game to play if they find a bean in the *gateau*.

Europeans also go out to sing and "wassail" or drink the health of their neighbours, animals and orchards on this night. "Wassail" is an old Anglo-Saxon word meaning "be whole," or "to your good health," and the Wassail-bowl, which was traditionally used by these luck-visitors, was the grandparent of our present-day punch bowl.

# Epiphany

*January 6*

Epiphany is the Twelfth Day of Christmas and the end of the Christmas season. To avoid bad luck, many people try to take down their decorations by this date. There are definitely a lot of used Christmas trees waiting for the garbage collection around this time, aren't there?

Epiphany comes from a Greek word referring to the baptism of Jesus and the arrival in Bethlehem of the Three Wise Men who came to worship Jesus. Greek Orthodox priests visit all the households in their parish on this day to bless the homes and family members with holy water. Polish homes are also blessed with holy water, and then the initials of the Three Wise Men and the year are chalked on the doorposts. This is what it looks like: 19 + C + M + B + 87. Can you decipher it?

Although Ukrainians do not celebrate Epiphany until January 19, their customs are similar. They have a big church ceremony to bless the water that will be used by the priests to bless the people, and the whole congregation has a procession. They call January 19 Little Christmas or Jordan Day, which refers to the Jordan River where Jesus was baptized. On the same day, Macedonians throw a cross into a pool of water. The young man who fishes it out will have good luck in the coming year. The water is used for blessing too.

In the Maritimes, Acadians call the Twelfth Day the Feast of Kings and treat it as a second Christmas. Spanish-speaking people call it Three Kings Day, and some families have three people dressed as the kings to bring gifts for the children, instead of Santa.

Some Italian-Canadians also give gifts to each other on Epiphany, although nowadays gift-giving is more common on December 25. The gifts are brought by an old woman called

Befana. She was so busy cooking and cleaning when the Three Wise Men went by in search of the baby Jesus that she couldn't stop to help them. When she finally was ready, the kings were far beyond her, and she has been wandering the earth trying to catch up ever since. She carries her broom and a basket of gifts, and she leaves something for every child, in the hope that he or she might actually be the Christ child.

In Labrador this date is called Nalujuk's Night or Jannies' Night. ("Nalujuk" is the Inuit word for someone who is ignorant or uninformed.) Children may hang up stockings at many different houses on January 5. They visit these houses and find their stockings full the next morning. There are also church services, which include an annual news report on the entire community.

In the evening, the Nalujuk (like Newfoundland's mummers) visit every house. They dress in furry clothing and ugly masks. Each Nalujuk wears a bag of goodies around his neck and carries some sort of weapon. Like the old German belsnickers, the Nalujuk use the weapons to smack children whose parents say they have been bad during the year. The Nalujuk also command children to listen to their elders and respect their mothers and fathers. Children have to sing a song or recite a poem and are rewarded with a present.

# Julian Christmas

*January 7*

The Ukrainians and many other people from the Eastern Orthodox churches celebrate Christmas on January 7. On Christmas Eve, January 6, they put a lighted candle in the window to guide travellers, in memory of Mary and Joseph's journey. The holiday begins with the first star on the horizon. If you are the child to spot it, you'll have especially good luck in the next year. Then the father in the family speaks an ancient blessing: "May God bring us all good fortune through-out the coming year, and let us thank him for his many bless-ings in the past. Christ is born!" The rest of the family echoes him with "Khrystos vodyvsia! Slavim yoho!" (Christ is born! Let us glorify him!)

Next the father puts a beautiful sheaf of wheat (called a *didukh*) in the corner of the dining room to symbolize the gathering of the family. After this, everyone sits down at the table, where hay has been placed under the cloth and on the floor. Do you remember what other group has a custom like this? (See page 35.) A Ukrainian family may also bring a goat, dog or some other small animal into the house, along with the wheat. After all, the animals in the stable in Bethlehem shared in Jesus' birth too.

Many Eastern Orthodox Christians have 40 days of partial fasting before Christmas. They do not eat meat or dairy foods such as milk, cheese and eggs — or anything made from them. Ukrainians say the fasting is supposed to remind them of the hardships endured by Mary as she and Joseph travelled to Bethlehem. And so, on Christmas Eve, the special Ukrainian "holy supper" consists of 12 meatless and milkless dishes.

The first of the 12 dishes is *kutia*, made of boiled wheat, honey, nuts and ground poppy seeds. It stands for family uni-ty and prosperity, and everyone, beginning with the father, must have a spoonful of *kutia* — even the pets in the house-hold! Another old belief about *kutia* was that some had to be thrown up to the ceiling. If it stuck, there would be good harvests in the coming year. Nowadays most Ukrainian-Canadians eat but don't throw *kutia*. After that dish the foods may vary, but usually include *borsch* (beet soup), cabbage rolls and *pyrohy* (dumplings).

After the Holy Eve meal, Ukrainian families sing traditional carols together or go out carolling from house to house. Then they attend midnight mass. This Christmas service, with deep

## Vasaloppet

*In many areas of Canada where there are large Scandinavian settlements, there is a 450-year-old Swedish cross-country skiing fest held in the late winter. People take part just for the fun of it, but it also commemorates a famous historical ski marathon in 1521 when King Gustav Vasa travelled 92 km (58 miles) on skis to gather his people to defend their country.*

- *In the Georgian Lakeland region of Ontario, the traditional* vasaloppet *festival is called Muskoka Loppet and takes place in mid-January. Skiers travel about 30 km (19 miles), making it the largest one-day cross-country ski event in the country!*
- *Quebec's February Canadian Marathon takes place on a course 160 km (100 miles) long. Fortunately skiers don't have to do the whole distance; they can choose laps of various lengths.*
- *In Nova Scotia, Scandinavians eat a traditional pea soup to warm up after their outdoor* loppet *party.*

## Snowsnakes

*This traditional Iroquoian game is played by racing long smooth sticks of wood along iced tracks in the snow. Snowsnakes tournaments are held in late January in London, Ontario, on the grounds of the Museum of Indian Archaeology, and in Brantford at the Woodland Indian Cultural Education Centre. Here's how to play it:*

*1. Make two tracks side by side in the snow about 15 cm (6 inches) apart and each about 10 giant steps long. You can form the tracks by dragging a tin can filled with ice behind you.*

*2. Spray the tracks with water to make them more slippery.*

*3. Find two broom handles to use as snakes. Two players stand at a "starting line" and throw the snowsnakes along the tracks. The one that goes farthest wins, and the winner challenges the next snowsnake thrower.*

voices singing all the prayers, is the most important part of their celebrations. After midnight mass, their meatless, milkless fast is finished. The next day, January 7, is spent visiting friends and relatives, singing, dancing and eating meat and milk again.

# Late Winter Festivals

After all the excitement of the holiday season, does winter seem unending and school boring? To break up winter's monotony, Canadians have come up with a number of festivals during January, February and March. Some of these are based on much older customs; others are more modern. Here are some examples:

- The most famous Canadian midwinter festival is Quebec City's Carnaval, which has taken place since 1954 in its present form. (Carnaval has been celebrated there off and on since before 1880!) Hundreds of tourists come to Quebec to enjoy winter sports and look at the ice sculptures, watch canoe races in the icy St. Lawrence River and generally have a good time. The name Carnaval gives you a clue to its origins in the old festivities before Lent began (see page 74). Quebec's Carnaval has been the model for other Quebec winter festivals. Some even manage to arrange for a visit from Bonhomme Carnaval, Quebec City's snowman mascot. Chicoutimi, for example, has Carnaval Souvenir, which recalls a different year from the past every winter.

- The Festival du Voyageur in St. Boniface, Manitoba (the French district of Winnipeg), lasts for eight days in late February. It was organized in 1970 to honour the *voyageurs* who transported the furs (Canada's first commercial product) three centuries ago. Voyageurs travelled over a huge area from Montreal to the Rockies, and from Hudson Bay down to the Gulf of Mexico. The Festival du Voyageur is now western Canada's largest winter get-together. It includes a grand Governor's Ball and a festival parade with participants dressed in red toques and blue *capotes* (blanket-cloth coats), which the voyageurs once wore.

- Also in Manitoba, the Trapper's Festival in The Pas, 700 km (435 miles) north of Winnipeg, celebrates the skill and hardiness of northern trappers. There are contests to do with every aspect of trapping life — fire-building, bannock-baking, tea-brewing, muskrat-skinning, snowshoe-running and, of course, dog-sledding! The festival began, in fact, with The Pas Dog Derby in 1915 and has been held without interruption since 1948. The World Championship Dog Race is now the focus of the festival and is run in three 56-km (35-mile) laps on three successive days.

- The Yukon Sourdough Rendezvous has been held every February in Whitehorse, Yukon, since 1962. Participants try their hands at sled dog-racing, moose-calling, packing flour the way the old Klondikers did and many other skills. The word ''sourdough'' refers to unmarried people who were not settled enough to keep yeast and bake yeast breads. Instead, they had to use fermented flour, called sourdough starter, to make things rise.

- Winter festivals in Regina, La Ronge and Prince Albert, Saskatchewan, feature King and Queen Trapper contests, jig dancing, animal and bird call contests, ice-sailing and a torchlight parade. These festivals are held in late February.

- Ottawa holds a ten-day Winterlude in early February. Centred on the ice-covered Rideau Canal, which runs through the heart of the capital, the festival includes sporting events, entertainment, ice sculptures and fireworks.

- In Manitoba the residents of Beausejour optimistically hold their Winter Farewell Festival on the last full weekend in February. (To be accurate, winter is not really over in Beausejour until the last frost date, which is in late May.)

## Homemade ice sculptures

*To make your own ice sculptures outdoors, all you need is a cold day (below freezing), a good imagination and lots of odd-shaped containers. You can pour water into any of these and freeze them outside:*

*a plastic funnel (block the end with Plasticine)*
*waxed cardboard milk cartons*
*a rubber glove (use an elastic band to close it tightly)*
*a doughnut-shaped cake mould*
*balloons (fill with water and use elastic bands to change the shape or blow up and put inside a larger container of water. When the water freezes, the air-filled balloon will leave a hole in it.)*

*Try adding food colouring to the water before you freeze it. And for even more special effects, freeze small objects such as bottle caps and buttons into ice cubes.*

*To remove your frozen ice pieces from their moulds, run them under warm water for a moment. Then start stacking and combining the pieces until the sculptor in you is satisfied. If it's very cold out, you may be able to use more water for glue.*

## Winter in Quebec

*Rudyard Kipling once wrote this limerick about Quebec winters:*

*There was once a small boy in
    Quebec,
Stood buried in snow to his neck.
When asked: "Are you friz?"
He said, "Yes, I is,
But we don't call this cold in
    Quebec."*

## Now that's cold!

*What's winter like in the Yukon? Here's Robert Service's description in his poem "The Ballad of Blasphemous Bill":*

*You know what it's like in the Yukon
    wild, when it's 69 below;
When the ice-worms wriggle their
    purple heads through the crust of
    the pale blue snow;
When the pine-trees crack like little
    guns, in the silence of the wood,
And the icicles hang down like tusks,
    under the parka hood...*

# Iroquois Midwinter Festival

*Before the January full moon*

What is the most important festival in the whole year for you and your family? For the Iroquois, it is the eight-day Midwinter Festival. It starts five nights after the new moon appears in January and marks their New Year. To launch the festival, two Big Heads, or special messengers, go from house to house, inviting everyone to special community centres called longhouses. They wear native clothes and kerchiefs wound around their heads like turbans to make them, literally, Big Heads!

The Midwinter Festival is, above all, a time to beg the Creator for life — to pray that everything be renewed and continued so life will go on. The first two days of the festival are used for a ritual called Stirring Ashes in the longhouse's two stoves. The Big Heads open and close the ritual, stirring the fire with long, wooden paddles. Then everyone joins in. Special songs go with the ritual, symbolizing renewal of the power of fire and of the whole culture.

The next two days are for individual curing ceremonial dances. These are not so much to cure people who are sick as to renew the power of the different traditional cures and to prevent sickness from returning. The ashes from the first two days may be used as part of a symbolic curing. The curing ceremonies finish with an announcement by someone playing the part of the Creator. He invites everyone to join in his sacred ceremonies, come in native costume and bring food to share.

The fifth day is for cleaning up and preparing for the rest of the festival. Faithkeepers wash themselves and scrub the longhouse and gather wood for the communal stoves. The sixth day is Feather Dance day, with songs and dances devoted to all the spirit forces. The first and third dances, held at dawn and just before noon, are done only by the chiefs and faithkeepers. The second dance at midmorning is for all the people to join in. The singers use turtle shell rattles to beat out the rhythms of the dance.

That afternoon, tobacco is gathered from all the participants for the Tobacco Invocation on the sixth day. This is a chant that has many verses. After each verse, a pinch of tobacco (symbolizing the entire community) is burned on a special fire. The chant thanks the Creator for what has been and also asks that each item will continue for another year. Here is a small part of the Invocation:

Let it be your thought
That the people are beseeching you, those living on the
   earth,
For it to be
As it was when the earth was young.
And now from the Indian tobacco
The smoke will rise
Carrying the message up.

On the seventh day, the Skin Dance is performed. For this dance, the lead singer uses a water drum covered with hide (or skin). Sometimes another singer accompanies him with a horn rattle. They begin their songs while the rest of the people wait outside. Gradually everyone enters and joins in, dancing counterclockwise around the singers' bench in the centre of the longhouse.

The sacred peachstone betting game begins on the eighth day and may last one day or continue for one or two more days, taking the festival right up to the full moon time. The game is a sign to the Iroquois that everything is still functioning as it was meant to be by the Creator. There are two teams, and they use 100 peachstones burned black on one side as players. People donate good clothes for the final prize, but the

## Star-watching

*In some cultures the year is based on the cycle of the sun; in others, on the cycle of the moon or a mixture of both. But some ancient people also watched the movements of the star constellations. The Iroquois New Year is celebrated during the period when the constellation Pleiades reaches the highest point overhead in the night sky. Do you know the Pleiades? It is a group of seven stars and is also called the Seven Sisters. It looks like this:*

*The Pleiades is part of the bigger constellation called Taurus, or the Bull. Look south and see if you can find it yourself on a clear winter night.*

# In the longhouse

**An Iroquois longhouse of 100 years ago**

The Iroquois longhouses today are community buildings where all their ceremonies and important gatherings are held. Longhouses are not exactly the same as churches, because lots of nonreligious events take place in them too, but they are a symbolic centre for the Iroquois culture.

The name "longhouse" gives you a clue about the building's shape: a long rectangle. Until about 1800, bark lodge longhouses were winter homes to family groups of Iroquois, as well as ritual centres. Later longhouses were made with logs. Today they are wooden buildings. An entrance door and wood-burning stove are located at each end of the longhouse, and people sit on long wooden benches arranged into two "moities," or sides. The two moities choose the best speakers to represent them. The speakers take turns saying familiar speeches. They don't memorize the speeches, only the sequence. The central area of the longhouse, between the two moities, is the focal point for speakers, singers and dancers.

The Iroquois have four sacred rites that are part of most of their religious ceremonies. These are the Great Feather Dance, the Men's Personal Chant, the Skin (or Drum) Dance and the Bowl Game (a peachstone betting ritual). Ceremonies both begin and close with "a thanksgiving address." And every ceremony is followed by the distribution of food among the participants.

losers don't feel unlucky — they think what they have lost goes to heaven!

In former times, Iroquois hunters stocked the longhouse with large supplies of meat for the Midwinter Festival. Reverence for animals is still shown by the importance of meat in the feast at this time. Everyone shares in boiled beef and venison, plus corn soup made from the leftover meat broth. Store-bought foods like cookies, doughnuts, bread and apples supplement the feast. All the food is served from large baskets or pails, taken around the longhouse.

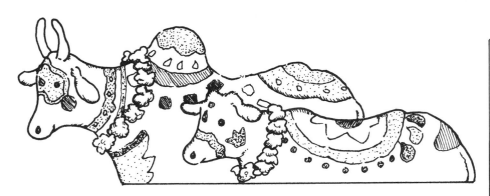

# Pongal

*January 13 or 14*

Holding a harvest festival in January may seem strange in frozen Canada, but in many parts of India, it is the time of the rice harvest. Pongal is a three-day-long harvest festival celebrating the new crop of rice. (The Sanskrit name Makara-Sankranti is used instead of Pongal in many areas.) In India, newly harvested rice is cooked in a special ceremony and fed to the local cows and bullocks, which are gaily painted for the festival. In Ontario, despite the cold, Indians usually have a cultural evening of singing and dancing to mark this time of thanksgiving.

# Chamishah Asar bi-Shevat, the Jewish New Year of Trees

*January or February*

On the Jewish calendar, there are actually four New Years: one for the months, one for the creation of the world, one for the kings and one for the trees. This last one is celebrated during the late winter. In Israel at this time, trees are beginning to bud, and children living there have tree-planting ceremonies. Usually separate trees are planted for boys and girls. In snowbound Canada, Jews often arrange for trees to be planted in Israel in their name on this date, and children eat fruit that has been imported from the Holy Land.

# Sun Nin, the Chinese New Year

*Between January 21 and February 20*

Chinese New Year is actually two celebrations in one: New Year's and a big birthday party. According to a Chinese tradition, everyone's birthday is celebrated on New Year's Day.

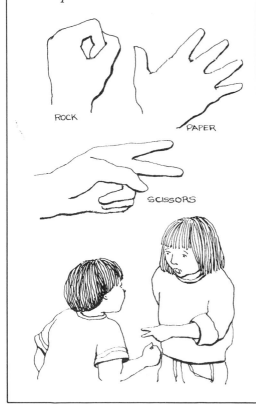

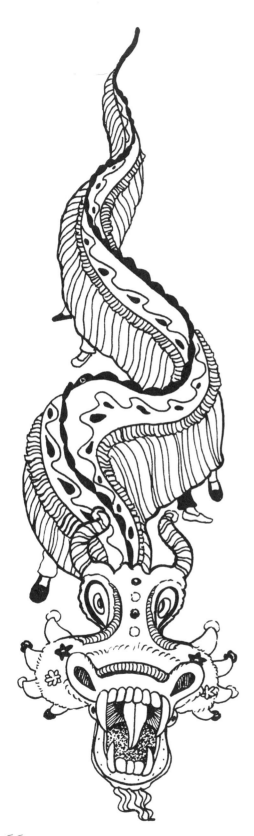

It is also the most important family get-together of the year, when you must see every family member face to face, and a time to ensure good luck for the future.

The Chinese calendar is lunisolar, which means it is based on the cycles of both the sun *and* the moon. The New Year is celebrated some time between January 21 and February 20; it does not have a fixed date.

The holiday starts on the first day of the second new moon after the winter solstice. Traditionally, this most important and merriest festival of the Chinese year lasted a whole month — it took that long to visit your whole family! In Canada today, a shortened version lasts for more than a week, with the biggest celebrations usually taking place on the weekend.

The Chinese have a saying that every time there is a festival, you think of your family and you double your thoughts and memories of your loved ones. It is sad to think that for many Chinese who came to Canada before 1947, New Year's Eve was the worst time of the whole year, because they had no families with whom to celebrate. Why not? For many years Chinese workers in Canada were forced to pay a "head tax" for each family member they brought here, and very few Chinese could afford to pay the tax. From 1923 to 1947, no Chinese were allowed into Canada at all. The Canadian government was afraid Chinese immigrants would add to the number of unemployed people or take over some industries, like the laundry business.

Because of people's suspicions, it's no wonder that Chinese-Canadians shortened their New Year celebrations. But even though it is short, Chinese New Year is still an important time for families to be united.

On New Year's Eve there is a huge feast for as many members of the family as possible. Families gather together to bid farewell quietly to the old year and to greet the new. At

midnight, the oldest person says the first New Year's greetings. The children are noisy all night, however, for the Chinese believe that the longer children stay awake, the longer their parents will live!

For this big reunion dinner, the table is covered with a red cloth and set with red candles, and the many vegetarian courses are served slowly: often there are 12, for the 12 years in the zodiac. No meat is served, because harm has to be caused to obtain it — the killing of animals. For good luck it is important to have so much food that there are leftovers for the next day, when no cooking may be done. Children play games and ask riddles while everyone eats.

The Chinese believe that whatever happens on Yuan-Tan, or New Year's Day, will influence the rest of the year. Family visiting begins, and visitors are given gifts of sweets and fruits (lichee nuts and kumquats are favourites). The greeting everywhere is "Kung hey fah choy," which means "I wish you a prosperous New Year." Older and married people give children presents of money in little red envelopes, called *lai-see*, so the children often say to each other "Lai see dao loy" (which means "Lucky money is coming soon").

After New Year's Day, you may visit friends as well as family — the important thing is to see one another. (A phone call would definitely not be enough!) During visits, children are given special rice cakes — as round as the family circle and as sweet as peace — or oranges, which mean good wishes for their happiness. All the treats of the holiday are meant to signify joy, peace and long life.

In Vancouver today, a huge dragon accompanied by firecrackers dances through the streets as part of the finale of Chinese New Year. Traditionally Sun Nin finishes after 14 days, with Deng Shih, the Feast of the Full Moon. Sometimes this is also called the Feast of the Lanterns. In China people decorate

## The Dragon Game

*With so many dragons around during New Year's you may want to try this Indonesian dragon game to get in the mood.*

1. *The players stand in a long line, one in front of the other. Each person holds firmly onto the waist of the player in front.*
2. *The leader is the head of the dragon. He or she tries to catch the tail, or last person. (In Indonesia, players sing a song and do a dance before the dragon tries to catch its tail.) The tail tries to avoid being caught. All the players making up the rest of the body try to help the head, and everybody has to hold on so the dragon doesn't break up as it twists and turns.*
3. *When the tail is caught, there are two ways to continue the game. Either the tail drops out and the body gets shorter and shorter, or the head moves back and becomes the tail, and the next person in line becomes the new head. The game stops when every player has had a turn to be head.*

their homes with paper lanterns for two or three days before it. On the feast night the lanterns are taken out for a parade. In Canada, the parade is more likely to be held around midday on the weekend nearest Deng Shih, and lanterns are less important.

The dragon leads the parade because he is the Chinese symbol of goodness and strength. He has a huge papier-mâché head and long cloth body. People hide under the dragon's body and move in a dancing rhythm. The dragon is thought of as the protector of humankind. To scare away anything bad, his face is very ferocious-looking. Firecrackers are set off to help frighten off evil. In front of the dragon, a single dancer carries a round sun symbol on a pole. Chinese people say that the dancing dragon is trying to devour the sun, but he never succeeds because now the New Year has come and the sun is growing too strong.

New Year's is also celebrated by many other Asian communities around the same time. This is because many immigrants from Viet Nam, Laos and Cambodia are of Chinese origin and share many similar customs.

In Toronto several Vietnamese groups combine to hold an all-day event called the Lunar New Year Tet Festival. This celebration involves games, displays, sales of food and crafts and crowds of people. For the Vietnamese, like the Chinese, New Year is the most important event of the year.

Tibetan New Year, called Losar, also comes at this time. Tibetans do a ritual housecleaning for Losar and decorate with good luck symbols, including prayer flags. On New Year's Eve they eat a special nine-dumpling soup, with tokens in it for telling their fortunes.

Some Tibetan Buddhist families in Canada have begun to celebrate Losar as Shambala Day, in memory of Gesar of Ling, the hero of the Tibetan national epic. Tibetans say that Gesar will return from the mythical land of Shambala if Buddhism and Tibet are in trouble.

GESAR OF LING

# Good luck!

Many of the special ceremonies and tokens used during Chinese New Year have to do with good luck for the coming year.

- Houses are swept and cleaned before the holiday, and then brooms are put away and washing is considered unlucky. Otherwise good fortune might be swept or washed away. Sweeping must be done inwards too, to keep good fortune in.
- The colour red is used everywhere, especially in the paper scrolls on doorways, because it signifies good luck. It is said that evil spirits fear fire, loud noises and the colour red.
- New clothes are worn, especially new shoes — bad luck will come to someone who steps on the ground in old shoes on New Year's morning!
- Debts are settled, for it is extremely bad luck to begin the New Year if you owe money or have kept something you borrowed.
- Any old quarrels are also settled, so that everyone can "begin again."
- A lion dance is performed to bring good luck and prosperity to the whole community. The lion (usually two dancers under a colourful papier-mâché head and cloth body) goes from street to street and door to door, accompanied by gongs, cymbals and firecrackers. People hang up gifts for the lion in their doorways: red packets with money inside or green vegetables like cabbages. If the lion "feeds" at your door, good luck will come to your home or business for the next year. Nowadays the lion may dance at other times of the year too, whenever future good luck is hoped for — for instance, at the opening of a new business.

---

# Make your own fortune cookies

Do you ever wonder how the fortunes get inside fortune cookies? It's easy! Start by writing fortunes on thin strips of paper. Here's how to make the dough for about two dozen cookies.

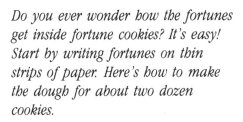

| | |
|---|---|
| 250 mL cake flour | 1 cup |
| 50 mL cornstarch | 3 Tbsp |
| 125 mL sugar | ½ cup |
| dash of salt | |
| egg whites from 3 large eggs (or 4 medium or small eggs) | |
| 125 mL vegetable oil | ½ cup |
| 50 mL water | 3 Tbsp |
| 2 mL lemon extract | ½ tsp |

1. Sift the first 4 ingredients into a bowl.
2. In another bowl, stir the egg whites and vegetable oil together with chopsticks or a fork. Add this mixture to the dry ingredients and mix until smooth. Stir in the water and lemon extract.
3. Heat the oven to 300°F (150°C). Lightly oil a cookie sheet and drop 4 rounded spoonfuls of the batter onto the sheet at a time. Use the back of a spoon to spread each spoonful into a circle about 7 cm (3 inches) across.
4. Bake until lightly browned, then remove the cookie circles one by one. Place your fortune in the middle, fold the circle in half and then bend it into a fortune cookie. The cookies will crack if they become too cool, so do the folding up while they're still warm.
5. Repeat until all the batter is used up. Don't forget to say "Kung Hey" (Happy New Year) when you give them away.

# Burns Night

*January 25*

Have you heard of Scottish "haggis"? It is a food, something like a huge sausage, that could almost be called the national dish of Scotland. Haggis plays a special part on Burns Night, the most celebrated Scottish event in Canada. All across the country, hundreds of Scottish clubs and societies meet to honour their favourite poet, Robert (or Robbie) Burns, who was born in 1759. Dinners held on this night begin with "piping in the haggis," a procession of people wearing kilts, led by a bagpiper. Then the master of ceremonies reads Burns's poem called "To a Haggis," cuts the haggis and says the famous Selkirk Grace, which Burns composed when he was a guest of the Earl of Selkirk in Scotland.

> Some hae meat, and canna eat,
> And some wad eat that want it:
> But we hae meat and we can eat,
> And sae the Lord be thankit.

The evening finishes with a famous Robert Burns song — "Auld Lang Syne."

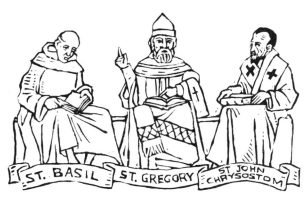

# Greek Day of Education

*January 30*

Greek-Canadian cultural centres all celebrate the Day of Education, or Three Hierarchs Day, on January 30. In Greece it is a school holiday because it is the anniversary for St. John Chrysostom, St. Basil and St. Gregory the Great. These saints, or "hierarchs," are honoured for their role in education in Greece. They combined ancient knowledge with Christian beliefs. Here in Canada, Greek teachers, educators and families attend special programs and performances in honour of the Three Hierarchs.

# Groundhog Day or Candlemas

*February 2*

Some people claim that watching for groundhogs is a very reliable way of predicting the end of the winter. However, scientists say groundhogs are only right about 30 per cent of the time. Here's the theory — try it yourself.

Groundhogs are supposed to come out of hibernation on February 2 to see how things are going above ground. If the sun is shining when they look out, their shadows are so dark against the snow that they are frightened back into their burrows. Those who believe in groundhog lore say this means there will be six more weeks of winter. However, if it is cloudy, the groundhogs are not frightened and do not go back into their burrows right away. This means that winter will be over before six weeks are out. The Iroquois have much the same idea, but they watch for bears instead of groundhogs!

February 2 falls halfway between the winter solstice and the spring equinox. It has been celebrated for thousands of years, since the time of the Celts. Today, Catholics call it Candlemas. See La Chandeleur next page.

# Black History Month

*February*

Black History Month was started in 1926 in the United States as Negro History Week. February was chosen because both Abraham Lincoln and Frederick Douglass have birthdays in February. (Lincoln was the president of the United States who freed the slaves during the Civil War, and Douglass was a black who worked to end slavery. He was a "conductor" on the "underground railroad," which smuggled runaway slaves out of the U.S. to freedom in Canada.)

A number of organizations across Canada observe Black History Month today, including the Ontario Black History Society, the Black Cultural Centre for Nova Scotia and the Black Historical and Cultural Society of British Columbia. Activities include performances and exhibits by black artists, storytelling, poetry readings, video screenings, lectures on early black history and even Caribbean song and dance parties.

# La Chandeleur

*February 2*

Newfoundland and the Maritimes once had a custom of house-visiting on February 2 called La Chandeleur. In Prince Edward Island, the custom was widespread among the Acadians until World War II. Today it is being revived in a few areas.

On La Chandeleur a group of house-visitors, dressed rather like mummers, go from house to house. The leader of the group carries a cane with a ring or a toy rooster on the top, decorated with ribbons. (Years ago the rooster was usually fake, but sometimes a real rooster was killed and used, then made into a stew for a feast later.) People give the Chandeleur

## Celebrate your heritage!

*A lot of provinces have declared the third Monday or the third week of February to be Heritage Day or Heritage Week. This is a time to enjoy your heritage by visiting a local historic site, making a family tree or recipe book or throwing a special heritage party or event. Why not try creating a whole new heritage celebration!*

visitors a gift of food and tie a ribbon onto the cane. Some of the food is donated to local people in need; the rest is eaten during a big party. It is customary to give the house-visitors a ribbon. To get it back, you have to go to the party — so the ribbon is a kind of ticket.

Pancakes were regularly served at these parties and still are today in French-speaking areas of Newfoundland and the Maritimes where Acadians live. These pancakes are sometimes made of potatoes, with a token cooked into them to predict the future. If a ring was a token of your coming marriage, and a coin was a token of wealth in the future, what do you think a bit of rag meant? You were in for a poor future! In northern New Brunswick, flipping the pancakes is an important way to tell your fortune. If a pancake falls on the floor while you flip it, you're in for bad luck too.

# Lent

*The seven weeks before Easter*

Lent is the period of 40 days (not counting Sundays) from Ash Wednesday until Easter Sunday. The word "Lent" is related to the old English word for spring and refers to the lengthening of the days. Lent used to be a period of fasting (or not eating) and great sacrifice for all Christians. These customs are a reminder of the 40 days Jesus spent alone in the wilderness, giving up his usual comfortable life, friends and food. So Lent is a time when many Christians fast and think about being like Jesus. Today it is not as strictly observed.

## Blessing the fleet

*In the village of Alert Bay, B.C., almost everyone depends on fishing for a living. The Nimpkish Band Council in Alert Bay organizes two ceremonies every year to bless the fishing fleet — one in June, when the salmon boats go out, and one in February, when the herring start to spawn. February can be awfully cold in Alert Bay — so cold that a fisherman's nets can freeze and prevent him from hauling in his catch. But somehow the herring, like the groundhogs, know that winter is on its way out. Blessing the fleet is a religious ceremony in which the whole community gathers to pray for the safety of the boats and a good harvest from the sea.*

## Out with winter!

*Swedish-Canadians have an old tradition of shooing winter out with the help of decorated birch branches. Brightly dyed feathers are fastened to the branches, probably in place of flowers. Today these are displayed during Lent, but at one time they were used symbolically, to sweep winter out of every house.*

## Football

*The game of football that we play today started out as a symbolic battle between winter and summer. These "battles" took place at Shrovetide. Players chased the ball (and each other) across fields and even through the middle of town. It was a rough-and-tumble game, and many townspeople boarded up their windows to keep them from getting broken.*

# Carnival, Shrovetide or Mardi Gras

*Before Lent begins*

Before the sacrifices of Lent begin, people have traditionally had rowdy celebrations to let off steam and use up food that has to be "given up" during Lent. Some of these were called Carnival, which means "the lifting off of meat," because meat was often given up for Lent. The festivities come when people are tired of winter and long for spring. At one time in Europe there were mock contests between the forces of winter and summer. People held big fairs and paraded through the streets in costume. Portuguese people in Canada still throw baby powder at each other or take aim with a water pistol during their Carnival!

The English called this time Shrovetide, which refers to being shriven, or making confession, in church. Mardi Gras, another name for these celebrations, is French for "fat Tuesday." It refers to the day you must use up cooking fats before giving them up for Lent. In Quebec today Mardi Gras celebrations are often held on the weekend before the beginning of Lent. Acadian Mardi Gras starts two weeks before Ash Wednesday. Dutch communities all across the western provinces have an annual Mardi Gras festival that moves from city to city.

There are lots of other names for this period before Lent. The Russians call the week before Ash Wednesday Butter Week because they try to use up all their butter. The Germans in Canada hold festivities called Fasching or Karneval. The Poles call it Zapusty. The Hungarians say Farsang, and hold a series of Farsang balls and suppers. Similarly, the Brazilian community of Toronto has an annual Carnival ball.

In Toronto a group of Swiss-Canadians have revived the old Carnival parade traditionally held in Basle, Switzerland. They make masks to wear and get a parade permit for 4 a.m.

on the Saturday night before Lent begins. Then they parade rowdily through the streets of Yorkville, a luxurious downtown shopping area, where they won't wake anyone up.

The Greeks call the final weekend before Lent Apokries, and they have festivities similar to Mardi Gras. On the Sunday it is customary for Greek young people to go to their elders and ask forgiveness for any wrongs they may have done in the past year. Macedonians do the same, and they call the day of forgiveness Prochtavanje. This is something like being shriven at Shrovetide, isn't it? All Orthodox Christians count Clean Monday (Kathara Deftera in Greek, Chist Ponedelnik in Macedonian) as the first day of Lent. They must clean up after the activities of Apokries and make sure no animal foods are left in the house.

## Shrove Tuesday or Pancake Day

*The day before Lent begins*

For many ethnic groups, Lent was traditionally a time to give up not only meat but also fats and dairy foods, especially eggs. To use up these foods before Lent began, the Italians cooked omelettes. Many British-Canadians still follow the old custom of making pancakes (or doughnuts or bannock breads) to eat at this time. So the day before Lent begins is often called Pancake Day, and many families and church groups in Canada have pancake suppers.

The Poles celebrate Shrove Tuesday with special doughnuts called *pączki*. The Portuguese make a pastry called *filhos malassadas*. The Germans make *Fastnacht Kuchen*, which means "cakes for the night before you fast." There is an old German superstition that good luck and a plentiful harvest will come to you if you eat *Fastnacht Kuchen* — which look like rectangular doughnuts — on Shrove Tuesday.

### Old Pancake Day customs

*At one time children took part in the general merry-making of Shrovetide by going "shroving" from house to house, asking for gifts of food and threatening mischief if they were refused. In fact, in some places in Britain, Shrove Tuesday was called Sharp Tuesday, because the children could throw stones or sharp bits of broken crockery at the door of anyone who didn't give them a handout! Some groups said:*

*Here I come, I never came before.*
*If you don't give me a pancake,*
*I'll break down your door!*

Memento, homo, quia pulvis est, et in pulverem reverteris.

If you don't, you may get boils, your hens won't lay and your crops will fail!

On Cape Breton, the old Scots idea was to eat as much meat as possible on Shrove Tuesday. If you didn't, your stomach would cry for meat continually until the next Shrove Tuesday. Vegetarians, get out your handkerchiefs!

## Ash Wednesday

*The first day of Lent, between February 3 and March 5*

Ash Wednesday is the seventh Wednesday before Easter. Some churchgoers are marked with ashes in the shape of the cross on this day, and this is how Ash Wednesday got its name. The ashes symbolize sorrow for things done wrong.

## Mid-Lent

*The fourth Thursday in Lent*

At one time, Catholic people in French Canada had a feast on the Thursday evening after the third Sunday in Lent, called Mid-Lent or Mi-Carême. This feast is an almost forgotten tradition today, except in some Acadian communities in Nova Scotia, such as Cheticamp on Cape Breton.

Long ago, children used to put on disguises on the evening before the feast and go from door to door asking for candies. The next night, after the feast, adults would take a turn wearing costumes and going visiting. In some Acadian communities in the Maritimes, an old woman called Mi-Carême was supposed to bring treats for Mid-Lent. The children stayed up late, waiting for her to pass through their village. Some would even hang up a stocking or a woollen hat before bedtime. Does she remind you of St. Nicholas?

Teenagers who went house-visiting would wear disguises so they could play tricks and make mischief without getting punished. Sometimes a group of Mi-Carêmes would arrive with snow hidden in their clothes. Then they began to dance — and sent snow everywhere! Or one dancer might be disguised as an animal to scare you. It seems rather like mummering, doesn't it?

Today in Cheticamp, Mi-Carême is celebrated on four or five nights of the Mid-Lent week. Costumes are elaborate and meant to disguise the visitors completely. Often Cheticamp natives living as far away as Boston will come home without telling their families, "pour courir la Mi-Carême." The challenge is to see if their own relatives and friends can recognize them beneath their masks and costumes! The whole community has fun during this sombre week in late winter.

# Valentine's Day

*February 14*

Valentine's Day is often called St. Valentine's Day. As you might expect, there probably was a person named Valentine who became a saint. What you might not expect, however, is that there seem to have been *two* St. Valentines. No one knows for sure why these two men, both of whom were imprisoned and killed for being Christians in the 3rd century A.D., should be associated with lovers. One story is that one of the St. Valentines wrote a letter thanking the jailer's daughter for her kindness, and signed it "your Valentine." A more likely story is that the two saints died on February 14, which in Roman times was the night before a festival called Lupercalia. The Roman festival had a lot to do with fertility, and probably some of those customs got attached to the saints' day once Christianity became the main religion in Europe.

Today, February 14 is the day to tell people that you love them. Many classrooms have valentine mailboxes, and all the

## Dear Valentine

*The very first valentine card is said to have been sent by the Duke of Orleans, imprisoned in the Tower of London, in 1415. Valentine cards were made by hand for centuries, until the first printed cards, sold in 1809, started a Victorian fad that continues today.*

*Some cards have old verses on them such as:*

*Somebody loves you, deep and true,*
*If I weren't so bashful, I'd tell you who!*

*Others have tricky verses, which take a bit of deciphering, like this:*

| Read | see | that | me. |
|------|-----|------|-----|
| up | will | I | love |
| and | you | love | you |
| down | and | you | and |

*This Valentine's Day try a new kind of card. Have everyone in your group fill in the blanks in this sentence: "I like (name of person) because _____." Write a sentence for each person in the group. When the sentences are cut apart, all the slips of paper for one person get glued onto a giant paper heart for him or her.*

Knock, knock

Who's there?

Olive.

Olive who?

Olive you!

children wait anxiously to see how many valentine cards they have been sent. Older people often give each other flowers, chocolates or other small gifts. It used to be the custom to send cards or give gifts anonymously, which means without signing your name or leaving a clue to your identity. In Quebec, people secretly delivered rude or insulting valentines, sometimes with caricature drawings, on St. Valentine's. No wonder many people never opened their mail on February 14!

## Sarasvati Puja

*Late January or early February*

Hindu students have a special day of worship called Sarasvati Puja in honour of the goddess of learning, whose name is Sarasvati or Saraswethi. On this school day they do no schoolwork! In fact, the tradition is to put your notebooks and pens around the image of this goddess on her shrine, to receive her blessing. Many Hindus believe that children should not learn to read or write before they turn five and have celebrated Sarasvati Puja.

Sarasvati, the goddess after whom the festival is named, is often shown riding on a swan. Hindus believe that swans symbolize the ability to tell right from wrong. Swans are thought to be so good at this they can even separate milk from water after they are mixed together!

## Hindu gods

Hindus believe God expresses himself (or herself) in the forms of different gods and goddesses (or "dieties"), each representing a part of life. There are essentially five different categories of deities: Surya, the ancient sun god; Shiva, the unchanging or destructive form of God; Shakti, the dynamic female aspect; Ganesh, who removes all obstacles; and Vishnu, the preserver (who has two famous incarnations, Ram and Krishna). Most Hindu deilies relate to one or another of these categories.

To make things more complex, however, different regions of India may give the same Hindu deity different names. For instance, Durga and another well-known, rather fearsome goddess called Kali are almost the same and are both related to Shiva, the destroyer. They may also be referred to as Shakti, the female version of divine energy. In a sense, these goddesses are like the Western idea of Mother Nature, both harsh and kind.

With all of its different divinities, Hinduism permits great freedom of worship. A Hindu prays to the particular form of God that appeals to him or her the most. The image for each stage of worship is called that person's ishtadevata. Even though you may have your own ishtadevata, you must respect the ones chosen by other worshippers. In Canada, in fact, many Hindu family altars include an image of Jesus Christ because of their respect for others' beliefs. Such tolerance of other ways and forms of life is an important part of Hinduism. It also explains why many Hindus are vegetarians.

All the great world religions include the idea of life after death, but Hinduism and Buddhism think of future life in terms of "reincarnation." This means to be born again in another body. Hindus and Buddhists think of reincarnation as a chance to come back to earth and undo any past wrongs, so that good will eventually triumph.

No one knows exactly when or how Hinduism began. Its tolerance and its ability to absorb other cultures has helped it survive for many hundreds of years. Over the centuries, many saintly Hindu leaders, or gurus, have found followers. Some of them have formed separate religions — Jainism, Buddhism and Sikhism, for instance, were developed by the followers of Mahavir, Buddha and Nanak, all originally Hindu. There are about 70,000 Hindus in Canada.

**Surya**     **Krishna**     **Vishnu**

# Nirvana Day

*February 15*

Mahayana Buddhists are one type of Buddhists. Many of them are Japanese. They celebrate this date as the anniversary of Buddha's death, or passing away. For Buddhists, this is not a sad day, just a time to remember that the Buddha moved from one state of being to the next. Some Mahayana Buddhists also join in the triple celebration held in May in Canada by all the different Buddhist groups (see pages 138-139).

# Shiva Ratri

*Mid-February*

All Hindus celebrate this "night of the great Lord Shiva" (*ratri* means night). To mark the holiday, they fast for 24 hours on Shiva Ratri and hold four worship ceremonies, or *pujas*, during the night.

An important item in the *puja* ceremonies is the leaf of the *bel* tree. (This tree doesn't grow in Canada so dried *bel* leaves are imported.) The *bel* tree is thorny, and its fruit is supposed to be very soothing for your whole body, especially to cool you in the heat. Despite the thorns, there was once a hunter who spent the night in a *bel* tree, having lost his way home — and also his food. At the foot of this tree there was a stone *lingam*, or shrine, to Shiva. The Hindu legend is that the hunter made some dew drops and leaves from the tree fall on-to the *lingam*. Although the hunter's action was accidental, Shiva was pleased to be worshipped. The idea behind Shiva Ratri is that even a little devotion is good and pleasing to the gods.

## Hamantashen cookies

These three-cornered cookies are traditionally baked at Purim. They're modelled after Hamen's three-cornered hat. This recipe comes from Sandra Kaminker.

| | |
|---|---|
| 125 mL butter | ½ cup |
| 125 mL margarine | ½ cup |
| 375 mL sugar | 1 ½ cups |
| 2 eggs at room temperature | |
| 5 mL vanilla | 1 tsp |
| 10 mL orange juice | 2 tsp |
| 5 mL orange rind, grated | 1 tsp |
| 750 mL all-purpose flour | 3 cups |
| 10 mL baking powder | 2 tsp |
| 2 mL salt | ½ tsp |

1. In a large bowl cream together the butter and margarine. Slowly add the sugar in a continuous stream. Beat until the mixture is light and fluffy.
2. Add the eggs one at a time. Beat well after each addition.
3. Add the vanilla, juice and rind.
4. Sift the dry ingredients together in another bowl. Using an electric mixer on low speed, gradually add the dry ingredients to the other mixture and mix until the flour disappears. Cover the dough with plastic wrap.
5. Chill the dough for at least one hour or overnight.
6. Preheat the oven to 350°F (180°C) and grease a cookie sheet.
7. Divide the dough into 3 parts and roll each out to ¼" thick. Cut in 3" or 4" rounds. Put a spoonful of filling in the centre of each and make 3-cornered shapes by bringing the sides together and pinching them together where they meet. Leave an opening in the centre.
8. Place on a greased cookie sheet and bake for 15 to 25 minutes or until lightly browned.

## Hamantashen filling

| | |
|---|---|
| 250 mL pitted stewed prunes | 1 cup |
| 125 mL raisins | ½ cup |
| 25 mL walnuts | 2 Tbsp |
| juice and rind of ¼ lemon | |
| 25 mL bread crumbs | 2 Tbsp |
| 50 mL sugar | ¼ cup |
| 10 mL honey | 2 tsp |

1. Put all the ingredients in a blender or food processor and purée.

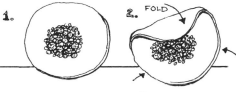

# Purim

*February or March*

Purim is a merry Jewish holiday, sometimes called the Feast of Lots. The Hebrew word *purim* means "lots." Drawing or casting lots is similar to rolling dice. The origin of Purim is found in the famous story about casting lots for the lives of the Jews, from the Book of Esther in the Bible.

Esther was a brave Jewish woman married to the Persian King Ahasuerus. The King had a mean prime minister named Hamen, who tricked the king into agreeing to kill all the Jews in his kingdom. Hamen decided the day for the killing by casting lots with the *purim*. But Queen Esther overheard his plan, told the Jews the date and helped them to be armed and ready to defend themselves. The Jews succeeded and Hamen was discredited. Purim is still held to celebrate that historic victory. It is a day when Jews remember that evil can be defeated if people of good faith work together.

*A gregger*

The celebration of the Feast of Lots includes a banquet at home, sending gifts of food to friends and to poor people, and a public reading of the Megillah, or the scroll of Esther. Children swing a very loud noise-maker (called a *gregger*) to drown out Hamen's name whenever they hear it read out loud — or they stamp, clap, boo or hiss. Everyone joins in. Outside the synagogue, people dress up like the various characters in this dramatic story, and sometimes the whole drama is acted out. As well as plays, there may be Purim masquerade balls and parades.

The special treat eaten at Purim is a kind of three-cornered, filled pastry called *hamantashen*.

## Ayyam-i-ha, Baha'i Intercalary Days

*February 26 - March 1*

"Intercalary" means inserted into the calendar — like Leap Year Day. Baha'is have four or five intercalary days every year, called Ayyam-i-ha. The Baha'i religious calendar is organized into months that are 19 days long. Each month is named for one of the attributes of God such as Baha, which means glory. And each is ushered in with a gathering called the 19-Day Feast. The Baha'i year is made of 19 of these 19-day months, with a few days left over for hospitality and charity. These extra days begin on the evening of February 26 at sundown, every year, and finish at sunset on March 1. In a Leap Year, there are five intercalary days; in other years, just four. The Baha'i intercalary days have no religious importance, but they do precede a month of fasting, as Mardi Gras precedes Lent. Baha'is exchange gifts and hold parties during the intercalary days and often host public meetings to share the Baha'i faith.

# Leap Year Day

*February 29*

Do you know anyone with a birthday on February 29? How does he or she celebrate it, and what happens when there is no 29th day in this month of 28 days? Leap Year Day is not an annual event — it occurs every fourth year, at the end of February, our shortest month. The proper name for a year with an extra day is "bissextile" — 1988 and 1992 are bissextile years.

No one knows for sure where the term "leap year" came from. It may have come about because February 29 had no legal status in the old courts and was thus "leapt over," or because all fixed dates such as birthdays that occur after February 29 "leap" forward, skipping one day.

There is an old tradition that women may ask men to marry them on this day — but the Scots believed women had to show their red petticoats to give warning! Supposedly this custom comes from the time of St. Patrick, in Ireland, who agreed to St. Bridget's idea that every fourth year it should be women's turn. Although he agreed to the idea, he turned her down in marriage!

# Prvi Mart

*March 1*

Macedonian-Bulgarians in Canada have an Old World custom of exchanging *marteniki* on or about March 1. *Marteniki* are little red-and-white tokens made of coloured threads, which people wear pinned to their lapels. *Marteniki* were once just little twists of red and white thread that were supposed to be thrown after a stork or swallow to help them build their nests. In Canada today, parents usually tell their children to throw *marteniki* down for the first robins they see.

Because *marteniki* are red and white and have old associations with luck and fertility, they have come to be rather like valentines. The custom is sometimes commercialized now, so you can get miniature belt buckles, bagpipes, shepherd's flutes, even figures of tiny men and women, all made of red and white thread! The pin may be attached to a greeting card that says something like ''Chestito Baba Marta,'' or ''Happy March First.''

## St. David's Day

*March 1*

St. David's Day is an important national day for Welsh people. St. David lived in the 6th century and probably died on March 1, 544 A.D. Today he is the patron saint of Wales. In Alberta and other provinces — wherever the Welsh community is big enough — St. David's Day is celebrated with storytelling, singing and banquets. Church services include lots of Welsh hymns as well. You may be able to spot Welsh men or women on March 1: the Welsh wear daffodils in their lapels or leeks in their hatbands as emblems of their homeland.

## Haru Matsuri, Japanese Spring Festival

*First weekend in March*

The Japanese Cultural Centre in Toronto holds a Spring Festival on the first weekend in March, long before the first day of spring and even before there are many signs of spring. It combines craft, dance and martial art demonstrations with two older festivals for Japanese children.

Hina Matsuri, or the Dolls' Festival, was traditionally held

on March 3. It is also called the Girls' Day of Japan, a day giving special attention to girls. Ceremonial dolls and miniature household objects are arranged in honour of the girls in each family on this day. Boys' Day, or Tango-No-Sekku, was the traditional day to honour the sons of each home. It was celebrated on May 5.

In Canada, many Japanese customs were lost and never reclaimed because of the sad time during World War II when Japanese-Canadians were interned, or forced to live in special camps. Many families today combine the two old celebrations in honour of their children and treat the event like a birthday party. In Toronto they also go to the Spring Festival at the Japanese Cultural Centre where a traditional doll display, called Hina-Dan, is arranged on tiered shelves covered with red cloth.

For more spring festivals, see the next season!

# International Women's Day

*March 8*

Every year in every major city in Canada, there are International Women's Day rallies, demonstrations and concerts on the Saturday nearest to March 8. On March 8 itself (the anniversary of the first protest march against terrible working conditions for women textile and garment workers in New York City, in 1857) there are also labour demonstrations and special activities related to women's rights. Women in Canada no longer struggle to gain the right to vote, but they do use March 8 as a time to celebrate women's history (often called "herstory"), to demand better day care or health service improvements and to express their concern for inequality everywhere in the world. In 1985, for instance, the Toronto International Women's Day theme was one of support for black civil rights in South Africa.

The song "Bread and Roses" has become a kind of theme song for International Women's Day. It was written by James Oppenheim in 1912 and commemorates a textile strike in Lawrence, Massachusetts. The third verse is especially strong poetry: "As we come marching, marching, unnumbered women dead,/ Go crying through our singing, their ancient cry for bread./ Small art and love and beauty their drudging spirits knew./ Yes, it is bread we fight for, but we fight for roses, too."

## St. Patrick's Day

*March 17*

March 17, the anniversary of the death of St. Patrick, is the day the Irish celebrate being Irish. Although St. Patrick probably came from England or Wales, he lived in Ireland at about the same time as St. David. Very little is known about him. He is said to have been captured by pirates at the age of 16 and held as a slave for six years. After other adventures and times of study, he settled in Ireland, supposedly banishing all the snakes from the land. The Irish claim him as their patron saint because he spread Roman Catholicism throughout Ireland.

You may have wondered why little green shamrocks have become associated with St. Patrick's Day. The shamrock is a clover leaf with three parts, called a trefoil, common in Ireland. Some people say that the three parts are the footprints of angels. St. Patrick used these three-leaves-in-one to

### Victoria's annual flower count

*For most of Canada, there is no sign of green leaves or flower buds outdoors when it is time to wear green for St. Patrick's Day. But in Victoria, B.C., things are different. Spring arrives before St. Patrick's Day. When it does, one entire week is declared Flower Count Week. All over the city, people go out into their gardens and count the number of flowers (like crocuses, snowdrops or early daffodils) and buds they see. Schools even give students an hour off to take part in the count. Everyone phones the numbers in to a special tallying centre, and every day the grand total is announced. There is even a special graph of the count at the Eaton Centre. It makes you wonder how people living in the Northwest Territories feel, doesn't it?*

explain the Christian idea of the Holy Trinity: God the Father, the Son and the Holy Spirit. However, the early settlers of Ireland, the Celts, had treated the shamrock as a sacred plant long before St. Patrick. Once again, old beliefs were borrowed for newer Christian celebrations.

Everywhere across Canada people wear a shamrock or something green in recognition of St. Patrick — even if they are not Irish! Irish clubs and associations have special dinners and celebrations, complete with green beer, and in Montreal there is a St. Patrick's Day parade.

## When does spring come?

The farther north you go in Canada, the later spring arrives. Way up in Churchill, Manitoba, in fact, they are still celebrating winter in mid-April. Although the days are longer and the sky is often bright, there is still snow on the ground, and so they play snow golf and enjoy fireworks at their annual Aurora Snow Festival. See Toonik Tyme on page 124 for even more details of how snowbound Canadians celebrate the coming of spring.

# SPRING

Look on your calendar and you'll see that spring officially begins on March 20 or 21. However, look out your window in most parts of Canada and you'll see snow! But even though it still feels wintery, the days are definitely longer and brighter: the sun is winning against the darkness!

The word "spring" comes from old English and German words meaning leap. When spring finally arrives, the plants leap up — and so do our spirits! But this leap comes late on the calendar in Canada.

On the prairies, spring is called "the reluctant season." "Reluctant" means rather unwilling — a good way to describe our spring. The poet E. E. Cummings has wonderful phrases for this time of year. In his poem called "In justspring," Cummings says that the world is "mudlucious" and "puddle-wonderful." The Iroquoian Cayuga also had descriptive names for the spring months. They called March/April "Frogs Peeping," April/May "Many Frogs Peeping," May/June "Prepare Cornhills" and June/July "Berries Ripening." What words would *you* choose to describe spring in your part of Canada?

Chances are that, wherever you live, as soon as the ground is dry enough, you'll join your friends outdoors, playing old and new games. Do you have a favourite spring game? How about marbles? Traditionally, in Europe, marble games were only played in the spring, during the 40 days of Lent. Hopscotch, ball-bouncing and jump-rope skipping are very ancient spring activities too. At one time people thought that by jumping or dancing or rolling on the ground, they could wake the plants up!

For Canadian farmers, spring means ploughing the fields and planting the crops — but they too have to wait for the ground to dry out, and that may be weeks after the equinox. When the ground is finally ready to plant, farmers must hurry to get their seeds in because our growing season is short.

In Canada, spring doesn't last long. Before we know it we

are catapulted into summer. But in much of Europe, spring lasts longer, and there is time to relax and celebrate the arrival of warm weather, the new plant life and newborn animals.

Many of the spring festivals still celebrated in Canada share some common elements. Here are some things to watch for as you read through the festivals in this section:

- *foods or decorations related to new life or rebirth:* Many holidays feature eggs, a symbol of new life. Trees or tree branches are also given special treatment. Many trees look dead in winter, but seem to come alive in the spring. Ancient people thought that was magical!
- *fire ceremonies:* These were originally meant to strengthen the sun at the equinox.
- *the colour white:* This represents purity. People used to whitewash their homes in the spring to freshen them after the winter. Also, many festive costumes are white.
- *water:* Nothing could grow without it so it is sacred to life. And in spring there is usually lots of it, mostly in the form of melting snow and spring showers. Several spring festivals include sprinkling — or showering! — participants with life-giving water. *Sources* of water such as springs and wells have also been honoured since the earliest times, especially in the spring. If you know of any wishing wells, this is a good time of year to throw a coin in and wish for good crops, as your ancestors did.

Even if you don't wear white or spray your friends with water to welcome spring, you probably do get spring fever. After months of winter, everyone feels restless, and change is in the air. For Inuit families in Canada's Far North, spring is the start of the traditional period to travel between camps and settlements, visiting relatives. Like the Inuit, we all want to get outdoors and be more active in the spring. Though it may be short, enjoy it!

## Spring detective

When does spring come in your *area?*
Start looking for "clues" in March:

* look at bushes and trees and watch for buds
* search for the green tips of bulbs and early plants
* note what birds and animals are around and what they are doing
* check the bugs and earthworms; they are worth watching
* observe other people. Are they wearing different clothes or spending their time differently? Who is doing spring cleaning or house-painting? Is anyone growing garden plants and flowers indoors?

Use the clues you have found to establish which day has been the real first day of spring.

## Ouch!

You may talk of the very mild
    weather,
You may speak of the birds how they
    sing,
But when a man sits on the point of
    a tack,
It's a sign of an early spring.

## Skipping rhyme

Springtime is skipping season. Here's a good rhyme to chant while you skip:

All in together, girls!
This fine weather, girls!
I spy a nanny goat,
Hanging by its petticoat.
If we call your name,
You must run out...

Then start calling out names. When the skipper hears his or her name, he or she must run out — or be out.

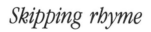

## Spring sing

This singing game can be played with a group of friends. It's sung to the tune of "Sur le pont d'Avignon." Here are the words:

*Won't you plant your seeds with care,
In the fields and in the gardens.
Won't you plant your seeds with care,
As they do in France so fair!*

You sing these words while you move around clockwise in a circle. But when you get to "France so fair," stop and stamp your feet three times, once for each word. Then sing new words for each verse, like this:

*Use your hands to plant them there,
In the fields and in the garden.
Use your hands to plant them there,
As they do in France so fair!*

Stand still for the verses and act them out, then circle around on the choruses. Remember to stamp on each "France so fair!" The fun part of the game is using as many awkward parts of your body as you can — try ears or even bums!

## Signs of spring

In Thunder Bay, spring is announced by the arrival of the first freighters coming up the Great Lakes as soon as the ice breaks up.

## Bad yolks

Teacher: Now if I lay three eggs here and three eggs over there, how many eggs will I have?
Student: Well, to tell the truth, I don't believe you can do it.

Q. What did the space cook see in the skillet?
A. An unidentified frying object.

## Anishnawbek Maple Fest

*Since the late 1960s, native people from as many as six reserves in the area have gathered on Parry Island, Ontario, to give thanks for the first sign of spring and life in the world. They meet on the last weekend in March for a time of solemn ceremonies, good food, contests and fun.*

*The weekend festival begins with the sweetgrass ceremony to give thanks to the Creator for the maple trees and to ask for blessing. Speakers address the trees and a symbolic first container of maple syrup. There are also ceremonial dances, which many festival attenders take part in.*

*Mr. and Miss Maple Fest are chosen every year, followed by the crowning of the Maple Queen. Then the comic old-time figures Mr. and Mrs. Sapsucker are chosen. All kinds of contests are held: cross-cut sawing, needle threading, snowshoeing, nail hammering, potato peeling — even pancake eating! There are children's and team races, fancy-dress competitions for both native and western-style clothes, a baby picture contest, craft displays and a talent show. A dance brings Saturday to an end. On Sunday morning there is a pancake breakfast before a special church service, and in the evening prizes are awarded for all the competitions. Finally there is a closing ceremony and a potluck supper with native breads, scones and corn syrup.*

# Sugaring-off Festivals

*March and early April*

Maple syrup season begins as soon as the sap starts running in the maple trees — usually early in March — and lasts three or four weeks. Nowadays the whole sap-gathering operation is streamlined, but at one time a group of workers or an entire farm family would camp out in the sugar bush. They worked for days, drilling holes in the maple trees, gathering the sap and boiling it down to make maple syrup. This process was called "sugaring-off."

Today maple syrup is thought of as a specialty, but a hundred years ago it was the only sweetener that many families had. Because sugaring-off was so important, children were often give a holiday from school in mid-March so that they could help with the task. Perhaps this is the origin of our present-day "March break."

The native people discovered the pleasures of maple syrup long before the settlers did. They would travel to the largest stands of maple trees during what they called the "sugar moon" or "maple moon." They camped in big groups, enjoying company after the long winter. They even held thanksgiving ceremonies for this springtime harvest. The Ojibwa, for example, celebrated their thanksgiving after the first flow of sap. Similar ceremonies are still held by the native people on Manitoulin and Parry Islands, on Lake Huron. The Iroquois hold two religious ceremonies: the Bush Ceremony to beseech the Creator to put the sap into the trees, and the Maple Ceremony to celebrate its flow. In the second ceremony everyone gathers to give thanks for the sap and to share a drink of "sap juice," followed by a feast that includes flint corn soup. A short version of the sacred peachstone betting game (see page 63-64) is also played.

When the buds on the trees finally burst open and the sap stops flowing, sugaring-off finishes with a glorious party. In

the Eastern Townships of Quebec, the celebrations are known as the Festival de la Cabane à Sucre, which refers to the little sugar house or shack where farmers do their boiling-down. Sugaring-off parties often include sour foods like pickles, to cut the sweetness of the syrup. Eggs boiled right in the maple syrup are another traditional food. French-Canadians have probably established the most lavish feasts for the season: they serve ham, omelettes, potatoes, cream, French bread and pancakes stuffed with bacon. And of course, every plate must be anointed with golden maple syrup!

In the Kitchener-Waterloo area of Ontario, the Mennonite farmers have a tradition of eating big farm sausages in long buns at sugaring-off time. Although these sausages look a lot like huge hot dogs, no one uses ketchup on them. Instead, they pour on the maple syrup.

Acadian French people in New Brunswick call their sugaring-off parties *licheries*. The tradition at these parties is to scoop up some very hot syrup on a big stick (when it is ready to turn to toffee), then scrape it off onto a little *palette* and lick it. In between all the sweetness, they eat salt cod and potatoes.

## Zoroastrianism

*This ancient religious system was founded by Zoroaster, a Persian, in the 6th or 7th century B.C. The Zoroastrian religion had a great influence on Judaism, and through Judaism, Zoroastrianism also influenced Christianity. The Three Kings, or Wise Men, who came from the East to worship Jesus when he was born were Zoroastrians.*

*The holy writings called the Zand Avesta set forth the principles of Zoroastrianism, based on the three truths: good thoughts, good words and good deeds. Zoroastrians believe in one true God, a universal spirit of good. They believe this spirit (Ahura Mazda) is always struggling with the spirit of evil (Ahriman). Zoroastrians teach that we can fight on the side of the good with our good deeds, and ultimately good will win. They also believe in life after death.*

*Zoroastrianism is followed today chiefly by two groups of Parsis, centred in Bombay, India. There are also Zoroastrians in Iran (once called Persia). Each of these three groups of Zoroastrians uses its own calendar. There are about 7 000 Zoroastrians today in Canada and the United States. In Canada there are about 200 families of Iranian Zoroastrians.*

# The Spring Equinox

*March 20 or 21*

The spring equinox and the fall equinox are the two days in the year when the hours of daylight and darkness are exactly equal: there are 12 hours of each. From March 20 or 21 until the longest day of the year (June 21 or 22), the nights will grow shorter and shorter. Many ancient people celebrated the new year on the spring equinox. In fact, the English (and therefore many early Canadians) had New Year's Day on March 22 until 1752. Today some groups still celebrate their new year at the time when the days start to grow longer.

# Ohigan

*March 22 to 29*

Ohigan is a week-long festival celebrated by Japanese Buddhists. To them, this time when night and day are of equal length symbolizes harmony in the universe. The idea of harmony encourages Japanese Buddhists to try to find their own inner harmony. So Ohigan is a time to remember the six perfections: charity, morality, endurance, endeavour, meditation and wisdom.

# Jamshedi Navroz

*March 21*

Zoroastrians call March 21 Jamshedi Navroz, which means new day of the month of Jamshed. It is a spring festival, involving a *jashan*, or thanksgiving ceremony. It is also an important time for Zoroastrian families to meet and enjoy special foods.

The month of Jamshed was named after an ancient king. Zoroastrians say that King Jamshed is the same person whom

Christians and Jews call Noah. Jamshedi Navroz is the anniversary of the time when Jamshed/Noah sent the animals from his ark out into the world after the flood. That was a new beginning, like a new year. Perhaps that is why Jamshedi Navroz is closely linked with Now Ruz, the Persian New Year (see below). Navroz is, in fact, just another way to spell Now Ruz.

## Now Ruz

*March 20 through April 2*

You have probably heard of Jack-Be-Nimble, who jumped over the candlestick in the nursery rhyme. But did you know that fire-jumping is an important custom for many groups of people? People with a Persian heritage (Iranians, Iraqis, Afghans and some others from the Middle East), for instance, jump over bonfires before their New Year celebration called Now Ruz (pronounced *no-ROOZ*). They do this to strengthen the spring sun and help it triumph over the dark and cold of winter.

Fire-jumping is just one part of the preparations for the Middle Eastern Now Ruz festival, which began more than 2 500 years ago. Although Now Ruz (which means new day) was originally a Zoroastrian festival, it is now celebrated on the first full day of spring, March 20 or 21, by people of every religion in Iran, Iraq, Afghanistan and some other parts of the Middle East. In fact, Now Ruz is a national holiday in Iran.

Many Canadians from the Middle East also celebrate Now Ruz around March 21. A celebration at the University of Toronto includes spring folk songs and dances from many cultures. At the heart of all Now Ruz celebrations are the ideas of creation — of life, the world and the first human being — and thanksgiving.

About two weeks before the equinox, preparations for Now Ruz begin.

- Wheat, celery or lentil seeds are scattered over water to soak and sprout. These are carefully tended in clay dishes so that they will be healthy and strong by Now Ruz Eve.
- A kind of clown called Haji Firuz makes people laugh at his antics and jokes at community gatherings. He sings and dances and wears a black face, as some mummers do. Also like the mummers, he pokes fun at everyone and criticizes the leaders or chief business owners. He gives out simple food gifts and often collects money from the crowds who watch him.
- Fire-jumping takes place on the last Tuesday of the Persian year, a few days before the equinox. It is called Shabe-Chahar-Shanbe-Souri, or "the night before the last Wednesday."
- People travel to be together with as many family members as possible for the holiday.
- Just before the equinox, the mother or oldest woman in each house breaks an old clay jar in front of the door. This means old quarrels are being thrown out, so that the New Year may begin in peace.

When these preparations are complete, everyone waits for the exact moment of the arrival of the equinox to begin the Now Ruz celebrations. They may even get up in the middle of the night if the equinox occurs then! At last the family gathers around a special table that is set with the *haft seen*, the seven symbolic objects whose names begin with the sound of "s" in the Persian language. These objects have changed as the years have passed, but often they include: sprouted seeds, for food and cultivation of the earth; coins, for wealth; sugar or candies and cookies, for sweetness in the New Year; vinegar, as a symbol of preservation; fruit such as apples, for happiness; flowers (*sonbol*, or hyacinths) growing in soil in a pot, showing the earth's productivity; and spices — for spice in our lives!

There are other symbols on the table too. A coloured egg symbolizes life and the world. An orange floating in a bowl of water is a similar symbol. Everyone hopes to see it move just at the moment when the New Year arrives because if the orange trembles, it proves the truth of the old legend that the earth trembles when the New Year begins. Every Now Ruz table also holds a mirror, because it is good luck to see your face and the faces of others. And there is always a candle for each member of the family. Finally, there is a holy book, such as the Zoroastrian Avesta or the Islamic Koran.

To make sure everyone is happy at the arrival of the New Year, it is the custom to eat a piece of candy while a passage is read from the holy book. Then people embrace and say, "Sad sal beh as in salha," which means "May you live a hundred better years!" Immediately after this, children must visit their parents. Parents often give small children presents of money, which they say comes from Baba or Amoo Now Ruz, or old Father (Uncle) Now Ruz. Does this sound like anyone else you know?

The early days of the New Year are meant for visits. Everyone holds an open house. First, the older people stay home to be visited by the younger ones. Then everyone visits people who had a death in the family in the past year; then newlyweds; then all their other friends and relatives. As in so many other New Year celebrations, this is a time for exchanging gifts, having new clothes and clean houses and resolving conflicts.

Every visitor is served sweets at Now Ruz, some of which are similar to the popular Middle Eastern pastry called *baklava*. Family dinners consist of rice, fish or chicken dishes. The most popular food is a dish of mixed vegetables, rice and fish. Every house will have this to share, or else *tachin* cakes, made of steamed rice and meat.

The Baha'i New Year is also called the Feast of Now Ruz. It

## Holi legends

*A legend about the Indian monkey god, Hanuman, explains the coloured water used at Holi. It is said that when Hanuman was a small child, he swallowed the sun, leaving the world dark and sad. The crops would not grow and the people didn't know what to do. So the other gods suggested that people try to make Hanuman laugh by rubbing colours on one another. Hanuman had never seen anything as funny as these squealing, laughing people, splashing colour about and running around like silly clowns. He gave a huge roaring laugh and up came the sun.*

*Another legend explains the bonfires at Holi. A demon called Holika ate all the children every spring. She even tried to destroy her nephew, a prince devoted to Krishna. Holika made a fire to throw the prince in, but by Krishna's grace, the prince was saved and Holika burned. When the Holi bonfires are lit today, many dirty things are thrown in to represent evil being destroyed. Its religious significance to Hindus is that God saves his devotees and destroys his foes.*

is welcomed with an 18-day fast during the last month of the Baha'i calendar, the Month of Loftiness. The fast ends with the feast on March 21, and the celebrations are similar to the ones described above.

# Holi

*March*

How would you like a day when you could squirt everyone with a water pistol or throw whole pitchers of brightly coloured water at your friends and family? That's just part of the fun on Holi, an ancient East Indian festival held at the time of the full moon in March. Although it is rather quietly observed here in Canada near the Indian date, it is the messiest festival of the year in India.

In northern India, March is when the winter grain is harvested, and Holi is a harvest festival. But Holi is also connected to the equinox, when the days begin to get longer. It marks the end of winter and the beginning of summer.

On the eve of Holi, Indians light huge bonfires to symbolically strengthen the sun. They shout and sing and dance around these fires until dawn. Then they pour water on the fires and make marks on their foreheads with the ashes, for good luck. After that, a wild coloured-water party begins, welcoming spring and summer. The fun and rejoicing may go on as long as three days. When it's time to clean up all the mess, it's also time to settle any old quarrels. To express their friendship, Indians eat a sweet and exchange hugs at as many houses as possible.

Children in India are given necklaces of yellow (the colour of spring) and white sugar for Holi, and everyone eats sweets and other delicacies. In Ontario these special foods are still enjoyed with much gaiety, and people often gather for evenings of dance and song. Everyone who attends wears a red

*tika*, a dot of coloured powder, on the forehead as a symbol of the spraying colours of Holi.

Holi is thousands of years old. One of the reasons it has survived this long is that people from every social group and religion can join in the fun. Laughing and playing, covered with different colours, people look the same.

Of course there is a religious element in this wild festival too. Hindus believe that the god Vishnu came to earth at one time as Krishna and played with the colours of life with his devotees. So in Hindu temples, people make offerings of coloured powders to Lord Krishna on Holi. In both India and Canada children make the same offering to their elders. They respectfully place coloured powders on their parents' feet.

# Greek Independence Day/ Evangelismou

*March 25*

Since 1821, the Greeks have observed March 25 as their national Independence Day. It commemorates the day they gained their freedom from Turkey. In Canada it is traditional to wear costumes in the style of Greek clothing from the early 1800s for Independence Day and to celebrate with programs of speeches and folk dancing.

On March 25 Greek-Canadians also celebrate another holiday — Evangelismou. This is the old Christian holy day to remember the Annunciation. (The Annunciation was the Archangel Gabriel's announcement to the Virgin Mary that she was to be the mother of Jesus.) In many European countries, it is called Lady Day.

Why was March 25 such a popular day for celebrating? At one time it was thought to be the date of the spring equinox. March 25 is also nine months before Jesus' birth on December 25. Nine months is the time it takes for a baby to be born

*Dance record*

*Did you know there are over 3000 different Greek folk dances? They have the biggest variety of any country in the world!*

## Waffle Day

*Swedish-Canadians call March 25 Waffle Day because of a mix-up. The Swedish word for Lady Day is Vårfrudagen, which sounds a lot like Våffeldagen, meaning Waffle Day.*

## Gandhi

*Have you heard of Mahatma Gandhi, the Hindu who had such a large effect on modern-day India? Gandhi was the leader of the non-violence movement from the 1920s through the 1940s, when India was struggling to be free of British rule and to find a solution to religious differences between Hindus and Muslims. Gandhi tried to establish the old religious idea of Ram-Rajya (which means the kingdom of Ram, or the kingdom of God) on the basis of non-violence. All Hindus look forward to Ram-Rajya, where, they believe, there will be no oppression of the weak by the powerful. India and Pakistan became independent, separate states in 1947. Less than six months later, Gandhi was assassinated, murmuring the name of Ram.*

(from conception to birth). How clever that early Christians added *their* celebration of the beginning of Jesus' life to the ancient celebrations of new life at the spring equinox.

# Ram Navami

*Late March or early April*

This Hindu festival celebrates the birthday of Lord Ram (see page 79 for more information on Hindu gods), also called Rama. On this day, devout Hindus fast, say special prayers and recite stories of Ram's life from the famous epic poem the Ramayana for 12 hours. Ram Navami is observed in all Hindu temples in Canada, where the emphasis is on thinking about how people can best help one another.

# April Fool's Day

*April 1*

Suppose you woke up one spring morning, turned on the radio and heard about this year's bumper spaghetti harvest in Italy. Would you suspect a joke? What if a radio reporter said she was watching a huge parade in Toronto, with the whole of Mount McKinley on a float? Would you realize that you were being fooled in honour of April 1? If not, you wouldn't be alone. The BBC once fooled hundreds of listeners with the spaghetti story, and lots of people called in to CKEY radio in Toronto to find out more about the parade.

Playing tricks on April 1 goes back a long way. As early as 1698 a London newsletter reported that several people had paid a penny each to see the annual ceremony of washing the white lions at the Tower of London's White Gate. Not only were there no lions, there has never been a White Gate at the Tower!

Even earlier in European history, there was an event called

the Feast of Fools. During this feast people switched their usual roles around. So a master might wait on his servant, and ordinary people — even boys! — got to be bishops or archbishops for the day. Sometimes the Feast of Fools included the Festa Asinaria, when people could act like "silly asses" in the church. For instance, an old shoe was once burned for "incense" to perfume the building! Although the Feast of Fools was held at Epiphany, it is thought to be one of the roots of April Fool's.

The tradition of April Fool's may go as far back as the early Holi celebrations (see page 100) or even to Noah and his ark. Jewish folklore tells that the first dove was sent out to look for land on April 1, and of course that trip was in vain. We still talk about people going on "a wild goose chase," and the Scots send April 1st messengers on meaningless errands. They call this "hunting the gowk," which means goose or fool.

Whatever the joke you play on April Fool's Day — switching salt and sugar, or setting the clocks to a false time — the fun is supposed to stop at noon. Otherwise, the tables will be turned on you, as this old English rhyme explains.

> April Fool's gone past,
> You're the biggest fool at last.
> When April Fool comes again
> You'll be the biggest fool then.

French- and Italian-Canadians sometimes call an April Fool an April fish — *poisson* or *pesce*. Why fish? Because at one time April Fool's fell in the zodiac sign Pisces, or the Fishes. Italian-Canadian schoolchildren sometimes cut out little paper fish and stick them onto another person's back. Then they laugh at the April *pesce*.

## Fool's soup

*Do you know the old story of stone soup? It tells of a group of wandering soldiers who trick some miserly villagers into sharing their food with them. First they borrow a pot, pour in some water and make a fire. Then they put in the first ingredient — a big rock. They taste this "soup" and pretend it is pretty good but just needs a few vegetables, some spices and a bit of meat to improve the flavour. The villagers are so intrigued that they gradually volunteer to bring all the things needed to make a truly delicious soup. The soldiers fool the people by starting with a stone, and in the end, everyone enjoys the soup together. Can you think of a way to turn stone soup into an April Fool's trick?*

## Good luck

*Next April 2, try this Sizdeh Bedar good-luck ritual. Tie blades of grass into a double knot and make a wish for the New Year. If you know someone who is old enough to marry, get him or her to tie a knot and wish for a good mate.*

HANS CHRISTIAN ANDERSEN

# Sizdeh Bedar

*April 2*

The 13th day after Now Ruz (see page 97) marks the end of the old Middle Eastern New Year celebrations. Thirteen was an unlucky number for the ancient people of the Middle East. Their Persian descendants today still think it's important to be close to nature and make a fun day on the unlucky 13th. So on Sizdeh Bedar, everyone leaves home for the day and goes on trips to the country or on picnics in nearby parks.

In Canada, April 2 is usually too cold for a picnic. But in spite of the weather, many Canadians with a Persian heritage follow the old custom of taking dishes of sprouted seeds from their Now Ruz tables out with them on Sizdeh Bedar and returning the seeds to nature, either by putting them in a field or by floating them down a stream. As you might guess, this custom was once a good-luck ritual for the crops. But there is another side to Sizdeh Bedar. Like April Fool's, it is a day to lie and play tricks on your family and friends. In fact these two special days are probably related.

# International Children's Book Day

*April 2*

April 2 is the birthday of the famous Danish storyteller Hans Christian Andersen. The International Board on Books for Youth (IBBY) chose this day to celebrate children's books around the world. Every year a special poster (with matching bookmarks) is made to commemorate International Children's Book Day. In 1990 it will be Canada's turn to design and produce the poster — watch for it! Celebrity author/illustrator tours and other events in honour of children's books are not held in April, however: they are usually clustered around Children's Book Week, the third

week in November in Canada. For more information about either of these special times, write to The Children's Book Centre in Toronto.

# Ch'ing Ming Festival

*April 5*

In China, Ch'ing Ming, the Clear and Bright Festival, is celebrated 106 days after the winter solstice, when the trees are budding and spring is definitely near. It is a time to wear pussywillows and visit family graves to clean them and make offerings. Probably these visits were a way of asking the blessings of the departed spirits on the coming farming seasons.

Chinese-Canadians also visit family graves on Ch'ing Ming, and there is often a family dinner afterwards.

# Hana Matsuri, or Buddha Day

*April 8*

Some Buddhists (mainly those from Japan) celebrate Hana Matsuri, the birth of Buddha, on this day. Hana means flower, and Buddha's birthday is a flower festival. One legend says Buddha was born in a lotus flower. In Canada these Buddhists also join in with another celebration of Buddha's birth in May (see page 138). This May celebration combines Buddha's birth with his enlightenment and death.

# Baisakhi

*April 13 or 14*

Baisakhi, known as the Solar New Year, is another spring New Year's celebration. Hindus, Buddhists, Jains and Sikhs from Sri Lanka, Bangladesh and India all celebrate this day.

Baisakhi is especially important to the Sikhs. It is a

## Sikhism

*Most Sikhs in Canada come from the fertile plains of the Punjab in northern India, where Sikhism began about 500 years ago. Its founder, known as Guru Nanak, was raised in a Hindu family and travelled widely, visiting many Muslim and Hindu holy men. After a divine trance, Nanak spoke these words, which form the basis of the Sikh creed: "There is one God, eternal truth is his name." Today Sikhs believe in one God, who considers everyone equal and does not divide people into social groups, as they were in the Hindu caste system (which forced people to live in certain ways and places, according to the caste they were born into). For Sikhs, devotion to God is the essential part of their religion, and service to other human beings is a practical way to show that love.*

## Kiri-bath (Sri Lankan rice squares)

*These tasty rice squares are traditionally served at New Year's by Sri Lankans. Rice and coconut, the main ingredients, are staple foods in Sri Lanka — and important fertility symbols.*

| | |
|---|---|
| 125 mL white rice | ½ cup |
| 375 mL water | 1 ½ cups |
| 125 mL flaked coconut | ½ cup |
| 25 mL sugar | 2 Tbsp |

1. Wash the rice and put it in a saucepan.
2. Pour the water over the rice and cover the pan. Bring the rice and water to a boil over high heat, then reduce the heat to low and cook for about 8 minutes, or until the rice is tender. It should look soupy at this stage.
3. Drain the rice in a strainer and save the water. Put the leftover water in a measuring cup and add enough cold water to make 250 mL (1 cup).
4. Put this water and the rice back in the pan. Add the coconut and sugar. Stir. Cook this mixture, uncovered, until all the water is gone.
5. Pour the mixture into a 2.0 L (8-inch-square) cake pan. Smooth it out with a spoon and let it cool for 20 minutes before putting it into the fridge. Chill for at least one hour.
6. When cool, cut into squares and top each one with a bit of jam or honey.

boisterous harvest festival in the Sikhs' homeland. Baisakhi is also the anniversary of the day their religious community was reorganized in 1699. At that time, Guru Gobind Singh, their tenth leader, initiated his first five disciples. So Baisakhi became the traditional day for people to be welcomed into the Sikh faith, in a ceremony called Amrit. Today, special music and hymns are performed on this date in Canadian *gurdwaras* (Sikh places of worship). Sikhs do not work on Baisakhi, and children are given special Baisakhi presents.

## Sri Lankan New Year

*April 14*

In Ontario the Sri Lankan community gathers for a ceremonial meal and a cultural program on the day after Baisakhi. They light traditional oil lamps and make speeches. It is a time for children to pay their respects to their parents and for families, friends and neighbours to exchange gifts and food. Sri Lankans from Sinhalese, Muslim, Tamil, Malay and Burgher groups all unite to celebrate their New Year together.

One Sri Lankan custom is the symbolic act of putting out every fire in the house at dusk, just as the old year ends. The next few hours are called *non-negathe*, which means "without fire," and it is a time for prayers and rituals. After that, the mother kindles new fires to prepare the first meal of the New Year. The special New Year curry requires seven different fruits and vegetables. Betel leaves are a traditional New Year's gift, symbolizing love and the seeking of forgiveness.

## Bon Chol Chhnam

*Around April 13*

People from Kampuchea (formerly called Cambodia) also celebrate their New Year, Bon Chol Chhnam, at this time. In Kampuchea (like Laos) April is the beginning of the rainy

season, when the work of harvesting the old crop is finished and the new farming season begins again. Everyone wishes for good crops in the New Year. As in many other New Year traditions, this is a time for presents, new clothes and being sorry for wrongs you have done in the past. Mothers are especially careful not to spank their children around the New Year.

Wherever Cambodians have settled in Canada, families and friends gather to celebrate Bon Chol Chhnam with prayers and a special meal. In Montreal, where there are more than 4 000 Cambodians, the Cambodian Association holds an annual religious program on the morning of Bon Chol Chhnam. As many as 1 000 people attend to hear their Buddhist monk make his ritual speech. This is followed by a ceremonial meal, eaten Eastern-style with fingers, while sitting on beautiful cloths spread over the floor. At night, everyone gathers for a party with more speeches, traditional food, music and dancing. Smaller Cambodian communities sometimes have to wait until a monk can visit them to have a formal gathering and officially welcome the Cambodian New Year.

# Songkran

*Around April 13*

Buddhists throughout Southeast Asia celebrate the solar new year at the same time as Baisakhi. The Thai New Year celebration, Songkran, is a three-day-long religious holiday. It involves lots of water play and ritual baths, rather like Holi (see page 100).

In Thailand homes are ritually cleaned to get rid of unwanted spirits before Songkran. And people sprinkle water on Buddhist monks who visit their homes, on statues of the Buddha and on one another for good luck too. Here in Canada,

## New Year's in April?

*Most Canadians celebrate New Year's in January. But people from Southeast Asia celebrate their New Year in mid April. Why? New Year's celebrations such as Songkran and Baisakhi are solar new years; they are based on the position of the sun in the sky. You might expect a solar new year to take place at an important sun day such as the spring equinox or the summer solstice — not some time in between those two dates. But because Southeast Asians base their calendar on the movement of the moon and stars as well as the sun, they celebrate their solar new year in mid-April.*

it's too cold for water play. Instead, Thai people gather for a party that includes traditional dance performances. People bless one another, especially the coordinator of the party! They wish one another long life, wealth, health and happiness. On the Sunday nearest to Songkran, Thai people in Canada attend a special religious ceremony to welcome the New Year.

## Bun-pi-mai-lao

*Around April 13*

The Laotian New Year is very similar to the Thai Songkran and sometimes even shares the same name. The temple service for Bun-pi-mai-lao includes washing the image of Buddha with a mixture of water, perfume and flower petals and then sprinkling the same mixture on everyone in attendance. The rainy season begins at this time in Laos, so people there get wet a lot!

## Pesach or Passover

*Late March or April*

Pesach is the Jewish festival of freedom, which is held every spring to celebrate the exodus of the Jews from Egypt, where they had been slaves, about 3 200 years ago. (The word "exodus" means going out or going forth. It is also the name of the second book of the Bible, which describes how the Jews escaped through the Red Sea and wandered in the desert for 40 years.)

Before this famous exodus, however, there were two much older Hebrew festivals at the same time of year. One was a feast held by wandering herdspeople in Judah, just when it was time to move their flocks from their winter pastures. At this festival, called Chag ha Pesach, every family killed a year-old sheep, goat or steer and ate it all during one night. To protect themselves from evil, they spread the blood of the sacrifice around their tent openings and did not break the bones. The idea was that one animal had been offered to God in order that the others might be protected, or "passed over." This is the origin of "Passover." Passover also refers to the passing over of the homes of the Hebrews in Egypt during a plague. Although the first-born sons of Egyptian families became sick and died because of the plague, the Hebrew children were unharmed.

The other ancient festival was called Chag ha Matzot, or the Feast of the Unleavened Bread. It was held in the farming regions of Palestine, north of Judah. In that area, spring was the time to harvest the barley, the first grain to ripen. The first barley sheaves to be harvested were ground into flour, baked into a ceremonial bread called *matzah* and eaten in thanksgiving. This special bread was made with just new flour and water. It contained no yeast or other leaven to make it rise. When the Hebrews left Egypt many centuries later, they were in too much of a hurry to let their bread rise. And so they ate a similar unleavened bread on their journey. Since then, the only bread Jewish people eat during Passover is *matzah*. Today *matzah* is like a big, flat, square cracker. It is the key symbol of the Passover festival and is often called the bread of freedom. Some Jews say that freedom is hard, and not easily won, and so their bread is hard.

Today Pesach is an eight-day holiday. Special dinners, called *Seders*, are held on the first two nights. Special ceremonies on the last two nights mark the end of the week of the festival.

Just before Passover begins, after the house has been thoroughly cleaned for the holiday, many Jewish families join in a traditional game. Carrying a candle, the father and the children search for any last traces of *chametz*, or leavened bread and cakes. They use a feather to brush up any crumbs, and every speck is burned at the end of their search.

The Passover dinner, or *Seder*, is both a meal and a worship service. Other symbolic foods besides *matzah* are eaten. The significance of each of these foods is explained as the evening progresses:

- salt water represents the tears of the Jews when they were slaves in Egypt.
- green vegetables such as parsley or celery to dip in the salt water are tokens of spring, the Pesach season.
- hard-boiled eggs to dip in the salt water are symbols of life and fertility.
- horseradish, called "bitter herbs" in Hebrew, is symbolic of the bitterness of slavery.
- a special mixture of grated apples and nuts called *charoset*, eaten between two pieces of *matzah*, symbolizes the mortar between the bricks of the buildings that the Hebrew slaves were forced to build for the Egyptians.
- a symbolic bone recalls the ancient sacrifice at Chag ha Pesach.
- wine, which is poured out at five times during the *Seder*, stands for the sweetness of life and the fruits of the vine.

The explanations of the foods and the whole story of the exodus are written in a special book, called the Haggadah. Everyone reads it aloud together. The children at the *Seder* ask four questions about why this night is different from all other nights. There are also Pesach songs to accompany the readings. The whole event is almost like a play, acted out around a festive table.

At the end of the *Seder*, there is another game, like the search for *chametz*. This time the children all hunt for a special piece of *matzah*, called the *afikoman*. In many families, whoever finds the *afikoman* gets to demand a prize from the adults at the *Seder*. What would you ask for?

**Seder plate**

# Coloured sand designs

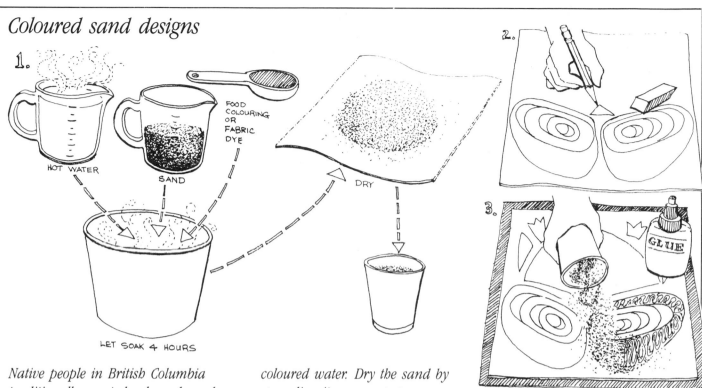

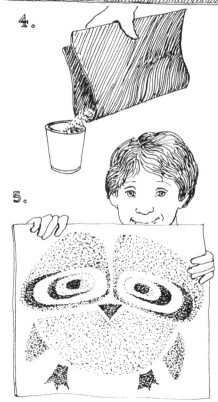

Native people in British Columbia traditionally created coloured sand designs on the ground to celebrate a natural event such as the beginning of spring. You could make similar designs on a piece of cardboard, using sand you dye yourself. This project must be done in stages. So pick a day when you have lots of time.

1. Start by making several colours of sand. To do this, mix 15 mL (1 Tbsp) of liquid fabric dye or food colouring with 250 mL (1 cup) hot water in an old plastic container. Use a separate container for each colour. Add about 125 mL (½ cup) sand and let it soak at least 2 hours. The sand will take on the colour of the dye and sink to the bottom of the container. After 2 or more hours, slowly pour off the coloured water. Dry the sand by spreading it on newspaper or paper towels in a warm place, then pour it into a paper cup.

2. Draw a design on a piece of cardboard. Use a pencil so that you can erase if you make mistakes.

3. Choose certain parts of the design to be all one colour. Cover these areas with white glue. Working over some newspaper, shake on one colour of sand let it dry for a few minutes.

4. Tilt the cardboard so that the loose sand falls onto the newspaper. Pour the leftover sand back into the cup.

5. Continue gluing and ''sanding'' different parts of the picture with different colours until it's finished.

## Ukrainian eggs

*Ukrainian* pysanky *are probably the most elaborately designed Easter eggs of all. They are tokens of love and respect and of a wish for health and happiness. At Easter, a pysanka blesses every Ukrainian home, bringing God's grace into the family. The colours and the designs of* pysanky *are all symbolic. Yellow, for example, is the symbol of light and purity. A star signifies God's love, and a straight line encircling the egg stands for the continuous thread of life. When Polish people make their* pysanky, *they believe the very first egg should be decorated with a plough design, because all farmwork begins with ploughing in the spring. The only words ever written on* pysanky *are "Khrystos voskres," which means "Christ is risen."*

*There is an old Ukrainian legend that claims the fate of the world depends on continuing the custom of making* pysanky: *otherwise a chained monster will be released who will devour us all! Certainly in Canada, the custom is very much alive. At the Ukrainian Museum of Canada, in Saskatoon, you can learn even more about this old, still living art. There are also Ukrainian museums in Winnipeg, Toronto and other cities.*

# Easter

*Between March 22 and April 20*

Many Christians believe that Easter is the greatest festival of the year. It is the holy day when Jesus came back to life, after being hung on a cross, or crucified, till he died. Easter celebrates the miracle of Jesus rising from his grave, called the Resurrection, after his death and burial. In the year 325 A.D., it was decided that Easter would be celebrated on the first full moon after the spring equinox. Why then? The idea was that pilgrims could travel late by the light of the moon to reach the Easter festivals.

In the northern hemisphere, Easter comes in the spring. Flowers and plants that have been buried under the snow begin to come back to life. Not only the plants are being reborn; young animals are being born and eggs are hatching. And so Easter — a religious festival celebrating Jesus' rebirth — also comes at a time of new life and rebirth in nature.

Easter and Passover are closely linked. Passover was celebrated just after the spring equinox for hundreds of years before the death and resurrection of Jesus. The Last Supper, which the Bible says Jesus attended the night before he was crucified, may have been a *Seder* meal, celebrating the Passover festival.

The early festival of Chag ha Pesach gave its name to Passover (in Hebrew it is Pesach) and to many of the later Christian Easter festivals. In Spain, Easter is called *Pascua de florida*, in France *Pâques*, in Italy *Pasqua*, in Scandinavia *Påsk*. Why do we use such a different word in English? The word Easter comes from the name of a Saxon goddess of the dawn, who was worshipped each spring. In Old English she was called Eastre or Eostre.

## Easter eggs

One of the best known of all Easter symbols is the egg. New life hatches from eggs, and so they have symbolized life and regeneration for many people. Centuries before the first Easter, the people of China, Greece, Persia and Egypt gave eggs to celebrate the annual revival of nature.

In some places an egg is the symbol of the sun, or of the universe itself. In one creation myth, the world began as chaos in the form of an enormous egg. Its contents were all disorganized, so that chaos finally split the shell. Then the upper shell formed the dome of our sky and the rest became the earth.

The early Christians saw eggs as emblems of Jesus' birth and adopted them as gifts for Easter. Down through the centuries eggs have been brought to church to be blessed before they are given or eaten, and many Christians in Canada, such as members of the Eastern Orthodox churches, still practise this custom.

## Easter rabbits

In Canada today Easter eggs are said to be delivered by the Easter Bunny. But in other parts of the world, they are brought by doves, cranes, even foxes. In France, children think that all the church bells fly away to Italy on Good Friday and bring the eggs back with them on Easter morning. Perhaps this idea came about because church bells in France are silent until Jesus' resurrection on Easter morning.

Where did the idea of an Easter bunny come from? The goddess Eostre had a hare (a rabbit cousin) as her sacred animal. Both rabbits and hares produce large litters of babies and often have several in one season, so they have always been associated with fertility. This is why they were connected to the early spring festivals and later to Easter.

## Egg games

*In Port McNeill, B.C., the whole community gets involved in a giant Easter egg hunt. But hunting for eggs isn't the only Easter game. Have you ever tried egg-tapping? The object is to see whose egg is stronger as you tap the end of your egg against the end of a friend's. The all-time record is held by an egg that cracked 16 others before it too broke. Can you "tap" that? Serbian and Romanian children get their tapping eggs from the priest in their churches, after he has blessed them.*

## Red eggs?

*Red is the favourite colour for Easter eggs in many parts of Europe. Why? Because of the old belief that red is a magic colour. Witches, for example, wore red petticoats. Some types of red berries were thought to keep away evil spirits. As far back as 900 B.C. the Chinese exchanged red eggs at their spring festival.*

## Mad wabbits

*Q. What do you get if you pour boiling water down a rabbit hole?*

*A. Hot cross bunnies.*

## Blown eggs

Easter eggs won't go bad if you blow out their insides. Here's how you do it.

1. Wash and dry an egg.
2. Bore a tiny hole with a darning needle at each end of the egg. One hole should be bigger than the other. Break the yolk inside with the needle.
3. Blow — hard — through the larger hole until the raw egg runs out (make sure you do this over a bowl) and the shell is empty. (Save all the raw egg for cooking.)
4. Decorate as you wish using felt pens, glued-on ribbons and feathers and so on.

There are lots of things you can do with blown eggs after you decorate them. Here are some ideas from other countries, but if you try them, be prepared to eat lots of scrambled eggs!

- String whole blown eggs like beads and hang the egg garland across a window. To string the eggs use wire or a big needle and thread. Or tie a thread to a small piece of toothpick and poke it all the way into the eggshell. This will anchor the thread.
- Polish people thread blown eggs onto stalks of dried wild grass. Start from the bottom of the grass stalk and tie ribbon bows between the eggs. Stand the stalks in a vase or bottle.

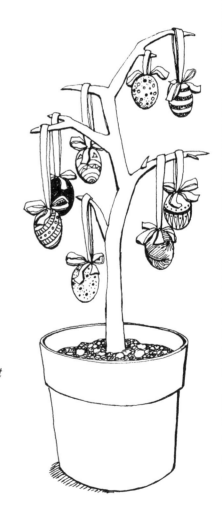

- Make an egg tree by planting a small tree branch in a flower pot and hanging blown eggs from it like Christmas-tree decorations. Many Central Europeans use pussywillow branches.
- If a blown egg breaks, make the parts into tiny baskets. Glue a short piece of ribbon or paper over the opening and fill the baskets with tiny treats. Then hang them on branches.

## Easter treats

The period of forty days leading up to Easter, called Lent, is a time of fasting for many Christians (see page 73 for more information on Lent). Many people give up eggs, dairy products and fats during Lent. When Easter comes, marking the end of Lent, it's time to eat all the things you've missed.

For many British people, the treats begin with hot cross buns. Most Easter breads are thought to be related to special wheat cakes prepared in pre-Christian days for the goddess Eostre, as offerings in her honour. Probably the crosses on hot cross buns were added in the early days of Christianity to make these old pagan treats appropriate to the Christian celebration of Easter. The Czechoslovaks have similar buns called Judas buns.

Breads and buns play an important part in Easter customs. The best known are probably the many variations of sweet egg breads, in lots of different shapes, often simply called *babka*. Hungarians make a giant double braid. Croatians twist their Easter loaves to look like babies in swaddling clothes. The Ukrainian *paska* is decorated with a cross and/or a braided circle. Italian loaves are shaped like a dove, the symbol of peace, and called *colomba pasquale*.

Some Easter breads also have eggs in the shell baked right into them. They become hard-boiled as the bread cooks. Southern Italians sometimes make wreaths of dough, with eggs at intervals around the circle. The Dutch make sweet buns shaped like nests, birds or flowers around an egg.

Puddings and cakes are also popular Easter foods. The Portuguese make a luxurious rice pudding, called *arroz-doce*, for an Easter treat, and the Finns make *mammi*, an orange-flavoured pudding with malt and flour. The Poles make cheesecake. The Romanians make a sweet cottage cheese and candied fruit dessert called *pasca* to eat along with their fancy bread. One Russian tradition is to shape this sweetened cot-

## Easter witches?

*When Swedish children think of Easter, they think of witches. Why? In northern Europe, people believed that witches rode out the night before May Day, or Walpurgis Eve, on April 30. May Day, like Easter, welcomes spring and the customs overlapped; witches became associated with Easter. Easter in Sweden includes:*

- *making a witch tree by hanging tiny home-made witches and birds, along with candies and blown eggs, on a painted tree branch*
- *dressing up like witches and leaving Easter Eve presents and messages in friends' letter-boxes*
- *going to fireworks displays, held to frighten off the witches*

*There is an old superstition that witches use empty eggshells as boats, and go out to sea to stir up storms. So when you eat a boiled egg, make sure you poke a hole through the bottom of the shell so the witch boat won't float.*

## Goodbye winter!

*Long ago in Bohemia, in eastern Europe, it was the custom to throw an effigy (a model something like a scarecrow) of winter into the water on Palm Sunday, singing:*

*"On the water flows death,
Summer breaks the spell of winter.
With Easter bread and red eggs
We celebrate summer."*

*What a lot of symbols!*

## An early Mother's Day

*If your mother is British, she might expect to celebrate Mother's Day on the fourth Sunday in Lent. In Britain that is called Mothering Sunday or Mother's Day. During the Middle Ages, it was the day to attend the main or "mother" church of the parish. You may be offered some simnel cake (like fruitcake made at Christmas) during coffee hour on this Sunday in Anglican churches in Canada. Simnel cakes are so much a part of Mothering Sunday in Britain that some people talk about Simnel Sunday instead.*

tage cheese into a tall pyramid or a tower. They use special wooden forms, bought through their church, to drain the cheese and mould it.

Greek-Canadian families exchange many different home-made pastries and breads on special visits before Easter. All the children long to taste the beautifully decorated treats, but they have to wait until Lent is over. They are told that, like Jesus, they have to suffer and learn to be patient. With all those goodies around, that's no easy matter.

# Palm Sunday

*The sixth Sunday in Lent, one week before Easter Sunday*

Palm Sunday is the last Sunday in Lent. It is the day Jesus entered Jerusalem on a donkey, surrounded by cheering crowds. Palm Sunday got its name because people tore green branches off palm trees to strew in Jesus' path, in celebration. In many churches today, little crosses made from palm leaves are given to the congregation on Palm Sunday.

Palm Sunday is celebrated in different ways by different people:

- The Germans have an old custom of giving every member of the family one brown egg from the *Palmhase*. If the *Osterhase* is the German Easter hare, or bunny, who do you think this *Palmhase* is?
- The Welsh call Palm Sunday "Flowering Sunday," because they have a tradition of tidying up family gravesites on this day. They decorate them with spring flowers, in preparation for Easter.
- In Canada, the Croatians prepare a bowl of special holy water and float some of the first spring flowers in it to wash away their sins on Palm Sunday.
- Czechoslovakian children take pussywillow bouquets to be blessed in church.

- The Syrian and Lebanese Christian communities in Ontario celebrate Palm Sunday in different special ways. Members of the Antiochian Orthodox Church watch the clergy and altar boys walk around the inside of the church carrying palm branches after the main service. And in the Maronite and Melkite congregations, Palm Sunday is referred to as the Children's Feast. The clergy and children also make a procession around the inside or outside of the church singing Easter hymns. The children all wear new clothes and carry lighted candles decorated with ribbons and flowers.

- Dutch children have a special Palm Sunday tradition that has been borrowed by some Girl Guides and Boy Scouts. They carry a branch or stick, shaped like a cross, decorated with greenery, little flags, oranges, strings of sweets, raisins and nuts and small bread figures. This *Palmpaasstok* may even have a bread rooster at the top, representing the cock who crowed on the morning of Good Friday. However, roosters, who crow to greet the sun, were probably symbols of the sun long before Christianity adopted them.

## Holy Thursday

*Four days after Palm Sunday, three days before Easter*

Jesus ate the Last Supper and washed the feet of his disciples on Holy Thursday, also called Maundy Thursday. ("Maundy" probably comes from the Latin word *mandatum*, which means a command and refers to the new commandment of love that Jesus gave to his disciples at the Last Supper.)

The Portuguese call this day Good Thursday. During a mass to honour the Last Supper, older church members in costume act out the story of Jesus washing the feet of his 12 disciples. The same people tend to take the same part year after year.

Macedonians read their 12 Gospels on Holy Thursday and

ring the church bells slowly. Italian-Canadians attend a service on Holy Thursday called the Last Supper Mass. After the mass, it is the custom to visit seven other churches to pray. The whole of Holy Week is also very important to Chileans, and on Holy Thursday they go to midnight mass, called Misa del Gallo.

Another name for this day is Green Thursday. German-Canadians call it Gründonnerstag. Some people eat only green vegetables; others think this is a good day to *plant* vegetables. It is probably too cold to plant in most of Canada, although you could try digging your garden over to prepare it.

The Greeks traditionally dye all their eggs bright red on Holy Thursday, while the Italians take colourless lupin bean plants to church and set them in front of the altar in a cross shape. These tall, pale plants were planted in the dark at the beginning of Lent. Like people fasting for Lent or Jesus in the wilderness, they endured 40 days of deprivation.

Holy Thursday is also the traditional day to clean the church altar and do Easter housecleaning. Some Europeans used to say it was a good day to be rid of any witches left over from All Souls' Day — maybe the housecleaning finally scares them out after a long winter's hiding!

## Good Friday

*Two days before Easter Sunday*

Good Friday was probably called God's Day originally. The Czechoslovaks call it "big Friday"; Macedonians refer to Velik Petok, or "great Friday." This is usually a day of sadness, remembering the crucifixion of Jesus. For many devout Christians, church services last several hours. There are no signs of joy, especially no bells. Ecuadorian Catholics, however, celebrate Good Friday as a feast day; to them it symbolizes the continuation of life. They eat a once-a-year-only soup called

*fanesca*, made of dried cod and many vegetables.

Members of the Eastern Orthodox church fast and attend a church service every evening during the week leading up to Good Friday. Some even sleep in the church overnight on Holy Thursday so that they can make what the Greeks call an *epitaphio*, a special place covered with flowers, on Good Friday. The *epitaphio* is meant to represent the tomb where Jesus' body was laid. In the evening, the congregation carries the *epitaphio* around the neighbourhood on a symbolic journey. The flowery tomb is held up on four poles. When the procession returns to the church, the *epitaphio* is set up in front of the church door so that everyone has to duck under it to get back inside. After the service, people take home a bottle of holy water and some flowers from the tomb. They dip the flowers in the water and sprinkle the whole house with it, for blessing.

Macedonians make a *plashtanitsa* for Good Friday. This is a picture of the dead Jesus painted on a large cloth embroidered with emblems and quotations from the Bible. The *plashtanitsa* is spread over a flower-decorated bier and later carried in procession.

Italian Catholics also have Good Friday processions, often called the Way of the Cross. More than 60,000 people stand quietly every year to watch this procession around the Church of St. Francis of Assisi in downtown Toronto. Sombre bands and choirs march between silent groups of people (some carrying statues) who act out scenes from the story of Jesus' betrayal and crucifixion. Year after year, the same people from the congregation are the actors and actresses.

## Good Friday luck

*Good Friday is the day for eating hot cross buns. If you have any leftovers at the end of the day, try following this old saying:*

*Hang a bun on a string*
*And good luck it will bring.*

*Early Canadian settlers believed that eggs laid on Good Friday would bring you good luck for a year. Other settlers believed that eggs laid on Good Friday could be saved and used to cure many different ailments all year.*

## Polish paper-cutting

*Polish country people once whiled away the long winter evenings making papercuts. Then when they whitewashed their houses in the spring, they used the papercuts to decorate the walls. You can use your papercuts on greeting cards or notepaper. You'll need:*

*pencil*
*assorted colours of origami papers*
*scissors*
*glue*
*notepaper or blank cards*

1. *Draw a bird, flower or other design on the back of a piece of coloured paper. Cut it out and glue it onto the card or notepaper.*
2. *Layer by layer, add details to your picture — for example, petals for the flower or wings for the bird. Each layer should be smaller than the one below so that the layers underneath still show around the edges.*

# Holy Saturday

*The day before Easter Sunday*

Some people celebrate Holy Saturday, which the Czechs call White Saturday, by attending a midnight church service in preparation for Easter. Greek-Canadians go to church at 11 or 12 o'clock, carrying new candles. Some services last until 2:30 in the morning! All of these services include a time of darkness when there are no lights or candles. The priest ends the darkness by announcing "Christ has risen" and lighting a candle to celebrate the Resurrection. The light is passed from candle to candle until hundreds of rejoicing faces are smiling in the glow. Greeks say "Christos anesti" and there are bells, sometimes even fireworks, to emphasize their joy. Syrians and Lebanese who belong to Melkite or Maronite congregations speak their Easter greeting in Arabic. The priest says "Al-Massih kam" (Christ is risen), and the people reply, "Hakkan kam" (Truly, he is risen).

Romanians attend a Mass of Resurrection on Holy Saturday. They stand outside the closed doors of their church, symbolizing the tomb of Jesus. At the 12th stroke of midnight, the doors are opened and the priest inside proclaims the news of the Resurrection three times. Everyone answers, and they march around the church three times in a candlelit procession before going in to celebrate the mass. Why do you think so many parts of the service are done in threes? Remember the idea of the Holy Trinity? "Trinity" means three, and the Holy Trinity represents the Christian God. After mass, the priests bless baskets of food that have been brought by parishioners.

After a midnight service, people go home to the first of several Easter feasts. Greek people eat *mayiritsa*, a rich soup made from the organ meats of a lamb (such as the heart and liver), eggs, rice and dill. Romanians finish their late Holy Saturday supper by cracking Easter eggs with friends. The last

person with an uncracked egg is supposed to have good luck for the next year.

## Easter Sunday

*Between March 22 and April 21*

Many Christians welcome Easter Sunday with a sunrise service. Ukrainians usually have a service at dawn on Easter and go outside just as the sun rises. Their priest lifts a cross, singing "Khrystos voskres" ("Christ is risen"). He is echoed by the congregation, who carry banners and lighted candles.

After the church service, the congregation stands in a circle around the church, while the priest circles the building three times and blesses rows of food baskets with holy water. There is a lighted candle in each basket, and the food is covered by an embroidered napkin. Ukrainian families begin their Easter breakfast by sharing one hard-boiled egg. The father passes the pieces, saying, "This is the symbol of life at Easter. Eat and rejoice." A dance called *hahilka* is often performed to welcome Easter too.

After their midnight services and feasting, Macedonians sleep in. They return to church at 3 o'clock in the afternoon for a one-hour service, followed by joyful dancing by the whole congregation.

## Easter Monday

*The day after Easter*

Have you ever had an egg-rolling contest on Easter Monday? Big public games such as egg-rolling or Thread My Needle were often played on the day after Easter in Britain. In much of eastern Europe, Easter Monday was very merry. Traditionally, it was a day for the boys to throw water on the girls, and there are many playful ways to do it. Some people call it

"Dousing Monday," others call it "Ducking Monday" because players had to duck out of the way! Does Ducking Monday sound like the East Indian Holi to you? Maybe these spring-welcoming celebrations are related.

The Polish name for Easter Monday is Dyngus Day. Poles sprinkle each other with water or try to whip one another with willow branches. The Czechoslovaks call this custom *pomlazka*, after the sort of whip made of braided twigs carried by the boys. The girls are supposed to be spanked by the boys with the whip so they won't be lazy, and they must give the boys coloured eggs. In the evening there is lots of dancing.

Here in Canada, Hungarian Boy Scout groups carry the water-sprinkling customs on in a much less rowdy way. Boys go from house to house and sprinkle eau de cologne on girls. They also recite short poems and receive painted Easter eggs in return.

## Low Sunday

*One week after Easter*

When Easter is past, there is a rather natural lull in people's lives. Maybe that is why the following Sunday was called Low Sunday in Britain.

Ukrainians call the Sunday after Easter the Sunday of the

Dead because a special memorial service for all the people who have died in the past year used to be held in Ukrainian cemeteries on that afternoon. They also call it Thomas's Easter to remember the Apostle Thomas, who wasn't present when Jesus appeared to the others after his resurrection. In Canada, a big community dinner called Sviachene, or Blessed Easter Dinner, held on this Sunday brings the Ukrainian Easter season to a close.

## Toonik Tyme

*Around the third weekend in April*

Around Iqaluit (formerly Frobisher Bay) in the eastern Northwest Territories, the snow stays on the ground until late May or June, and some deep snowbanks don't disappear until mid-July. However, by late April the days are warmer (though not above freezing) and longer, and so the 2800 residents give themselves a "spring break."

Toonik Tyme is named after a legendary Inuk named Toonik who lived long ago. He was a giant of a man, with such long arms and legs he had to sleep with his legs propped up on the walls — every room he entered was too small for him!

A lot of the Toonik Tyme activities are centred on the Frobisher Bay Arena, which claims to have the northernmost artificial ice-making unit in Canada. (Seems a bit silly to *make* ice in the Arctic, doesn't it?) Inside the arena there are broomball competitions with team members wearing one skate and one sneaker, tugs-of-war on ice and hockey games with teams of mothers and fathers. In 1986 a new event was added — the first Eastern Arctic Indoor Human Dog Team Championship. Each of the 12 teams that entered had five human members, four to pull a rope fastened to a round "flying saucer" sled and one to ride and mush the others!

There are lots more hilarious competitions. Have you ever heard of a Four-legged Race? Three people try to run with two single and two tied-together "double" legs. What about a Backwards Parka Race? Contestants hurry to see who can reach their partners first — with their hoods over their faces. Maybe you'd like to try the Slope Climb, with plastic bags tied over your boots. No one gets very far up the slope, but everyone laughs a lot. Better yet, you could try the Honeybucket Fling — "honeybucket" is the misleading name for a chamber pot....

Because Iqaluit is the focus of the largest Inuit population in any area of Canada, traditional Inuit games are a major part of Toonik Tyme. There are fishing and hunting contests; dog team races for both children and adults; igloo-building races; harpoon-throwing, whip-cracking and seal-skinning competitions; and high kick contests. In addition to the games, many Inuit folk artists perform. There are throat singers, drum dancers and folk singers who sing in many different Inuktitut dialects. There are also craftspeople displaying local arts and crafts.

Prizes are given for the most warmly dressed hunter in traditional Inuit gear and the seal hunter wearing the best and most traditional seal-hunting gear. Contests similar to those at other Canadian winter festivals are held too — ice sculpture, tea-brewing and bannock-making, snowmobile races, beard-growing and so forth. The RCMP hosts a car rally; the Boy Scouts hold a Saturday morning brunch; and the whole festival opens with an interdenominational church service.

On top of all these activities, Toonik Tyme has talent shows for children as well as adults, a dog show, big concerts, fireworks, parades, a new annual Eastern Arctic Marathon and a traditional Inuit feast, with caribou, char, seal and other meat served raw — for those who like it. The Royal Canadian Legion sponsors an Elders' Dinner, and the Francophone Society brings in maple syrup from the new crop "down south" to make real maple snow cones out of local snow — there's plenty of that!

## Rizvan

*April 21 to May 2*

This 12-day festival is the holiest time of the year for Baha'is. To them, Rizvan (which means paradise) is the "king of festivals." It is a time for them to think about why they hold their faith. And it is a celebration of the Great Teacher Baha'u'llah's announcement that he was the prophet whose coming had been foretold. Baha'is treat the first, ninth and twelfth days as especially sacred, and they do not work or go to school then. The festival of Rizvan is marked by joyful gatherings at which prayers are offered. There are also picnics, special parties and outings for the children.

## Mahavir Jayanti

*Some time in April*

The 24th leader of the Jain religion was Lord Mahavir, or Mahaviraswami, who was born in 599 B.C. His birthday, or Jayanti, is celebrated in April with special prayers, temple worship and public meetings in his honour. This is one of his teachings:

> Live, let live and help others to live.
> Be kind to birds and animals by not eating them.

Kill not, cause no pain.
Nonviolence is the greatest religion.

For more information on Jainism, see page 189.

# Arbour Day

*April or May*

Have you ever been part of a special tree-planting ceremony in the spring? If so, you may have been observing Arbour Day. The Latin word *arbor* means tree, and the idea of a particular day or week for planting trees came to Canada from the United States.

Tree-planting ceremonies have been around for a long time. Long ago they took place during spring festivals; planting a tree was a way to celebrate spring growth. This ancient idea took on new meaning in the prairie state of Nebraska at the end of the 19th century. A man named J. Sterling Morton wanted to plant trees in his almost treeless state. He knew that trees would benefit the farmers by providing windbreaks and helping to prevent soil erosion. People would also enjoy the shade and beauty of the trees.

Morton promoted the idea of Arbour Day, and in 1885 his birthday, April 22, was declared a legal holiday for planting trees. That year almost one million trees were planted where there were almost none before! The idea spread rapidly and was adopted by many American and Canadian communities.

# St. George's Day

*April 23*

When people emphasize their words with the expression "By George" they actually mean "By St. George." St. George was a famous knight who, according to legend, slayed a dragon

*What is it?*

*In spring I look gay,*
*decked in comely array;*
*In summer more clothing I wear.*
*As colder it grows,*
*I fling off my clothes,*
*And in winter quite naked appear.*
*What am I?*

*A tree*

## Children's Days

*Canada does not have a national Children's Day, but there are local festivities in some areas. In Saskatchewan, for example, the Cut Knife Elks Club has held an annual Children's Day in early June for over 30 years. It includes ball tournaments, children's races and pony rides. Also the Tibetan Buddhists and Vietnamese in Canada honour children on two other days — see Tibetan Children's Day (page 42) and Trung-Thu (page 211).*

*Many countries have Children's Days. In India, for example, former prime minister Nehru's birthday is now celebrated as Children's Day on November 14. Here are some other Children's Days around the world:*

*May 5 in Japan*
*May 27 in Nigeria*
*June 1 in China, Poland, East*
*    Germany and the Soviet Union*
*June 17 in Indonesia*
*August 16 in Uruguay*
*October 12 in Brazil*

*Feeling left out? You could always celebrate Universal Children's Day on the first Monday in October. It was established by the United Nations in 1954. The idea is that each country celebrates its Children's Day on the date and in the manner it feels is most appropriate.*

and saved a princess. He also converted many people to Christianity, about 300 A.D.

St. George wore a suit of armour and a white tunic with a red cross on it. This cross is the symbol of the International Red Cross and forms part of the Union Jack, the flag of the United Kingdom of Great Britain and Northern Ireland. His own flag flies from the many churches and cathedrals that have been dedicated to him. No wonder this famous saint is remembered in church services on the weekend nearest to his day.

St. George's Day is the most important of all the Greek name-days (see page 12). Greek families with fathers, grandfathers, uncles or sons named George have a party in honour of *their* George or St. George. If your family does not have a George, visit a family that does. According to custom, you should pull all the Georges' ears for good luck!

St. George is the patron saint of the Greek community in Halifax and of Coptic (Egyptian) Christians everywhere. St. George's Day is also an important holiday for Bulgarians and Macedonians, but because they use the Julian Calendar, they celebrate it on May 6 instead.

## Turkish Children's Day

*April 23*

Wouldn't it be wonderful to have a special festival just for children? Turkish families in Canada celebrate one, called National Children and Independence Day. It is held on April 23, because on that date in 1923 the new Republic of Turkey was officially founded. Turkish President Ataturk dedicated the day to the children of Turkey and of the world.

To celebrate National Children and Independence Day, the government invites at least one boy and one girl from every country in the world to a special reception each year. Dressed in their national costumes, these children attend the inaugur-ation of a young Turkish "president" and other leaders who will govern the country for the day. Everyone feasts and shares folk songs and dances. There are speeches about how important children are to the future of the world, as well.

In North York, Ontario, the public library hosts a special children's party on the Saturday nearest to Turkish Children's Day. The Turkish Culture and Folklore Society invites one boy and one girl from every ethnic association in the Toronto area to attend. There is lots of singing and dancing, and the chil-dren are given special sweets and barbecued meats to eat, plus Turkish flags and trinkets made from copper as souvenirs.

# May Day

*May 1 or later in the month*

Have you ever seen a May Day march or a maypole? Watch for them around the first of May. For about 3000 years, May 1 has been a day to welcome in the summer. Today May Day is also an international labour holiday in many countries, especially those with Communist or Socialist governments. In many Canadian cities, labour and other groups have special rallies and meetings on May 1. May Day became a labour holiday in the late 1800s when the Socialist Party declared May 1 an in-ternational workers' celebration. But long before that, May 1 was another kind of labour day — a traditional day for hiring servants and farm labourers.

How did maypoles become associated with this holiday? A maypole symbolizes a tree. It is decorated with ribbons, and dancers circle it on May Day or later in the month. For hun-dreds of years maypoles have been linked with freedom and the rights of the common people because they were erected

## Magic dew

*The fair maid who, the First of May,*
*Goes to the fields at break of day*
*And washes in the dew from the*
*    hawthorn tree,*
*Will ever after handsome be.*

This old rhyme refers to the superstition that May dew will make you more beautiful and prevent ageing. To be magic, the dew must be gathered just at dawn. It's worth a try! Magic May dew is yet another kind of sacred water used in spring rituals.

Both Acadians and Québécois collect l'eau de Mai on May Day to use for special healing and beautifying. City people have to go out to the country to find a suitable source for this magical water.

## Ancient May Days

*When the Celtic people dominated Europe, before Christianity, their summer began on May Day, which they called Beltane. Beltane dawn was often observed with huge bonfires to strengthen the sun. These fires are now usually lit for the summer solstice, but some Europeans still burn them, supposedly to "keep away the witches," on April 30, the night before Beltane.*

---

## May Day food

*Does your family have a special food on May Day? French-Canadians traditionally make dandelion salad with the new green leaves from those pesky plants. Some English people make special May cakes, and others a kind of egg nog.*

---

on common land and the whole community celebrated around them.

Maypoles were erected in some parts of French Canada long ago. They are also remembered in some parts of the United States. In most of Canada, May Day and maypoles are no longer important, partly because our short spring and summer are times of hard work for our farmers. They have less time to relax and enjoy the warm weather after they get their seeds planted than European farmers (and their Celtic ancestors) did. However, on Vancouver Island and the west coast of British Columbia, where the spring season is long and mild, English maypole dancing and other May activities still go on. They are kept alive by the many people of British descent in that area.

In Victoria, B.C., the dancing is performed in front of the provincial Parliament Buildings on Victoria Day weekend. There is also maypole dancing on Quadra Island and a May Queen contest and parade on the far end of Vancouver Island, in Port McNeill. In New Westminster, south of Vancouver, the annual Hyack Festival includes crowning a May Queen as well as maypole dancing, usually held on the Wednesday before Victoria Day. Even Prince George and Kaslo, both in the B.C. Interior, celebrate May Days around the same time.

## Carnival Day, Vappu

*May 1*

Usually Carnival means the time before Lent, but Finnish-Canadians hold Carnival Day, or Vappu, on May 1. Originally Vappu was a celebration for labourers and students. Now it is a social gathering in a gaily decorated hall. Under bright streamers and balloons, the Finns dance and share traditional food. They drink lemon-flavoured *sima* and its complementary sweet bread, called *tippaleipä*.

# Morris dancing on May Day

In Toronto, Morris dancers, their families and friends get up before dawn on May Day morning and gather on the highest hill in High Park to "dance the sun up." Although it has been known to snow on these hardy dancers, and it is always cold, the morning is a merry one, with lots of singing and lively music. After a huge group breakfast, some dancers continue around the city, while others go off to a normal day of work — unless it is a weekend, when the celebrations last all day — rain, shine or snow!

Morris dancers in London and Ottawa, Winnipeg, Vancouver and Victoria are also out celebrating.

They are all part of a revival of an old English kind of folk dancing. The Morris, as the dance is called, was traditionally done in the late spring to make the crops grow. Now it is performed on May 1 and all through the warm months.

Morris dancers, dressed in white shirts and trousers, wear bells on their legs and carry long sticks or white hankies to emphasize their movements. Each team has its own colours and arrangements of ribbons.

Some Morris teams have an accompanying mascot, a dancer usually dressed as a hobby-horse. However, unicorns or even lobsters have been seen! Although they are all comic characters nowadays, at one time these animal dancers represented fertility in the springtime. Sometimes mummers dressed as animals for similar reasons.

There are all kinds of dances for welcoming the spring. Some are variations of Morris or maypole dances, to make the seeds grow or to honour the trees; others are processions. Some dancers even parade in and out of the doors of everyone's houses! Why not try it yourself in your school or community on the first good day of warm weather to really give spring a welcome!

## Fruit crosses

*People from South and Central America also celebrate May 3 as the Day of the Cross. One El Salvadorean custom is to make a table decoration out of fruit arranged around a cross on this day. The more money a family has, the more elaborate this fruit cross will be.*

# Santa Cruzan Day

*May 3*

In the Philippines, May 3 is considered the first day of spring. It is also a special day in the Filipino Catholic Church, the Day of Commemoration of the Holy Cross, or Santa Cruzan. On this day in the 4th century A.D., St. Helena (the mother of Emperor Constantine of Rome) found the holy cross on which Jesus was crucified. She had a church built on the very spot where it was found. Emperor Constantine was the first Roman emperor to grant freedom of worship and recognition to the early Christians, so he is now known as St. Constantine.

In Toronto, three Filipino groups organize a parade and spring festival for Santa Cruzan Day every year at Harbourfront. Two people dressed as Emperor Constantine and Queen Helena lead the parade. Young Filipino women are sponsored by a patron at Santa Cruzan. The patrons also appear in costume for the parade. They dress as famous women, such as the Queen of Sheba. After the parade, the young women are escorted to church, dressed in their best. Later they go back to their patrons' homes for a special meal.

# Other spring festivals

*Throughout May*

In Ontario, two well-known events are the Festival of Spring in Ottawa in mid-May and the Romanian Spring Festival in Kitchener on the weekend nearest to May 24. These come about two months after the official first day of spring, when true spring weather has finally arrived in much of the province, and the outdoors really does begin to look green.

Ottawa's festival is known as the Tulip Festival, because the whole city is bright with millions of tulips. Do you know why Ottawa has so many of these spring bulbs? During World

War II, Princess Juliana of the Netherlands lived in Ottawa. As a token of their appreciation, the Dutch people sent the Canadian people a present of their national specialty, tulip bulbs — over 4 million of them! Every year when they bloom it seems as if the gift has been given anew. Ottawa celebrates spring — and the tulips — with more than 70 events around the city, including a marathon race and firework displays.

In Saskatoon, the annual Vesna Festival (Vesna means spring) is a huge, three-day Ukrainian celebration, held the weekend before Victoria Day. In Chateauguay, Quebec, there is a somewhat earlier Festival du Printemps. Do you know of any other spring festivals in Canada?

# Santo Cristo

*The fifth Sunday after Easter*

St. Mary's Roman Catholic Church in Toronto celebrates the Portuguese festival of Santo Cristo on the fifth Sunday after Easter, or Rogation Sunday. This old church, in Portugal Square near the shores of Lake Ontario, is the "mother church" to thousands of Portuguese people in Canada and the United States. Many of them come to Toronto for the festival, which is the largest one of its kind in North America.

Santo Cristo has a history that goes back more than 500 years to the Azores Islands, off the coast of Portugal. It is said that two nuns there were so devoted in their care of a statue of Jesus that it showed signs of life, and anyone who prayed to it was sure to be miraculously healed or helped. Portuguese immigrants have continued to celebrate the miracle of Santo Cristo here.

On the Saturday evening before the festival, a small procession is held for devout Catholics doing penance. Men in red tunics carry the Santo Cristo, a large statue of Jesus in a

flower-covered stall, out of the church and around Portugal Square. Many followers carry big white candles, more than half their own height in length. These will be used by the church in services during the year and represent promises made to God in return for blessings such as good health. Some people in the procession do penance by walking barefoot or even on their knees.

As many as 100,000 people gather on Sunday afternoon to join or watch a bigger procession move through the surrounding streets to a nearby park. Again, the Santo Cristo is the focus of the procession. Clergy, marching bands, children in angel costumes or confirmation clothes and faithful worshippers, some with candles, all join in. They move slowly and solemnly along the crowded streets, while the bells in the tower of St. Mary toll again and again.

When the religious services finish, the festival becomes more of an outdoor concert, with music, rides, games and food. Portugal Square and the church itself are specially decorated for the whole event. The general fun does not stop until after midnight.

## Dia de Nossa Senhora de Fatima, or Our Lady of Fatima Day

*May 13*

On May 13, 1917, something unusual happened to three shepherd children in Portugal. They thought they saw and talked to the Virgin Mary near the town of Fatima. She appeared in the same place, on the 13th day of the month, for six more months! By her last appearance on October 13, 1917, more than 70,000 people had gathered to see the vision of Our Lady of Fatima. She is said to have performed a miracle with the sun for all to see, and she gave the children messages telling the world to pray for universal peace.

At first a chapel was built on the spot where she appeared. Now millions of people go to pray every year at the church that stands on that holy site. Many are crippled or diseased and hope for cures.

In Canada, Our Lady of Fatima Day is celebrated with a special mass on May 13. Some Portuguese Catholic churches hold annual processions for Our Lady of Fatima in May, while others wait until October 13, the anniversary of her last appearance.

There are other pilgrimages in Canada. For example, Forget, Saskatchewan, is the site of an annual pilgrimage to the shrine of Our Lady of Salette on the second Sunday in June. At nearby Cudworth, pilgrims go to the shrine of Our Lady of Sorrows on the third weekend in June every year.

# Mother's Day

*The second Sunday in May*

Mother's Day is a little more than a hundred years old. It started after the American Civil War in the early 1860s, when Julia Ward Howe launched a Mother's Day for Peace. Best known as the author of "The Battle Hymn of the Republic," Julia Ward Howe nursed the wounded during the Civil War. It made her determined to put an end to all wars. The first Mother's Day for Peace was held in 1872.

In 1907 Anna Jarvis of Philadelphia had the idea of holding a special church service in honour of mothers. She began by arranging for a service to be held in a local church in memory of her own mother, who had recently died, on the anniversary of her death. Anna Jarvis asked everyone who attended to wear a white carnation. By 1914 her campaign had been so successful that the President of the United States declared the second Sunday in May Mother's Day. In some places it is the custom to wear a red carnation if your mother is alive and a

## Other Mother's Days

*The last Sunday in May is Mother's Day in Sweden and France. In South Africa it is held on the first Sunday in May. Yugoslavians celebrate Mother's Day two Sundays before Christmas. Yugoslav children have a custom of tying up their mother's feet in order to ransom a present from her. Serbian Mother's Day customs are similar, only they take place on the last Sunday in December. In case you're wondering, mothers don't mind being tied up and having to give presents. They see the presents as a symbol of God's gift to the world at that season — his son Jesus.*

white one if she has died.

Do you go to any Mother's Day events? Do you know of any official celebrations of mothers? If you don't, maybe you could start one and make a new tradition in your part of the country. Here are two examples:

- In Alberta, some native people have a special ceremonial dance in honour of Mother's Day, as a part of a big spring pow-wow.
- In Ontario, the Polish-Canadian Youth Club of Kitchener-Waterloo holds an annual Mother's Day banquet.

## Pentecost or Whitsun

*Seventh Sunday after Easter*

This Christian festival celebrates the renewal of faith that Jesus' apostles (followers) felt after his death. The 12 apostles found it hard to continue spreading the words of Jesus after his death, and they rejoiced when his holy spirit was felt among them. (There is also a Jewish festival called Pentecost — see next page.)

Pentecost is a customary time for new members of a church to be baptized. Baptism is a ceremony performed in many churches to admit you as a member of that group. To be baptized, you must be dipped in water, or at least sprinkled with it. You may need to wear white clothes to show that you are pure in spirit and ready to be baptized. That's why Pentecost Sunday came to be called White Sunday or Whitsun in English. The Ukrainians call this Sunday "the green holiday" and use lots of new spring greenery in their decorations.

Many Catholic churches in Canada have special processions for Pentecost, especially Portuguese, Italian and Greek congregations.

The Russian name for Pentecost is the Feast of the Holy Trinity (referring to the Christian idea of God the Father, the Son and the Holy Spirit). They think of Pentecost as a time of new life, and here in Canada they scatter green leaves and new grass on the floor of the church and decorate with flowers and birch branches. (Using birch decorations is a very old custom related to new life. Birch has been a favourite tree for maypoles and spring decoration for centuries in Europe — long ago it was sacred to the Celts.) These signs of spring remind Russian worshippers of the new life around them and are meant to encourage them to think about their spiritual lives.

# Shavu'ot, or the Feast of Weeks

*May or June*

The Jews celebrate the 50th day after the beginning of Passover as the end of the Passover period. It is called Shavu'ot, the Feast of Weeks, or Pentecost. (*Pente* is the Greek word for five, and *pentecost* means 50.) Long ago in the Holy Land, it was a harvest festival. It marked the wheat harvest just as, seven weeks earlier, Passover was held at the time of the barley harvest. Today the biblical Book of Ruth is read in the synagogue at Shavu'ot because of its harvest story.

Later Shavu'ot became a festival to remember God's gift of the Torah and the Ten Commandments. These were given to Moses as he and other Jews wandered in the desert at the time of Shavu'ot. (The Torah is also known as the Five Books of Moses, which are the same as the first five books of the Old Testament. The word Torah is best translated as "teaching," for these books teach Jews about the creation of the world, their history, their laws of right living — their religion.)

*The Torah*

In Canada today, many synagogues hold confirmation exercises at Shavu'ot. These mark the beginning of one stage of religious education — learning the Torah — in a Jewish child's life. Houses and synagogues are decorated with lots of greenery, in memory of the miracle of the rushes, when the baby Moses was found in his basket among the bullrushes of the Nile. Do you know that story? One legend says that the baby would not nurse, or suck milk, from the breast of any but a Hebrew woman. Supposedly that is why fancy milk and dairy dishes are prepared for this holiday. Also, Jews say that "honey and milk are on your tongue" if you have learned the Torah — and Shavu'ot is the time that the Torah is celebrated.

## Wesak, Buddha's Birthday Festival

*Around the second Sunday in May*

All Buddhists, no matter what country they live in, celebrate three main events in the life of Buddha; his birth, enlightenment and *paranirvana* (see box next page). In Canada many Buddhist groups join together to celebrate the three festivals of Buddha's life as one event. They do this on the day of the fourth full moon after the lunar new year, or the Sunday closest to that day. Usually this is some time in mid-May.

The joint celebrations include various rituals, prayers and meditation, refreshments or a vegetarian feast and a multicultural program of singing and dancing. The 1986 Wesak service in Toronto included a *kambutsu* ceremony in which a statue of the Baby Buddha was bathed with holy water. Wesak participants approach the Buddha and make their own personal *kambutsu* wishes.

Newly arrived Buddhists may remember other traditions from their home countries:

- Some Vietnamese Buddhists call the festival Phât-Ðan, or Buddha's Birthday, and it is the most important day of the

## Buddhism

*Buddha was a spriritual teacher whose original name was Prince Siddhartha Gautama. He lived in India about the 5th century B.C. As a young man, he sat and meditated under a now-famous Bo Tree and "attained enlightenment." Buddhists say this means he understood the true nature of the world.*

*Using the wisdom he gained at that time, Buddha taught others to follow his example, and Buddhism gradually became one of the great world religions. Buddhism is now widespread in central and eastern Asia. Many people from China,*

*Japan, Korea, Viet Nam, Laos, Thailand, Kampuchea (formerly Cambodia), Malaysia, India, Nepal and Sri Lanka are Buddhists.*

*Buddhists believe that being open-minded brings peacefulness and that meditation brings enlightenment, as Buddha found. Enlightenment leads to a feeling of oneness with all living beings, animals and humans. Enlightened Buddhists can escape the cycle of death and rebirth, a cycle they believe we all go through repeatedly, and attain nirvana. Then they are free from ignorance, desire and hatred, which Buddhists believe*

*cause bodily pain and sorrow. Buddha was the first to attain paranirvana, which means death without being reborn. Since then, many have followed his example.*

*In Canada today there are more than 24 kinds of Buddhism. Most Buddhists are recent refugees from countries such as Viet Nam, and have settled in Vancouver, Montreal or Toronto. Some groups, like the tiny Tibetan communities in Lindsay and Belleville, Ontario, or Lethbridge, Alberta, are affiliated with bigger Buddhist groups in the United States.*

year for them. One of their traditions is to buy captive animals and set them free on Buddha's Birthday. The most popular pets to release are turtles, birds and fish.

- Sri Lankan Buddhists celebrate all three events on Wesak. After their religious services, they light special Wesak lanterns.
- Korean Buddhists have a lantern parade and put up paper lanterns outside their homes.

## Ball-bouncing game

*Try bouncing a ball as you say this rhyme:*

*Twenty-fourth of May,*
*Firecracker day!*
*Kiss the girls, kiss the boys!*
*Oh, boy, what a joy.*

---

### Victorians in Victoria on Victoria Day Weekend

*In Victoria, B.C., celebrations of Queen Victoria's birthday are especially lavish. For many years hundreds of children have gathered on Friday morning for maypole dancing on the lawns in front of the Parliament Buildings. In the evening there is a May Queen Ball.*

*Next day there are all kinds of Victorian events, such as a contest for the best period costume, a rally and display of vintage cars and beard and moustache contests. After Sunday-morning church services, there is a huge sailpast in the harbour. Decorated boats parade past the admiral of the fleet from the nearby naval college. Sunday evening a new teen May Queen is crowned.*

*The highlight of the holiday weekend is a three-hour parade on Monday. About 40 different bands take part, and most of them warm up all weekend with concerts across the city. Plus there are floats, clowns, decorated cars and horses and costumed citizens. Now that's some birthday bash!*

## Citizenship Day

*The Friday before Victoria Day*

Citizenship Day has been held on the Friday before Victoria Day since 1958. Canada's Citizenship Act came into force on January 1, 1947, and the first official Citizenship Day was May 23, 1950. This is a day for all Canadians to think about their rights and duties, privileges and responsibilities as Canadian citizens.

## Victoria Day

*The Monday before May 24*

Since 1952, the Monday before May 24 has been celebrated with fireworks and festivities as Victoria Day even though Queen Victoria, whose birthday is being honoured, has been dead for many years. Throughout the British Empire in the 19th century it was the custom to celebrate the monarch's birthday officially. Queen Victoria ruled for so many years that Canadians got very accustomed to having a holiday on the 24th of May. And so her birthday has become a permanent Canadian holiday, except in Quebec where the holiday is called Fête de Dollard des Ormeaux. We now honour Queen Elizabeth II as well on this day, although her actual birthday comes earlier in the spring, on April 21.

On the Six Nations Reserve, near Brantford, Ontario, Victoria Day is called Independence Day, or Bread and Cheese Day. Every year the residents of the reserve line up outside their community centre in the morning to receive gifts of bread and cheese from government agents. This is an old custom, begun by agents of the Queen on May 24, 1837. In the afternoon, the day is celebrated with cultural displays, horse races and ball games.

In southern Canada, the Victoria Day weekend is the time

to plant the family garden — the last frost date is often May 24. In New Ross, Nova Scotia, an official Pumpkin Planting Party is held over this weekend, on the historic Ross Farm. You might want to go help, if you're not busy in your own backyard.

# Canadian Ploughing Championship

*Last weekend in May*

Stewardship of the soil, or how we look after the soil in which our food grows, is very important. Ploughs are the tools for turning the soil over in the spring, and good ploughing is a skill crucial to farmers everywhere. For more than 40 years, several Canadian provinces have competed in an annual ploughing competition which moves from province to province.

In 1986, the Canadian and World Ploughing Championships took place in Olds, Alberta. Whalley Marr from Brooks, Alberta, was the national winner (he and his brother Doug have been sharing the championship for a few years), and Northern Ireland won the international competition. In 1987 Quebec will host the Canadian Ploughing Championship, and Austria the World Ploughing Championship.

To be the champion, you first must win within your province. At the World Ploughing Championships, entrants have fifty-horsepower tractors and moldboard ploughs — the ploughshare cuts the soil, and the moldboard turns it over. They have 30 minutes to "make the opening split" in a plot of land. This means they make the first trip up and down the field, and cut two furrows. Then those furrows are judged. After that, they have two and a half hours to finish. They are judged by the straight, level and even appearance of the soil — it will dry out if not done properly.

## Fiddlehead Festival

*Have you ever eaten fiddleheads? They're the young curled-up shoots of the ostrich fern. They got their name because they look like the head of a fiddle. Fiddleheads are a traditional food of many native Canadians. Long ago they showed the early settlers how to get their vitamins from the fiddlehead "crop" before their gardens were planted. Today fiddleheads are a famous Canadian delicacy.*

*The Maliseet Indians of New Brunswick once used to gather fiddleheads and feast together at their first spring pow-wow. More recently, the St. Mary's band of the Maliseet organized a Fiddlehead Festival on the Victoria Day weekend and began a new tradition. The festival opened and closed with Indian ceremonies and included foods such as salmon and buffalo meat (from Alberta!) to eat with the fiddleheads. Local dignitaries attended and a Fiddlehead Queen was crowned; there were concerts and special dances. Unfortunately, the festival lapsed in the 1980s, although some people still hope it will be revived. If you are in the Fredericton area when fiddleheads are poking through the wet earth, ask if there are any celebrations...if not, fiddlesticks!*

## Happy Father's Day

Here's a Father's Day card that shows Dad how much you love him.

1. Start with a long strip of paper. Fold it into five parts.

2. On one side, write this:

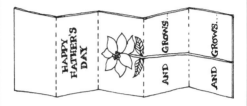

3. On the other side do this.

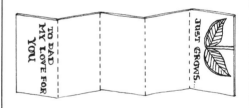

4. Fold the card up like an accordion. Fold the top flap over the rest of the card. When you lift this top flap, the first thing you should see is the beginning of your flower.

# Annapolis Valley Apple Blossom Festival

*Last weekend in May*

Nova Scotia's Annapolis Valley is famous for its apple orchards. Every year since 1932, apple trees have been the centre of celebrations during the Annapolis Valley Apple Blossom Festival. All the local towns get involved, especially Kentville and Wolfville. So does Acadia University and even the Canadian Forces Base at Greenwood (they observe Armed Forces Day at the same time).

There are a number of local suppers and sports events, plus fair rides and games, concerts and fireworks. There is a Blossom Tea and a Blossom Church Service — even a Via Rail Apple Blossom Special and Apple Blossom River Boat rides! On Saturday both a children's parade and a regular street parade go from New Minas to Wolfville. The high point of the festival is crowning Queen Annapolisa, who reigns over the Friday evening Queen's Ball and Saturday's Princesses' Ball. (The Apple Blossom princesses are chosen by each local town.) There is also street dancing, square dancing and maypole dancing during the weekend. On the last day of the festival Queen Annapolisa and her princesses make official "royal party" visits to many valley communities and schools.

# Father's Day

*Third Sunday in June*

Many Catholics call St. Joseph's Day, on March 19, Father's Day, because Joseph was the father of Jesus. But most people celebrate a more modern version of Father's Day. It began in the United States, but no one knows quite where and when. Some say that a Mrs. John Dowd of West Virginia began Father's Day to honour her own father, who raised his family alone after his wife died. Others say it was launched in Spokane, Washington, in June 1910 by a Mrs. John Bruce Dodd. The names sound suspiciously similar, don't they? Whatever the true origins, Father's Day is now widely observed in Canada.

Do you do anything special with your father on "his" day? Children in Wynyard, Saskatchewan, can take their fathers to the World Championship Chicken Chariot Races, held annually on Father's Day. Small chariots weighing less than 500 g (about a pound) are attached to the tails of the chickens. Then they race down a 15-m (50-foot) enclosed track.

# SUMMER

What do you think of as the beginning of summer? The time when school closes? That's logical, but it varies across the country. Strictly speaking, summer begins with the summer solstice on June 20 or 21. But many people start their summers a month earlier. For lots of Canadians, the Victoria Day weekend in late May marks the beginning of the season. (It's the time when many people open their summer cottages, for instance.) After this date more and more typical summer events are held — picnics, sports days, summer trips, outdoor parades and festivals of one kind or another.

Every summer festival in Canada shares one thing: warm weather. If all goes well, it should be sunny; it may even be sweltering hot! And when the weather is good, Canadians go outdoors. Perhaps that's why most summer festivals are held outside. Even religious services are conducted under the open skies.

Our warm weather is due to the sun. It shines for more hours *and* more directly in the summer than at any other time of the year. We get the most sunshine (because the days are longest) during June and July, in the weeks just before and after the summer solstice. Above the Arctic Circle, the sun shines all day and all night, never leaving the sky during much of June and July. Ice and snow disappear, although frost may linger until late June. But summer is short so far north in Canada, and the life cycle of Arctic plants and animals is often compressed into a few brief weeks. The frost may return to the Arctic by the middle of August, when people on the prairies are still baking in heat waves.

The Inuit who live in the Arctic call July "mosquito month." The sun also warms up the insect world! Clouds of these little buzzing creatures plague every living creature on land. Nonetheless, summer is the Inuit people's favourite season.

Until quite recently the Inuit made long summer migrations overland, despite the mosquitoes. Do you travel during the summer too? Some children go away to summer camp for two weeks or a month. People make long journeys to family reunions or religious gatherings.

Wherever you visit, there is sure to be a summer festival. Many of these celebrate the first appearance of a local food. There are strawberry socials, corn roasts, even oyster-shucking championships! Other festivals feature a special heritage or culture, sometimes including a national day of remembrance. Still other festivals will focus on skills and outdoor activities, such as rodeos, Highland Games and threshing contests. Most of these festivals are local, not national, and several have roots in very old customs, as we shall see.

## Summer

The word "summer" is related to many similar old English and Germanic words such as sumor and sumar, which all mean this season of the year. The old Sanskrit word sama means a half-year or a season.

The Iroquoian/Cayuga names for the summer months all have to do with growing things: May/June was called "Berries Ripening," June/July was "Many Berries Ripening," July/August was "Beans Ripening" and August/September was "Many Things Ripening."

## Summer stories

Who can resist a summer campfire? They're great places to sing, toast marshmallows and tell ghost stories. You may be surprised to learn that one group of Canadians used to forbid storytelling in the summer. The Iroquois, or Longhouse people, thought it was important to stick to farming and building in summer.

They feared that plants and animals would be bewitched by summer storytelling and forget to prepare for winter. What if a passing animal were so entranced by a legend that he forgot to find his winter home before snowfall? Or a bird didn't fly south because it listened too long? Even the plants might forget to let

down their sap before frost, if they got too involved. The Iroquois believed there were fairy guardians of this summer silence who would send a snake under your bedcovers or a bee to sting your tongue if you dared to tell a story even in secret.

## Sonshine

Once a farmer had a large hay field and a son who was not happy living in the country. So the son moved to the city and looked for a job. All he could find was work shining shoes, so now the farmer makes hay while the son shines!

## Who's out?

Try saying this rhyme next time you need to settle who gets the last slice of watermelon:

Bee, bee, bumblebee,
Sting a man upon his knee.
Sting a pig upon his snout,
I declare that you are out!

## Summer reading

There are always books to read in the shade, as this poem by William Cole, called "Summer Doings," points out.

Some at beaches
  Are sand-castling
Some are silly —
  Fighting, rasseling!

Some are swimming,
  Camping, hiking;
Some say stick-ball
  Is their liking.

Some on bikes are
  Gaily speeding;
Some are smarter —
  SUMMER READING!

## Pateca

*Here's a Brazilian-Portuguese game called* pateca *that you can play on Dia de Portugal. Traditionally it's played with a sand-filled cloth bag shaped like a cone, with a feather at the peak. However, you can play it with a ball. Players stand in a circle and start volleying a ball around, counting "A...B...C...D..." and so on for each time it is hit aloft. No one can touch the ball twice in a row. If the ball drops to the ground (or touches the ceiling, if you're playing indoors), the counting starts from the beginning again. See if you can reach the letter Z!*

# Dia de Portugal

*June 10*

Have you ever read a history book written entirely in rhyme? Portuguese-Canadians have. They celebrate their poet-historian, Luis de Camões, on June 10 every year. This is the Portuguese equivalent of Canada Day. The date is extra-special because it is dedicated to the great Portuguese poet who wrote *The Lusiads*, a book about the history of Portugal — in poetry.

Dia de Portugal is celebrated in various ways. Often celebrations include writing contests, formal events and dance programs. In Nova Scotia, the Halifax Portuguese community usually holds a huge picnic. In Toronto the Portuguese-Canadian community began a new tradition in 1985 by holding a parade from City Hall to Ontario Place on Dia de Portugal.

# Scandinavian National Days

*May or June*

May and June seem to be the months for Scandinavian celebrations! Not only does each of the four Scandinavian countries have a national day or flag day during this time, but they also all celebrate Midsummer Day, or St. John's Day as it is sometimes called. Here are some of the Scandinavian national days celebrated in Canada:

- May 17 is the anniversary of the Norwegian Constitution of 1814. Dinner-dances, followed by speeches, are the usual way Norwegian-Canadians celebrate.
- Danish-Ontarians have observed Danish Constitution Day since 1849 on June 5, or the Sunday nearest it, with an outdoor church service and lectures.

- Until 1983, June 6 was Swedish Flag Day. Special church services were held to honour their blue flag with a yellow cross. Now it is called Swedish National Day, and ceremonies are held in Canada on the Sunday nearest June 6th. The Swedish flag dates from 1663 and has been described as "the gold of the sun on the blue of the heavens" — very appropriate in June!
- June 17 is the anniversary of Icelandic independence from Denmark in 1944 and the birthday of a famous Icelandic statesman, Jon Sirgudsson. Around the time of this National Day, many Icelandic-Canadians hold picnics featuring sporting activities popular in Iceland, such as foot races, tugs-of-war, ball games and *glima* (Icelandic wrestling).

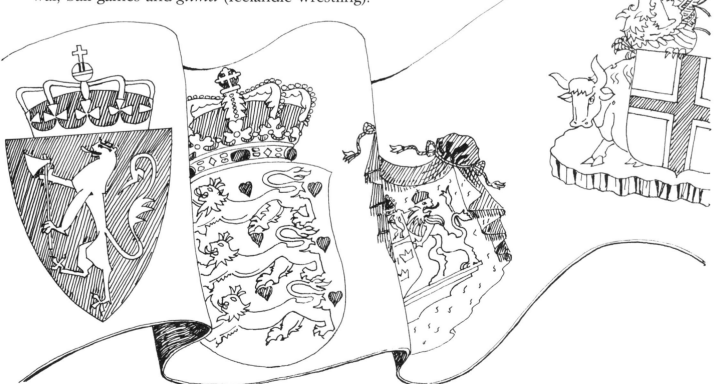

## Chinese Dragon Boat Festival

*May or June*

Once this ancient Chinese festival was an exciting outdoor boat race. Dragon-shaped boats raced, symbolizing a real dragon fight in the heavens, to bring heavy rains. The festival took place after the spring planting, when people had time to relax and, of course, needed rain for their crops. Today in Canada, there are no dragon-shaped boats racing down Canadian rivers. Instead Chinese-Canadian groups celebrate with community picnics near the fifth day of the fifth moon on the Chinese calendar.

The Dragon Boat Festival also reminds the Chinese of a statesman who lived about 2 300 years ago. His name was Wut Yuen, and he drowned himself in protest against his corrupt government. His friends searched in vain for him by boat. To keep the fish from eating his body, they dropped some food into the river for them. Today Chinese-Canadians eat the same food, called *joong*, made of rice wrapped in lotus leaves, during the Dragon Boat Festival. You can buy *joong* from a bakery, but it is traditional to make them at home. There are lots of ways to make the filling for *joong*, and each family has its own recipe. Whether the *joong* are sweet or salty, flavoured with peanuts or pork, everyone gathers together to wrap them up. In fact, tying the lotus leaves around the filling is an art that is passed down through generations in a family.

Vietnamese and Viet-Chinese call this the Fifth of Five Moon Festival. They hold a feast and eat rice cakes in honour of their dead ancestors, and they bathe with medicinal leaves. The water used to bathe is specially blessed by the Dragon in heaven at this time. Dragons are the most important symbol of good fortune in Chinese tradition.

## Hot stuff

*The south-central prairies have the sunniest days in all of Canada.*

# The Summer Solstice

*June 20, 21 or 22*

The sun shines for the greatest number of hours on this day. In many parts of Canada it's light until about ten o'clock in the evening. The farther north you go, the more hours of daylight there are. The sun reaches its highest point above the horizon at noon on the solstice. Wherever you live across Canada, at noon on the solstice your shadow will be the shortest it will be all year.

The summer solstice is the longest day of the year. It occurs exactly six months after the shortest day of the year, the winter solstice. Remember how many customs were meant to strengthen the sun during the winter solstice? (See pages 22-23.) Ancient people thought the summer solstice was an important time for ceremonies to worship the sun, too. Summer solstice ceremonies were meant to honour the sun at its fullest strength.

Many groups still hold celebrations or festivals around the time of the summer solstice. In Montague, P.E.I., the weekend closest to the summer solstice is a big celebration for the whole community. It is called Welcome to Summer and features a parade, raft race, softball tournament, contests of all sorts and the local high school graduation ceremonies.

In Prince Albert, Saskatchewan, runners from across western Canada gather for three long-distance races on the Saturday closest to the summer solstice. About 300 people enter 5-km, 10-km or 20-km races that begin at 6:30 p.m. Do you think they finish before sunset?

In Falmouth, Nova Scotia, the local community association has begun a new annual event on the Saturday closest to the solstice. They hold a huge teddy bear picnic and supper, to which everyone brings their teddy bears. There's a concert, square dance, craft fair and flea market, but the real

## Ancient sun monuments

*The Celts of Europe, the Mayans of South America, the ancestors of our native people and other ancient people were keen sun-watchers. They built special structures out of stone and earth to keep track of the passing of the year just as we have watches to keep track of the passing hours. In fact, these structures were often circular like watch faces — only much bigger. Stonehenge on the Salisbury Plains in England is probably the best-known example. In Canada there are at least two prehistoric rock configurations in Saskatchewan that have been shown to be aligned with the sun at the summer solstice. They date from around the first century A.D.*

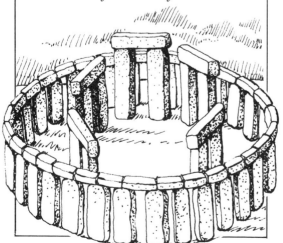

excitement has to do with the bears. There are parades and displays and competitions with such categories as much-loved bears, old bears and celebrity bears. How would *you* decide on the best teddy in a crowd of thousands?

# Midsummer's Eve

*June 23*

The night before Midsummer's Day is called Midsummer's Eve. It is a time for fairies and magic, according to old European traditions. Gather fernseed on this evening — it will make you invisible. Then the fairies and spirits will not be able to see you, and you can watch their festivities.

Midsummer's Eve is also a night for foretelling the future and for discovering who your true love might be. Scatter rose petals before you at midnight on Midsummer's Eve, and the next day your love will visit you, some say. This rhyme will help the process: "Rose leaves, rose leaves, rose leaves I strew. He that will love me, come after me now." Roses picked at midnight on this eve or the next day and wrapped in paper are supposed to keep fresh until Christmas. (For best results, wear a blindfold while picking the roses.)

Scattering hempseed (which also has magical properties) was also thought to let you see your true love. Say this poem as you scatter the seeds in a churchyard:

> Hempseed I sow, hempseed I mow,
> He that will my true love be
> Come rake this hempseed after me.

The magic will work better, the English say, if you walk 12 times around the churchyard without stopping, saying the rhyme over and over.

On Midsummer's Eve you can dream of the future if you hang a special pincushion in your sock at the end of your bed.

Stick pins in it first, to outline the initial of the person you hope to marry. If you see him or her in your dream, then you will be successful. Or you can make a "dumb cake" (the old meaning of the word "dumb" is unable to speak) with a friend, without talking! Once it is cooked, break it in half and say: "Two make it, two bake it, two break it." Then go to bed without another word and put the piece of dumb cake under your pillow. You should dream of your future love.

One old Swedish custom is to sleep with seven different flowers under your pillow. Then girls will dream of their future husbands, they say. Others say you must climb nine fences and pick nine kinds of flowers to put under your pillow. All these bits of midsummer magic were supposed to be done by girls, but times have changed and today boys could try them too.

One not-so-old way of predicting your love is to write down the name of your supposed lover and then cross out all the letters that appear more than once. In "*Richard*," for example, you are left with i-c-h-a-d. Then you say these words, one for each letter: "Love, friendship, marriage, hate." Repeat the words until all the letters have been used up. The last word you say tells you what will be the fate of that relationship. How did poor Richard fare, can you tell?

## Fire on the Mountain

*You'll need at least 11 people to play this game. You should always have an odd number of players. One person stands in the middle of two circles of players. Both circles should have the same number of players. To begin the game, the player in the middle (the leader) starts to clap. The players in the outer circle walk around those in the inner circle. The players in the inner circle stand still and follow the leader, clapping hands until the leader shouts "Fire on the mountain!" and throws his or her hands up in the air. The "insiders" do the same thing. That is the signal for the "outsiders" and the leader to try to get a place in front of an insider. This creates a new double circle, but leaves one person out. He or she becomes the new leader and the game begins again.*

# Dragon kite

Kites and breezy early summer weather seem to go together. Here's a Chinese-style jointed kite, in three sections. You'll need:

12 plastic straws
tissue paper in several colours
felt-tip markers
glue
strong thread or kite string

1. Thread your string through four straws. To do this, start the string into a straw and suck on the other end. The string will be sucked through. Tie the string ends together and form the straws into a square. Repeat until you have three straw squares.
2. Cut three tissue-paper squares slightly larger than the straw squares. Put each straw square on a square of paper, fold over the edges of the paper as shown and glue the edges over the straws.
3. Tie these squares end to end as shown.
4. Cut long strips of tissue paper to make a dragon's tail. Glue these to the bottom edge of the last square.
5. Use the felt-tip markers to draw a dragon's head and body and to decorate it.
6. Attach strong thread in three places to the head of the dragon as shown. Attach the flying string.
7. FLY IT!

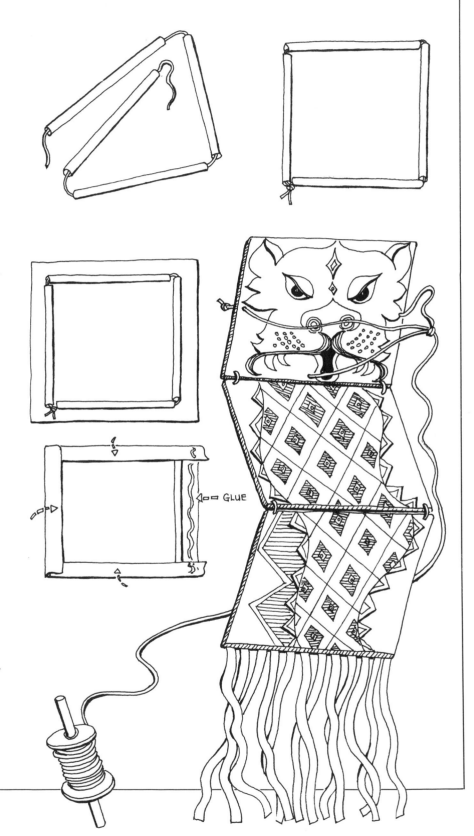

GLUE

# La Fête de la Saint-Jean-Baptiste, Fête Nationale

*June 24*

St. Jean Baptiste (St. John the Baptist in English) is the patron saint of French-Canadians. June 24 is his feast day, celebrating his birth, and it is an official holiday in the province of Quebec. There are parades throughout the province, in which one float often features St. Jean as a shepherd boy with a pet lamb by his side. The lamb is snowy white, with a ribbon tied around its neck. Other festivities include sports and games and special foods for sale.

The night before the parades, the sky is lit by St. John's fires across Quebec. First a town along the St. Lawrence River lights its fire. That bonfire is the signal for the next village to light its fire, and so on. Early French-Canadian settlers brought the midsummer bonfire custom with them from France. However, with the rise of the Quebec nationalist movement in the 1970s, the old practice took on new meaning. June 24 is now called Fête Nationale and the "fires of joy" have been called "an act of faith in our national destiny." In 1978, for example more than 1,500 fires were lit. Often fireworks are also part of the festivities.

La Fête de la Saint-Jean is an important festival wherever there are francophone communities in other parts of Canada as well. For instance in La Broquerie, Manitoba, it is celebrated on the weekend closest to June 24.

# Midsummer's Day or St. John's Day

*June 23 or 24*

Scandinavians in Nova Scotia have a big picnic and a bonfire in a park near Halifax and Dartmouth on the Saturday closest to June 23. On the same weekend, at the other end of the

## Midsummer fires

*People have lit midsummer fires in honour of the sun for centuries. They believed that when the sun was blazing at its strongest, bonfires would help keep it that way. Later, fire gods were worshipped with burning sacrifices, maybe even human victims. As Christianity spread across Europe, the old midsummer fires came to be called St. John's fires. Cats were sometimes burned in these fires in France. Poor cats, they represented evil to be cleansed by fire! (Today Danish-Canadians gather around a huge bonfire and pretend to burn a witch.)*

*In many parts of Europe, it was the custom for couples to jump through the flames for blessing, or for cattle to be driven through them for protection from evil. Sometimes during celebrations, flaming sticks were thrown into the air, in imitation of the sun. After these fires burned down, the ashes were used as fertilizer. The fireworks that are a part of many summer festivals today are descendants of these midsummer fires.*

*French-Canadians are not the only people to celebrate with fire at this time of year. In Newfoundland, the Irish-Canadians around St. Mary's Bay light bonfires for the solstice and call it Bonfire Night. The Poles call midsummer's eve Sobotka and light bonfires too. One old Polish custom was to set candlelit wreaths afloat on rivers.*

## Good apples, or bad?

*In the area around the Conquerall Banks, Nova Scotia, there is an old superstition among people with German backgrounds that if it rains on St. John's Day, June 24, the season's apples will all be wormy!*

## Discovery day

*Did you know that St. John's, Newfoundland, got its name because the explorer John Cabot sailed into its harbour on the eve of St. John's Day, 1497? In Newfoundland, June 24 is more important as a provincial holiday called Discovery Day than as Midsummer's Day or St. John's Day.*

country, there is a Scandinavian Midsummer Festival in Whistler Village, B.C. And the Calgary Danish-Canadian Club holds a St. Hans Festival on June 23 or the nearest weekend. In Ontario, the Finns and Norwegians have similar festivities, with singing, dancing, storytelling and general all-round merriment.

Many Swedish midsummer festivals include putting up a tall, decorated pole, or symbolic tree, in the centre of the dancing. It is often called a Maypole — in June! But it has no ribbons for dancers to weave around it. Instead it is more like an old-style English Maypole, from before the 1800s. At that time, English people just did country dances near or around a very tall pole covered with garlands of flowers and greenery. The Scandinavians still do these dances.

Latvians in Canada call June 24 John's Day and celebrate with a picnic and a bonfire. Estonians celebrate John's Day on the last weekend in June and combine the celebrations with a religious service in memory of the soldiers who died in their war of liberation against Russian and German forces, from 1918 to 1920.

Spanish-Canadians call John's Day San Juan. They make a delicious tart called *coca* every year on San Juan.

## Sommerfest

*Late June*

Can you figure out what the German word Sommerfest means? All the German-Canadian organizations hold a huge gathering called Sommerfest on the last weekend in June, usually in Kitchener, Ontario. This summer festival includes dancing, singing and gymnastic performances. Performance groups from West Germany are often invited to attend and add to the show. Canadians from many groups attend and enjoy the festivities and the sun.

# Lesbian/Gay Pride Day

*Last Saturday in June*

The gay liberation movement, championing every person's right to choose the way he or she expresses his or her sexuality, was born in New York City in 1969. During the 1970s various lesbian and gay groups in Canada began to observe Pride Day along with groups in the United States. They chose the weekend nearest the June 29 anniversary of the so-called Stonewall riots in New York to celebrate. In Toronto a police crackdown on gay activities in February 1981 generated enough support for the lesbian and gay community to make Pride Day an annual event in June — it's too cold to demonstrate in February! Each year since then, Lesbian/Gay Pride Day has been a combination of entertainment, political speeches and a parade.

# Ratha Yatra

*June or early July*

Ratha Yatra is the Hindu chariot festival that represents the travels of Lord Krishna. In India, a decorated chariot or huge cart is taken on a symbolic journey. A similar festive cart is taken out in Montreal, Vancouver and Toronto. An image of Krishna with his hands cut off is inside the cart. The missing hands are symbolic. They are meant to show that Krishna does not need to act to be powerful; the divine principle is everywhere. Indians from Bengal and Orissa and many members of the Hari Krishna movement celebrate Ratha Yatra. It occurs on the second day of the new moon of the third Hindu month.

## Krishna

*Krishna can be thought of as another name for Vishnu. Hindus believe Krishna is the most prominent incarnation of Vishnu. Like Ram, another incarnation of Vishnu, Krishna stands for the protection of the innocent and righteous people from evil forces. Krishna's story is told in the great Hindu epic called the Mahabharata. You may have heard of its famous section describing Krishna's words to his chariot companion on the field of battle. It is called the Gita or Bhagavadgita.*

## Prairie haiku

*Have you ever written a Japanese haiku? A haiku is a three-line verse that creates a mood or a picture about nature using strong, vivid words:*

*<u>The</u> <u>bees</u> <u>and</u> <u>flowers</u>*
*<u>Dancing</u> <u>in</u> <u>the</u> <u>summer</u> <u>breeze</u>*
*   <u>Against</u> <u>the</u> <u>blue</u> <u>sky.</u>*

*The underlines show you the syllables. There must be five syllables in the first line, seven syllables in the second and five in the final line. These are the "rules" of haiku-writing. Now that you know them, try writing your own summer haiku.*

# Iroquois Strawberry Festival

*Early summer*

What fruit do you look forward to most in early summer? Some people would say cherries; others, gooseberries. The Iroquois people say strawberries. They hold a Strawberry Festival, which is a "first fruits" ceremony to celebrate the coming of summer.

The Iroquois hold several religious ceremonies to mark the stages in planting, growing and harvesting food crops. They used to hold even more — including a raspberry festival. They think of themselves as part of an interlocking chain of obligations between humans and the Creator. At midwinter, for example, they ask him to give life to the plants; when he answers their call they have ceremonies to thank him. The Strawberry Festival is one of many times to give thanks.

The Strawberry Festival begins with a thanksgiving address and closes with a shorter version of the same speech. After the opening address, the Great Feather Dance is performed, with prayers directed to the appropriate spirit forces for the plants. Next a solemn sharing of strawberry juice takes place. A pail filled with crushed berries and juice is carried from person to person, and each one sips from a ladle and silently says thanks. Then another set of the Great Feather Dance is done before the closing and the final feast.

The Strawberry Festival is also the anniversary of the time when the famous 18th-century Seneca prophet named Handsome Lake had visions. Sometimes preaching from Handsome Lake's "code" (his advice about how to live) is done just before the festival starts.

# Canada Day

*July 1*

Canada's national day is like a giant birthday party, celebrated all over the country on July 1. Until recently these celebrations were known as Dominion Day. The first Dominion Day, on July 1, 1867, was the result of a vote by the British House of Commons giving the Canadian provinces permission to unite and form a confederation. The formal name for the law that gave this permission was the British North America Act. In September 1981 the name of this Act was changed. It was called the Constitution Act and was "patriated" (brought home to Canada from Britain).

Canada Day is the official date when we celebrate our unity as one country. The ways in which it is celebrated are as diverse as our people. Many, many different ethnic groups are involved, sharing their songs, sports, games, dances, crafts and foods. You name it, someone is probably doing it in honour of our national birthday! Some of the most common activities are parades, sports days, folk or film festivals, street dances and citizenship ceremonies.

But there are also air shows and puppet shows, lobster dinners and Inuit feasts. In Montreal there is a cruise to Cap-de-la-Madeleine, and in Whitehorse there is a recreation of a Klondike boat crossing. Richmond, B.C., holds the Steveston Salmon Festival. And in Eston, Saskatchewan, there is the World Championship Gopher Derby. Every year Prairie enthusiasts catch 64 gophers, name them and race them in eight races at the local fair.

At Flin Flon, in northern Manitoba, an annual trout-fishing festival is held over the Canada Day weekend. For those who don't want to fish, there is a Queen Mermaid contest and a Gold Rush Canoe Derby. The Flin Flon Trout Festival began in the 1950s to commemorate the opening of Highway 10,

## Privateer Days

*In Liverpool, Nova Scotia, and all around the South Shore area, the Canada Day weekend is the beginning of a local heritage celebration called Privateer Days. The privateers were men who smuggled supplies, instead of serving in the Royal Navy, during the American Revolution, the Napoleonic Wars and the War of 1812. Fireworks are lit over the Liverpool harbour in their memory on Friday night. On Saturday there are two parades. In the morning, the children of Liverpool march down Main Street, dressed according to a theme such as dolls or gingerbread. In the afternoon, the adult parade features lots of pipe bands. The weekend also includes a softball tournament and an old car competition.*

*One week later, on Sunday afternoon, Privateer Days reach a quiet finale. The local Queen's City Museum holds a Privateers' Tea on the lawn of a historic privateer's home, the Simeon Perkins House.*

## A big bang

*What does it take to put on a fireworks display for a whole country? To celebrate Canada Day in 1981, about 300 boxes of fireworks and 50 cannons were sent to 16 Canadian cities.*

which links Flin Flon with the rest of the province.

What is the most unusual or exciting activity you have ever taken part in for Canada's birthday? In 1981 the Japanese community in Winnipeg made 1 000 paper birds and launched them into the sky as part of an Air Spectacle!

Of course, no national birthday party is complete without fireworks, which are the special evening feature of Canada Day festivities everywhere. Staging a fireworks show takes a lot of work, but it is especially difficult in Canada's North. The sun shines 24 hours a day at this time of year in the North, so ordinary fireworks won't work. Instead northern fireworks

## Cake!

*Birthday parties usually include a cake, but did you know that we have an official Canadian cake? The recipe, which uses maple syrup, was created by Joanne Young of Nova Scotia. Canada's birthday cakes are baked in special tins shaped like giant maple leaves and are often used for prizes or holiday ceremonies.*

## Canada Day "Dip in the Bay"

*In Churchill, Manitoba, there is an annual Canada Day relay race, with the last runner taking a plunge into Hudson Bay. The water temperature is usually no more than 10°C (50°F)...brrrr! The day also includes games, contests, a parade, a food fair and a dance.*

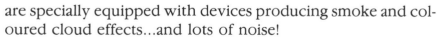

are specially equipped with devices producing smoke and coloured cloud effects...and lots of noise!

The biggest display of fireworks of all goes off at the International Freedom Festival, jointly sponsored by the cities of Windsor, Ontario, and Detroit, Michigan. The fireworks actually are set off on the night of July 2, because the festival is celebrating both Canada Day and July 4, Independence Day in the United States. All kind of events — from concerts to contests — take place during the last week in June and the first week in July.

# Our national anthem for a birthday present!

"O Canada" officially became Canada's national anthem on the country's 100th birthday in 1967. It was composed by a Québécois, Calixa Lavallée, to words written by Quebec Judge Adolphe-Basile Routhier. There are several English versions — with entirely different words from the original French — but the most common one is by a Toronto schoolteacher, Robert Stanley Weir. Weir used a line written by Alfred, Lord Tennyson, the English Poet Laureate at the time, describing Canada as "That true north." Some people feel Weir's reference to Canada as "our home and native land" leaves out the growing number of Canadians who were not born here. What do you think?

## Confederation

The idea of a Canadian union, or confederation, was first discussed in 1854 in the Assembly of the province of Nova Scotia. Then, in 1864, a conference was held on Prince Edward Island to consider uniting the Maritime provinces. But Upper and Lower Canada (the regions that became Ontario and Quebec) wanted to be included, and so a second conference was held that same year. The people who attended this meeting and approved of the plan for a wider federation are known as the Fathers of Confederation.

At the time of Confederation, everyone argued about whether to call this new union the "Kingdom" or the "Dominion" of Canada. In a letter written in 1889, Sir John A. Macdonald explained that "Dominion" was chosen because the former name "would wound the sensibilities of the Yankees." Naturally enough, the United States would not like to have a kingdom for its northern neighbour, after rebelling against one!

Despite their agreement to unite, the original four provinces were not all equally happy with the arrangement, for the benefits to them were not all the same. It was said that "Ontario was jubilant, Quebec doubtful and expectant, New Brunswick sullen, Nova Scotia rebellious." In fact, Nova Scotia was so angry that it did not celebrate Dominion Day until 1898!

At the historic meeting of 1864, both Newfoundland and Prince Edward Island refused to join the new confederation. Prince Edward Island did come into Confederation a few years later, in 1872, but it took until 1949 for Newfoundland to agree to join. In the meantime, British Columbia had joined in 1871, and in the same year the province of Manitoba was created and joined. The provinces of Alberta and Saskatchewan were formed from two territories and admitted to the Dominion in 1905.

# Czechoslovak Day and Sokol Slet

*First Sunday in July*

Have you noticed how some special days — the Fête de la St-Jean-Baptiste is an example — have a combined religious and political significance? Czechoslovak Day is another festival like this. It occurs on the first Sunday in July. The celebrations include a religious service, the laying of memorial wreaths and speeches (about the struggle for liberty in the area of Europe now known as Czechoslovakia) and Sokol performances.

Sokol is a patriotic athletic organization, something like the Scouting movement. The word Sokol means "falcon," a bird that is both strong and swift. Falcons are also intelligent and accept discipline. Members of Sokol try to be good citizens and patriots. Instead of meetings, they attend meets and practices for calisthenics, track and field, apparatus work and certain sports. The first Sokol unit was formed in Prague in 1862, and the first one in Canada started in Frank, Alberta, in 1912. Sokol Toronto was formed in 1931. When many different Sokol units get together it is called Sokol Slet. (The word *slet* means "flying together in one place.") One place in Canada where Czechs and Slovaks gather together to observe Czechoslovak Day and Sokol Slet is Scarborough, Ontario.

# Louis Riel Day

*Early July*

The day before the Saskatoon Fair and Exhibition is called Louis Riel Day in Saskatchewan. Riel was the famous Métis leader who helped his people (in what is now Manitoba) form a government and become part of the newly created Dominion of Canada in 1870. His skill and courage were instrumental in helping the young Red River Settlement become the province of Manitoba.

LOUIS RIEL

## The trial of Louis Riel

*In Regina, Saskatchewan, Canada Day has been the opening day of a special play about the life of Louis Riel for more than 20 years. The dramatic story of the Northwest Rebellion of 1885 is staged all over the province throughout the summer.*

## Back to Batoche Days

*For ten days in late July, the Métis lands near Batoche National Historic Site (88 km/55 miles north of Saskatoon) are the site of many activities related to Riel. There are ball tournaments and music festivals, fiddling and jigging contests, as well as a native rodeo. On the last Sunday, there is a commemorative church service for the Métis and native people who died in the rebellion. The traditional Feast of the Dead, honouring those who died, is held that evening. For the 100th anniversary in 1985, there was also a special native peoples' conference and an international pow-wow, featuring native dancers from many parts of the world.*

In 1885, Riel led a rebellion against the Canadian authorities in the West because he feared that more and more Métis lands would be lost to new settlers. The rebellion began in northern Manitoba and spread to Saskatchewan, but it failed. Riel was convicted of treason and hanged. Today his name is a symbol for native independence.

On Louis Riel Day a race is held in which eight-member teams demonstrate traditional Métis skills. They must run, ride horseback *and* canoe to the finish line! There is an old European flavour to Louis Riel Day as well: the world championship for eating *holubsti* (cabbage rolls) is held at the same time. Do you suppose it is possible to be both the world champ *holubsti*–eater *and* on the winning race team?

# Tanabata

*June, July, August or September*

Tanabata, the Japanese Star Festival, was traditionally held on the seventh day of the seventh moon on the lunar calendar. Often nowadays it is celebrated on the seventh of July, the seventh month on our calendar. In Canada, it may be held in late August or September. The Japanese Cultural Centre in Toronto celebrates Tanabata with demonstrations of Japanese dancing, judo, karate, origami and flower-arranging during Toronto's multicultural festival, Caravan, in late June.

The date of Tanabata may change, but the legend behind it remains the same. It is said that the weaver-princess star, named Shokujo (also known as Vega), fell in love with the herdboy star, Kengyu (or Altair), who came to earth where Shokujo and her sisters were weavers for the gods. The two star people lived so happily together on earth that they forgot the tasks they were supposed to perform. After three years the gods became angry because their herds were left untended and they had no new clothes. The lovers were separated on opposite sides of the river called the Milky Way. But they were so unhappy that Shokujo's father, the heavenly king, relented and allowed them to meet one day a year. Now each year as the constellations of Vega and Altair draw near in the skies, it is said that Shokujo is crossing over the Milky Way on a bridge made by a flock of joyful birds to meet her lover. Some Japanese say that if you can find a grape arbour on this night and stand under it, you will hear the happy laughter of Shokujo and Kengyu.

The Chinese also celebrate the seventh day of the seventh moon but call it the Seven Sisters Festival. Chinese-Canadians from Singapore and Malaysia observe the festival as a special time for women and sisterhood.

## Weather permitting...

*In Great Britain July 15 is St. Swithin's Day. St. Swithin was a 9th-century monk who has come to be called the "rain saint" of England. Although he became Bishop of Winchester, he was so humble he asked to be buried outside the cathedral when he died, so the rain could fall on him. When a later bishop tried to move this grave on July 15, it began to rain and didn't stop for 40 days!*

*Since then there has been a superstition that the weather for the next six weeks can be foretold on July 15. The Scots made a rhyme about it, which goes:*

*St. Swithin's Day, if thou dost rain,*
*For forty days it will remain;*
*St. Swithin's Day, if thou art fair,*
*For forty days 'twill rain nae mair.*

# Japanese Obon Festival

*July 15*

Japanese Buddhists celebrate Obon on July 15 in honour of the spirits of their departed ancestors. They believe these spirits make an annual visit to the family home, and so a festival of lighted lanterns is held to guide them. The festival ends with a circular folk dance. In Toronto it is now customary for Buddhist dancers to perform at Nathan Phillips Square, in front of City Hall, on the evening of July 14. Another place where the Japanese Obon Festival is celebrated is Richmond, B.C.

Vietnamese Buddhists call this festival Vu Lan. They remember their deceased ancestors with reverence and hold ceremonies in Buddhist temples for several days, starting on the 15th day of the seventh moon.

Cung Co Hon, or the Chinese-Buddhist Feast of the Lonesome Souls, is similar to the Japanese and Vietnamese Buddhist festivals held at this time. On the eve of the festival, families hold a feast for all lonesome souls, so that these souls will not harm them. People lay out food — rice, boiled chicken and cakes — and burn paper specially printed with pictures of money and warm clothes — all meant for the spirits!

# St. Anne's Day

*July 26*

St. Anne was the mother of Mary, the mother of Jesus. In the Middle Ages she was a favourite saint in Brittany (part of France) and England. In early Canada she was thought of as the special guardian of all who lived or worked by the sea. In 1658 a chapel was built in the name of St. Anne at Beaupré, east of Quebec City on the St. Lawrence River. It is said that some sailors from Brittany vowed to build the chapel if they were saved from a terrible storm. They were and they did. Then one of the men working to build this chapel was miraculously cured of his rheumatism. The news spread, and lame or sick people made pilgrimages to Beaupré from all over. Native people came as well to seek the blessing of "Good Saint Anne."

In the past 300 years, the original chapel of St. Anne at Beaupré has been rebuilt and enlarged eight times. Thousands of worshippers visit Sainte-Anne-de-Beaupré every year, with as many as 15,000 coming on July 26. Most visitors come to be healed and stay for nine full days of prayer to St. Anne.

The first big event of the pilgrimage is a candlelight parade to the Stations of the Cross on July 25, the eve of St. Anne's Day. While the church bells peal, a slow-moving line of pilgrims winds out of the church, across the road and up the hillside. Their lighted candles glow inside shades made of red paper. The next afternoon the bells toll again and summon everyone to the Ceremony of the Blessing of the Sick. Hundreds of people gather in orderly rows of wheelchairs, hoping to be miraculously cured. The candlelight processions continue for the next eight nights.

One special group of visitors to Beaupré at this time are the Rom, or gypsy people. They come for Santana (notice the similarity to St. Anne) from all over Canada and the United States. However, the Rom are not particularly concerned with healing; they do not bring their sick to be blessed, but say prayers on their behalf and toast St. Anne with whiskey during the processions. For the Rom, Santana is an annual reunion and social time marked by special feasts called *slavi*.

The Rom camp on the grounds around the church, turning the area into an old-time gypsy encampment. At the *slavi* on July 26, in honour of St. Anne, lamb is barbecued over many open fires. Each family prepares a lavish outdoor *slava* table,

## Summer contests in Manitoba

The name Manitoba is a native word that means "the god who speaks." Perhaps the god who speaks in Manitoba is a very playful, if not downright crazy god, for this province has a greater number of silly festivals and contests than any other in Canada, and they almost all occur during the summer. There are frog jumping championships early in August (see page 179), and in mid-July there are two more worthy of mention:

- The Canadian Open Wellington Boot Throwing Championships are held on the third weekend in July in Dugald, Manitoba. The event seems pretty self-explanatory...but what happens if it rains and people need to wear their boots?

- The Canadian Turtle Derby takes place in Boissevain, near the Canada-U.S. border, around the second weekend in July. The derby, started in 1972, pits Western painted turtles against one another in a race. It is so well established now that the town boasts an 11-m (36-foot) statue of Tommy the Turtle plus the world's only electric starting gate for turtles. On Friday there are children's turtle races and on Saturday both Canadian and American championships. The finals and the world championship take place on Sunday.

For each of the more than 40 different heats, turtles are placed under separate cages at the centre of a 14-m (46-foot) circle. When the cages are lifted, the turtles are supposed to start moving towards the outer rim of the circle — but they may not, or they may be distracted! The first to finally reach the outside edge is the winner. The world record (prior to 1985) of 23.69 seconds is held by a turtle named Adam I, owned by Adam Burke of Emerson, Manitoba. People come from far and wide to bring their entries — others rent turtles. Not surprisingly, the entire town of Boissevain turns into a carnival for the duration of the derby.

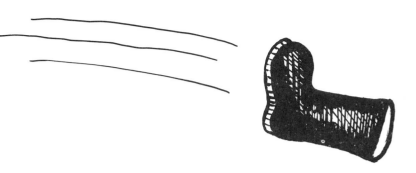

and everyone eats at everyone else's table in turn. Guests say to the host: "T'al baxtali ki slava, t'al baxtali ki Santana." This means "May your *slava* be lucky, may your St. Anne's Day be lucky." The host answers, "Te pomozil tuke e Santana," which means "May St. Anne bless you." Feasting begins at two o'clock, and the men are served first, according to Rom tradition. After them, the elderly are served, then the married women, unmarried young people and finally the children. But there is plenty of food for the main course, followed by cake decorated with candles for St. Anne.

After the *slava*, the dancing begins. There is time to renew old friendships and talk with relatives. For most Rom, their main church-centred activity is the nightly candlelight processions on the shrine hill. Some carry religious banners, some hold candles, and others stand and watch. Santana is a time for solidarity, when Rom people say, "We have to be together and celebrate all night." Singing, preparing food together and camping out are all part of the "peace of St. Anne."

## St. Ann's Missions

*July*

St. Ann is considered the patron saint of many Christian native people, who spell her name without the "e." She is lovingly called the grandmother of the Micmacs in Nova Scotia and New Brunswick. St. Ann's Missions are festive religious gatherings held by the Micmacs during July. At the most well-known mission, on Chapel Island off Cape Breton Island, native people gather for ten days. Chapel Island is a sacred place to the Micmacs, and many families travel there hoping to be healed. The Mission is a time for special religious ceremonies for children and adults, as well as for meetings of the Native Grand Council.

St. Ann's Day itself, July 26, is called Procession Day. A crowd of native people carry the statue of St. Ann out and around the church and up a small hill. At one time, guns and cannons were fired constantly during this ceremony. Later on Procession Day, there is a special dinner, dancing and the acclamation of chiefs, or Grand Captains. Another old custom at the Mission on Chapel Island is "crawling to St. Ann." Devout people crawl on their hands and knees to the feet of the statue of the saint to kiss them. They begin outside the church and crawl together, stopping to pray every three or four paces. They believe that any sickness you have can be cured by "going to see St. Ann on your knees."

## Pile O'Bones Sunday

*Late July*

The City of Regina sits on land that was once called Pile O'Bones because Plains Indian hunters left a pile of buffalo bones there to mark the place to cross Wascana Creek. It was renamed Regina in 1882 after Queen Victoria (*regina* is Latin for "queen"). Now Canada's largest outdoor picnic (or so they claim in Regina) is held on the last Sunday in July. It features a Buffalo Days costume contest and lots of good food. (Chances are there's a good-sized pile of bones left over after the picnic too!)

## The Sun Dance of the Native People

*Various dates in the summer*

Think of fasting and dancing for hours in one place, with your eyes fixed on a sacred symbol. What a lot of discipline it must take! That is what native people do in the Sun Dance, in the hope of gaining spiritual wisdom. The Iroquois hold their Sun Dance in their longhouse, in the late spring. In Saskatchewan, the Plains Cree Sun Dance is held in a special encampment for about four days every summer, during the full moon.

Many native people direct their prayers to the Great Spirit through the medium of the sun. They say the sun is the nearest thing to the Great Spirit that humans can see. It causes the grasses and trees to grow; it causes the animals, which feed upon the grasses, to grow; and so it causes humans to live, because they feed upon both the plants and the animals. The Sun Dance is really a prayer.

The Plains Cree offer their prayers every year in a newly built Sun Dance lodge. The lodge is a shelter made of cottonwood poles, with a centre pole symbolizing the sun. This pole is carefully chosen from trees in the woods, then prepared for its eventual position in the dance. While still in the forest, a red circle is painted around it. Next, its trunk is wrapped with bright cloth. On the second day, the tree is purified by burning sweetgrass and everyone smokes the ceremonial pipe around it. Then the sacred tree is cut, stripped of most of its branches and dragged to the centre of camp. There the symbols of moon, thunderbird and buffalo are cut into the bark, and the whole tree is draped with coloured cloth. After this, 28 other poles are cut to construct the lodge itself. At noon a ritual meal of rice and raisins is made and served to everyone, for the sharing of food and tobacco is a traditional sign of goodwill.

Finally it is time for the ceremony of raising the centre pole. Offerings of tobacco and black cloth are put into a hole in the ground, and a prayer is said, asking the tree to preside over the camp. Near the top of the sacred tree where it forks into a "V," a bundle of cottonwood branches is tied to represent the thunderbird's nest. Then the branches are shaken, as if to drive the thunderbird from his nest. A shrill whistle is blown to sound like him, and the tree is quickly raised into

# Sun dancers

Before Europeans came to North America, the Sun Dance was the major religious ceremony of the Plains Cree, Blackfoot and other tribes. Summer for the native people, as for other Canadians, was and is the time for large gatherings. Tribal alliances were made, friendships renewed and major religious rituals held. Scattered bands met for communal bison hunts, the Sun Dance or the Medicine Dance. The old pattern for the Blackfoot people, for example, was to begin to gather in June, hunt in July and dance in August for eight to ten days at a Sun Dance encampment. Then the bands dispersed again for the autumn hunting season.

The Sun Dance represented a traditional way of life that European settlers and Christian missionaries attempted to crush. As native people lost more and more land and freedom, their sense of pride in themselves was also lost. Their frustration came to the surface during the Sun Dance gatherings. By the late 19th century these were often marked by violent, drunken brawls. By the 1920s the Sun Dance was thoroughly suppressed.

Fortunately, some native people refused to abandon their old religious beliefs, and the Sun Dance was never totally forgotten. The Blackfoot-Peigan reserve outside Lethbridge, Alberta, is one place where the Sun Dance was preserved. In recent years, as North American native peoples have reclaimed their culture and customs, the Sun Dance has been revived. Today, true to its origins, it is a ceremonial quest for spiritual vision and supernatural power. Native groups now ban alcohol at their celebrations.

position. Men and boys pull on the attached ropes while the women shout:

> "Hurry! Hurry! May the tree go up safely and remain firmly in the ground, Great Spirit, for we do not wish misfortune for the coming year!"

The base of the tree is wedged into position, the bright cotton cloth flaps gently in the wind, the other poles are set in place and the lodge is ready.

Ceremonial drumming, dancing and singing begin on the third day and continue through the fourth. Dancers gaze steadfastly at the pole, perhaps fixing their eyes on the carving of the thunderbird, and move in time to the music. Some hold firmly to the ends of brightly coloured material radiating from the centre pole. That way they hope to establish a connection between themselves and the source of spiritual power. All the dancers pray to receive a vision or a dream to strengthen or guide them in their lives. The vision ends the ceremony.

When the Sun Dance finishes, the lodge is dismantled except for the centre pole. It will stay up in the encampment area as a memorial, along with previous years' centre poles. Rain at any time during the four days is a favourable sign that prayers have been heard. Unless it rains, many participants will fast throughout the Sun Dance.

# Tish'ah Be'av

*July or August*

Tish'ah Be'av is the traditional day on which Jews mourn the catastrophes that have befallen their people, from the destruction of the First and Second Temples in Jerusalem to the Holocaust. It occurs in July or August and is a fast day. Jews believe their mourning will give them spiritual strength as well as help them to remember both the past and their responsibility towards the future.

# Swiss National Day

*August 1*

How good are you at throwing heavy rocks? You might find out if you celebrated August 1 with Swiss-Canadians. On this date in 1291, all the Swiss territories, or cantons, were united; the event was a bit like our Confederation.

In Alberta, the Swiss celebrate this ancient national day with traditional folk music, dancing and sports, such as crossbow competitions. They also hold a heavy-rock-throwing contest! This comes from an early 19th-century competition among Swiss Alpine herdsmen. (It is still held at a festival in Interlaken, Switzerland, once every four years.)

On the night of August 1, Swiss-Canadians light bonfires to symbolize the preservation of a free Swizerland. Centuries ago, bonfires were signals of rebellion across the country. Swiss National Day celebrations also include fireworks and a children's lampion parade by night. Can you guess what a lampion is? The word means "little lamp." The lampions are made of red paper and are often decorated with the Swiss cross or the coats of arms of the different cantons.

# Carifesta and Caribana

*The first weekend in July or August*

Have you ever heard a steel drum band from the West Indies? They make a very loud, distinctive sound. Imagine the sound made by *dozens* of steel bands, add summer weather and many wildly happy people, dressed in fantastic costumes, and you have a parade straight out of Carifesta and Caribana.

People from the Caribbean Islands began Caribana in 1967 in Toronto, as an expression of black community life for Canada's Centennial. At first it was put on by Canadian blacks and West Indian immigrants from the English-speaking islands such as Trinidad, Barbados, St. Kitts and Jamaica. They wanted to continue many of their home islands' pre-Lenten Carnival celebrations with costumes, steel drum bands, reggae music, colour and excitement. But Caribbean Carnival (see

## Edible garden flowers

*Do you like salads in summer? Try adding new colours and flavours to summer salads with petals from the following garden flowers: marigolds, roses, sweet peas, dandelions, nasturtiums, pansies, day lilies, violets or borage. (You can also eat the leaves of dandelion and nasturtium flowers.)*

*If you like soup with your salad, marigold petals are good for seasoning. For sandwiches, try thinly sliced white or brown bread and butter with a filling of fresh-picked nasturtiums. Use two flowers and one leaf to start. If you like the taste, increase the amount you use, in the same proportion of two to one.*

*Finally, for dessert, try a cake decorated with sugared rose petals or mint leaves. Beat an egg white with a fork until it begins to froth. Dip the petals or leaves into the egg white, then sprinkle with very finely ground white sugar (not icing sugar). Spread the sugared petals and mint leaves on wax paper and leave them to dry for two to three days. Store in an airtight container until you're ready to eat.*

page 74 for more Carnival information) falls in Canada's winter. Caribana's organizers wisely rescheduled the Canadian Carnival to summer.

Soon blacks from every background were joining in the festivities in Toronto on the August long weekend. Montreal started to hold its own Carifesta, on July 1, a few years later. Other similar Carnivals developed in New York and London, England, too.

Today Caribana and Carifesta are uniquely Canadian events. The centrepiece of the festivities is a huge parade. Steel bands glide by on trucks with friends and supporters clustered around them, and other parade-goers dance by in costumes that have taken months to make. This colourful, energetic Caribbean celebration is the highlight of a week of related activities, such as concerts, dances and beauty pageants.

## August Civic Holiday

*First Monday in August*

August is the supreme vacation month! And to start things off right, the first Monday in the month is a civic holiday (that means it has no religious importance to any group) all across Canada except Quebec. In different provinces, it has different names. In British Columbia, for instance, it is B.C. Day. It is named Simcoe Day in Ontario, for the first Lieutenant-Governor of Ontario, John Simcoe. In Alberta and Saskatchewan it is Heritage Day.

In Halifax, Nova Scotia, the August civic holiday is known as Natal Day. It is the birthday of Halifax, which was founded in 1749. Today, more than 200 years later, the birthday party includes fireworks, a parade and a free rock concert on Citadel Hill. Lots of towns and cities across Canada have similar birthday celebrations at this time. Do you know of any?

# Islendingadagurinn

*August long weekend*

If you noticed that the first part of this holiday sounds like Iceland, you're right. Since 1890, there has been an Icelandic Festival, or Islendingadagurinn, in Manitoba on the August long weekend. This gathering, which means Icelanders' Day, was begun in Winnipeg by an Icelandic newspaper editor named Jan Olafson. After 1932, it moved to Gimli, where the park was bigger. During the 1960s it changed from a single-day event to two and then three days. Islendingadagurinn is attended by Icelandic-Canadians and their friends from across the country on the long weekend. (Manitoba has the largest Icelandic community outside Iceland itself.)

The weekend features reunions and all the usual trappings of a good fair — delicious food (in this case Icelandic rolled pancakes), a tug-of-war, fireworks, a concert and a parade, which features a replica of a Viking longboat. A Maid of the Mountain, Fjallkona, representing both the motherland and motherhood, is elected to give an annual speech. But one of the most popular Islendingadagurinn events is the Viking Challenge. It's a pillow fight between two contestants who sit on a pole stretched over water!

# Frog Follies/Folies Grenouilles

*August long weekend*

Every year on the August long weekend in Manitoba children in St. Pierre-Jolys beg their parents to take them to the Frog Follies. No wonder. The highlight of the festival is the Canadian National Frog Jumping Championships.

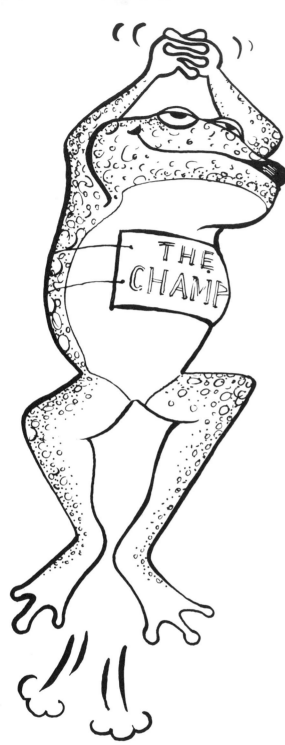

_rrribbit!_

THE CHAMP

The Frog Follies began in 1970 as a way to draw people to the town's annual country fair. Now they have become far more important than the parade, agricultural exhibition, tug-of-war championships _or_ entertainment over the three-day fair. Both children and adults may be "jockeys" and enter a contestant. Frogs can be rented if jockeys can't catch their own.

The winner is the frog that covers the greatest distance in three hops — three hops only, and only in one direction. The frogs aren't very good at sticking to these rules, but the most their jockeys are allowed to do is pound the platform behind them to encourage them. In 1985, the longest overall jump was made by a frog named Tequila, owned by a man from the Liquor Control Commission. Do you suppose he helped his frog jump 449 cm (14 feet 9 inches) by getting him drunk?

## Festival of Freedom or Emancipation Day

_August long weekend_

Emancipation means "setting free" — it was a very significant word in North America during the 1700s and 1800s. At that time, most black people were the slaves and servants of white people. Some tried to buy their freedom; others ran away. Many black slaves escaped to Canada from the United States by travelling on the "Underground Railroad." This was a secret chain of people willing to smuggle slaves north to freedom. The Underground Railroad ended in southern Ontario, and some former slaves decided to settle there.

In southern Ontario, a special celebration for the freedom of former slaves was held as early as 1814. It was called "an anniversary of African emancipation." After slavery was abolished throughout the British Empire in 1834, Emancipation Day was observed each year. The first Emancipation

Day event was in St. Catharines on August 1, 1835. Soon Hamilton and Toronto were both holding large celebrations, but Windsor, Amherstburg, London, Owen Sound and Oro Township also organized annual events. These usually included parades, picnics and thanksgiving services.

In Windsor from the 1930s through the 1970s, Emancipation Day celebrations over the August long weekend were huge — as many as 200,000 people attended. In the 1950s both Eleanor Roosevelt and Martin Luther King spoke and received awards as part of the festival. Recently the name has been changed to the Festival of Freedom. It is organized by the North American Black Museum and Cultural Centre, in Amherstburg, near Windsor, and features a fashion show, beauty contest, dance, parade and church services.

Other towns in southern Ontario — such as Chatham, Dresden and Wallaceburg — that had early black settlements, once had or still have similar celebrations.

## Ilinden

*August 2*

Macedonians honour the prophet Elijah on this day. They also remember a not-so-ancient event, the unsuccessful 1903 uprising against the Turks to free their country. More than 20,000 Macedonian-Canadians in the Toronto area attend a huge annual picnic for Ilinden. It is usually held on the August long weekend.

## The Feast of the Transfiguration

*August 6 or 19*

The word "transfiguration" is similar to "transformation" — they both mean a change. But when someone is transfigured, the change is supposed to be to something better. Several of

## The Shadow Project

*Strange white shadows of ordinary people and trees, lamp posts or parking meters appear on the night of August 5 all across Canada. In 1985, 43 Canadian cities took part in this unique protest against nuclear war. Organized by Performing Artists for Nuclear Disarmament, the project is a way of showing what would happen if a nuclear bomb exploded. Close to the centre of the explosion, people and things would simply "evaporate," leaving only a ghostly shadow behind.*

*Using a paint made of chalk and water, and a cut-out silhouette of themselves, a friend, pet or object, hundreds of people took to the streets to make shadows of the world they love. In Toronto, for example, 1 000 painters made 25,000 shadows — there were shadows of dogs, cats and children with doll carriages. There were even shadows of people carrying pizzas outside a pizza parlour and commuters with briefcases outside a subway station!*

Jesus' disciples said they saw him transfigured, standing on a mountain top, at one time in his life. He looked like a glowing angel and stood with Moses and Elijah on either side of him. The Transfiguration is important to Christians because it shows that Moses and Elijah recognized Jesus as the Messiah.

The Feast of the Transfiguration celebrates the change in the appearance of Jesus on the mountain. The feast originated in the Eastern churches, where it is celebrated on August 19, the Julian Calendar equivalent of August 6. The ceremonies are a bit like Thanksgiving; they celebrate the abundance of nature and the changes that are taking place in the natural world.

In Canada, people of Ukrainian background sometimes observe a Thanksgiving-like ceremony too. They believe that every living thing needs blessing on this day, and so fruits and flowers are all taken to church to be blessed. A special flat cake, called *poloneytya*, made with honey and poppyseed, is served.

# Hiroshima Day

*August 6*

Hiroshima Day is observed in many parts of the world and in Canada with special vigils and peace marches. It is held to commemorate the dropping of the first atomic bomb on the Japanese city of Hiroshima on August 6, 1945. Three days later, a second nuclear bomb fell on the city of Nagasaki.

It was hoped that the use of nuclear bombs would help bring about the surrender of the Japanese and the end of World War II. Although the attacks on Japan did indeed help end the war, the problems that were both created and revealed by the nuclear explosions, such as radioactive contamination and illness, are now the biggest challenges facing humankind.

August 6, 1945, has come to be called the beginning of the Nuclear Age. Can you tell why? People from many different backgrounds unite on this day to declare their commitment to never letting another nuclear bomb be used against any humans, anywhere.

## The story of the paper cranes

When the atomic bomb exploded over Hiroshima in 1945, Sadako Sasaki was only two years old. She did not have any apparent after-effects of the explosion, although her brother died. However, ten years later, when Sadako was 12, she developed leukemia. An old Japanese legend says cranes will bring long life, health, happiness and good luck. And the Japanese art of paper-folding (called origami) is also an old tradition. So Sadako started folding a thousand origami paper cranes in the hope that she would become well. Sadako said to her cranes, "I will write peace on your wings and you will fly all over the world."

Today paper cranes have flown around the world with the message of world peace, even though Sadako died before she could fold all 1 000 cranes. Her classmates began to collect one-yen coins (worth about half a penny) from all over the country to build a monument to her and to all the children in Hiroshima who died as a result of the atomic explosion. They raised the equivalent of $25,000! The money went towards the construction of a children's monument in the Peace Park in Hiroshima.

This memorial to children everywhere has a statue of Sadako on the top, holding a huge outline of a paper crane above her head. People often hang strings of paper cranes at the base of the memorial. Written on the base are the words, "This is our cry, this is our prayer: peace in the world."

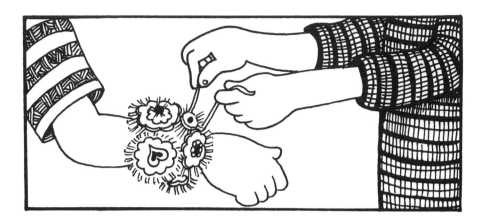

# Raksha Bandhan

*During August*

In your family, is there any special way or time to show that you love your brothers or sisters and want to protect them from harm? Many Hindu families have a summer ceremony to do just this, called Raksha Bandhan. It is based on an old legend.

Hindus say that when their gods warred with demons, the god Indra was helped by his wife. She tied a silk charm around his wrist to protect him from evil. After that, Indra was able to defeat his enemies and win back his home in the heavens. Today, Hindu girls give their brothers woven bracelets called *rakhi* in a special ceremony. Brahmin Hindus also change the sacred threads that they wear year-round on this day.

Some girls and women weave the *rakhi* they give their brothers; others buy them. *Rakhi* are often made of red and gold thread, but whatever the colour, they are always bright with tinsel. They represent the bond between brothers and sisters and are meant to give protection. When a sister ties a *rakhi* around her brother's wrist, she also gives him a candy or something sweet to eat. Brothers are very proud to wear their *rakhi* and give their sisters a present in return. Hindus think that Raksha Bandhan is a very sad day if you have no sisters. However, boys without sisters can be "adopted." If a girl ties a *rakhi* on a boy, he will try to protect her like a brother.

# Janmashtami

*During August*

Janmashtami is a joyful day-long religious event, held on the eighth day of the waning moon in the Hindu month of Bhadra. It celebrates another event in the life of Lord Krishna — his birth and rescue from potential death. Families and temples make tableaus displaying all the details of this period — rather like the crèche scenes Christians make about Jesus in December. Krishna's story is very dramatic too: exactly at midnight on this day, his father carried him out of prison, where he had been born, and swapped him with a cow herder's baby daughter for his safety.

Hindus try to relate to Krishna in various forms — they adore him as a little boy called Balakrishna, as a lover or as a friend. For this festival, the most common image is of Balakrishna crawling and stretching out his right hand for an offering. Everyone makes an offering to Krishna, either at a home shrine or in the temple, and then gives a push to a swinging cradle, made specially for the occasion in the god's honour.

In Canada, many Hindus hold a dinner on Janmashtami, followed by all-night prayer vigils and singing and dancing devoted to Lord Krishna. At midnight it is traditional to make lots of noise by blowing on conch shells in celebration.

# Ganesh Chathurti

*Late in August or September*

Have you ever seen a picture or statue of a Hindu god who looks like an elephant? He is called Ganesh or Ganapati. On the fourth day of the new moon in the Hindu month of Ashvin, Hindus from central and south India celebrate a day in honour of this elephant-headed god. Ganesh is actually one of Lord Shiva's sons. He is known as the "remover of all

obstacles,'' or the god who gives you what you need to accomplish a certain task or goal. The round belly on statues of this god is often shiny, because people rub it for his blessing as they say their prayers. All Hindus worship Ganesh. Since he removes all obstacles, Hindus must perform a *puja*, or act of worship, for Ganesh before they pray to any other Hindu god or goddess.

## The Assumption of Mary

*August 15*

The Acadians' national holiday is August 15, the feast day for Our Lady of Assumption, their patron saint. It is the most important day of the year for them. (The Assumption refers to Mary's death and ascent to heaven.) The Festival Acadien is also held around this date. It is a big homecoming time, with lots of music and drama and other special events.

Acadians first arrived in what is now Nova Scotia from France in 1604. A hundred and fifty years later, they were expelled by British soldiers and had to find homes elsewhere. They slowly returned and in the 1880s Maritime Acadians adopted their own flag, as well as their own patron saint. Today there is an Acadian community proud of its heritage.

The most exciting — and noisy — part of the August 15 holiday is called *tintamarre*. This is the bedlam of sounds made by banging pots and pans, beating drums and blowing whistles at exactly 6 p.m.

On the Sunday nearest to the 15th, there are special church services and picnics in the Acadian community. In Caraquet, New Brunswick, this is also the day for the annual blessing of the fleet. To a slightly quieter accompaniment of sirens blowing, decorated boats sail past the main dock in the harbour, where a priest blesses them.

Many different Catholic congregations also celebrate

August 15 as a religious holiday for the Assumption of Mary. The Portuguese call Mary "Our Lady of the Angels" at this time. Greek-Canadians may undertake a partial fast before celebrating the Assumption. Spanish-Canadians call the holiday Asunción. It is the name-day for all Catholic women called Mary. For more information on name-days, see page 12.

On the Sunday following August 15, Sicilian-Canadians in Toronto hold a special mass for Our Lady of Assumption, whom they call the Madonna del Assunta, after a huge outdoor procession. About 10,000 people join in, as the statue of the Madonna is carried from the church to Monarch Park. The rest of the day is busy with soccer games, other sporting events, singing, dancing and eating. The Madonna del Assunta is the patron saint for many Sicilians too.

Other Catholic congregations have pilgrimages around this date. For instance, in Kaposvar, Saskatchewan, the Our Lady of Assumption Pilgrimage is held on the Sunday closest to August 15. In Rama, Saskatchewan, there is a candlelight procession on August 14. The next day there is a procession to the Stations of the Cross, at the grotto beside St. Anthony's Roman Catholic Church. Held on the anniversary of Mary's Assumption for almost 50 years, it is called the Our Lady of Lourdes Pilgrimage.

Polish-Canadians celebrate a kind of early harvest festival on August 15, which they call the Feast of the Mother of God of the Herbs. People bring fruits, vegetables and other foods to the church. The main ceremony involves blessing these foods. After being blessed, the food is given to poor or needy people.

People of Armenian Orthodox background don't celebrate the Feast of the Assumption of the Virgin Mary until August 28 because they use a different calendar. As part of the Feast, the first grapes of the season are blessed and distributed. Originally this was an ancient harvest and New

Year's festival. The Ukrainians celebrate August 28 in a similar way, taking flowers to church to be sprinkled with holy water and blessed by the priest. Then the flowers are taken home as blessed objects. These celebrations of the Assumption are very similar to those of the Transfiguration, held earlier in August (see page 181). This is probably because August is the beginning of the harvest.

## Pateti and Navroz

*Late August*

Pateti is the last day of the Zoroastrian year for Parsis (see page 95 for more information on Zoroastrianism and Parsis). It is the time to repent (be sorry for) any wrongs you may have done in the past year — Pateti means Repentance Day. The next day is Navroz, or the Parsi New Year. It is celebrated by holding a *jashan*, or thanksgiving ceremony, similar to the one at Jamshedi Navroz, March 21 (also known as Now Ruz, see page 97). Parsi Zoroastrians celebrate both New Years, but Iranian Zoroastrians do not, because they use a slightly different calendar.

In 1987, Pateti will fall on August 24, and Navroz on August 25. In 1988 these will move to August 25 and 26. This is because the Zoroastrian calendar is neither lunar *nor* solar. It is made of 12 months, each with exactly 30 days. Five "extra," or intercalary, days are added at the end of every year, just before Pateti. So every four years, the Zoroastrian calendar jumps ahead about one day.

# Paryushana Parva

*August or September*

The Jains observe this religious festival for eight days about a month before their New Year (see Divali, page 239). The fifth day is devoted to reading the life story of their 24th saint, Lord Mahavir, from their scriptures. The last day, called Samvatsari, is the holiest day of the Jain year, the day of universal forgiveness. Jains fast, meditate, pray and confess any bad deeds they may have done. Every Jain asks pardon of everyone else, and they forgive each other for wrongs done during the past year. This sounds similar to Pateti, doesn't it? Do you know what other religion has a similar day? If you guessed the Jewish Yom Kippur, you're right.

# Italian Feast Days

*Throughout the summer*

Many Italian community and parish groups hold feast days for various saints during the summer months. These are both social and religious events. They include an outdoor procession and mass plus lots of food, games and music. Back in Italy, each town or region had its own saint's-day celebrations. But here in Canada, Italian-Canadians from different regions of the old country get together to celebrate.

In Willowdale, Ontario, the feast of St. Gabriel of the Sorrowful Virgin (the Festa di San Gabriele dell'Addolorata), is a "new" Italian-Canadian religious holiday. It has been organized to appeal to a wide range of Italian immigrants in all of eastern Canada. It is held without the traditional games and food-sellers. The organizers want the event to be a spiritual one for the whole Italian community. The procession is short, and the central feature of the mass is a special sermon called a *panagirico del Santo*. This is a talk showing how the life of St.

## Jainism

*The Jains are a religious group with roots in both Hinduism and Buddhism. Jains seek* moksa — *perfect liberation. Their sacred book is called the Kalpa Sutra. Jains celebrate most Hindu festivals, but they have their own 24 important saints as well as the Hindu gods, whom they honour at the same time. They believe Lord Mahavir was the last of these 24 saints.*

*Jainism is a religion of complete peace. It began about the 6th century B.C. Jains do not believe in violence and will not kill any living thing, not even insects. For this reason they are vegetarians. There are about five million Jains in India and another half-million elsewhere, including Canada. The Jain Society of Toronto has built a Jain temple in Etobicoke, Ontario.*

*In Jainism there are many categories, such as the five central vows, the four forms or pillars of behaviour, the three divisions of the world, the six substances from which the world is created, and so forth. The four forms are good guides for any human being, Jain or not, don't you think?*

- *To perform a kind act without expectation of reward.*
- *To rejoice at the well-being of others.*
- *To sympathize with distressed people and relieve their suffering.*
- *To pity criminals.*

Gabriel is relevant to living a good Christian life today. Afterwards everyone feasts on traditional foods and enjoys Italian folk music.

## Heritage Festivals

In a country with such a mixture of people and traditions as Canada has, it's no surprise that there are hundreds of summer heritage festivals. Heritage means different things to different people. Here are some ways Canadians celebrate their various heritages.

### The National Ukrainian Festival

For more than 20 years, Ukrainian-Canadians have said "Vitaemo, vitaemo" (Welcome) to thousands of people attending the National Ukrainian Festival near Dauphin, Manitoba, on the August long weekend. The festival includes a parade, colourful singing and dancing, amateur talent shows, traditional craft workshops and sales, local history and, of course, lots of traditional foods. In the ritual bread-baking competition you can see the special breads made for each seasonal festival of the year, and then some, all at one time!

The National Ukrainian Festival begins with the old Ukrainian welcoming ceremony of presenting bread and salt. Visitors are formally greeted with a *kolach* loaf and a salt-shaker (sometimes the salt is baked into the top of the loaf in a special lump instead). These symbolize warmth and hospitality because bread is the staff of life, the symbol of plenty, and salt is the additive, the spice of life that makes it pleasant. The greeters give the visitors a wish for their health, love and happiness along with the bread and salt.

In 1985 the festival moved to a new site in Riding Mountain National Park that has been specially set aside as a permanent Ukrainian heritage park. The new site (called Selo Ukraina, or Ukrainian village) should be a complete, year-round cultural complex by the year 1991, which is the 100th anniversary of the arrival of the first two Ukrainian settlers in Canada. What a celebration there will be then!

## Scottish Festivals

In several areas of Canada, but especially in Nova Scotia, Scottish groups hold summer Highland Games, Gaelic Mods or gatherings. These are another kind of heritage festival, including both cultural and sporting events, with plenty of bagpipe music thrown in, naturally! In Fergus, Ontario, the Games include haggis-hurling — beware, Robbie Burns!

## Multicultural Festivals

How would you like to go to a different heritage festival every day? You could, if you took part in one of Canada's new multicultural festivals such as Caravan in Toronto, Folklorama in Winnipeg or Mosaic in Regina. These have much in common: various ethnic groups organize pavilions that showcase their heritages through food, crafts, music and other arts. People buy "passports" as tickets to the different pavilions — as many as 40 in Winnipeg — and "travel" from country to country every evening.

## Old-Time Festivals

Contests and celebrations featuring the skills needed by the early settlers, such as rodeos, Pioneer Days and Threshermen's Days, are also a kind of heritage festival for Canadians from farm backgrounds. The Calgary Stampede, the "Big M" Morris Stampede in the Red River Valley and the Edmonton Klondike Days are probably Canada's best-known rodeos. However, there are dozens of rodeos all across the western provinces in the summer:

- the Mule Rodeo takes place in Miami, Manitoba, in mid-July
- in early September, Virden, Manitoba, is the home of the Canadian Firefighters Rodeo
- and the Wood Mountain Stampede, in Saskatchewan, is the oldest continuous rodeo in Canada.

Threshermen's Days are held all over western Canada. They are a kind of country fair with the emphasis on contests of farming skills. Less than a hundred years ago, the speed with which people could thresh their grain was very important. Harvesting wheat was not done by machines then, and it had to be done quickly and efficiently at the end of the short Canadian growing season. The Saskatchewan Tractor Pulling Championship, held in Moosomin in late July, is another example of a festival featuring farm skills.

Pioneer Days are held from one coast to the other in Canada, and not only in the summertime. They can be held any time at reconstructed pioneer villages. For example, the Mennonite Village Museum at Steinbach, Manitoba, celebrates Pioneer Days on the August long weekend each summer.

Of course the oldest heritage in Canada is that of our native people. They celebrate with summer pow-wows in dozens of places. These pow-wows usually involve native dance competitions plus arts and crafts displays.

# Food Festivals

*All summer long*

Food festivals are a time to rejoice in the abundance of seasonal food. The festivals themselves are as plentiful as the foods. Strawberry festivals, for instance, are found from Clearwater, B.C., in early July, to Portage la Prairie, Manitoba, in late June, to Concession, Nova Scotia, again in July. In British Columbia, the Penticton Peach Festival lasts for a week in late July and early August. In the Maritimes, the Bear River Cherry Carnival goes on in late July in Nova Scotia. There's even an ice cream festival in Tupperville, Nova Scotia, around the same time.

Fish festivals often follow ceremonies to bless the fishing fleet. Lobster suppers, for instance, are especially popular in the Maritimes, with variations such as the annual lobster-eating contest at Stanhope, P.E.I., or the Lobster Carnival at Summerside, which includes the Miss P.E.I. Pageant. Lobsters aren't the only ocean creatures that rate a festival. Solomon Gundy suppers happen in Blue Rock and all around Lunenberg County, Nova Scotia. (Puzzled about Solomon Gundy? It's a traditional German fish dish of herrings marinated in sour cream.) In Murray River, P.E.I., the Northumberland Provincial Fisheries Festival during late July features a scallop-

## Bathtub races

*One crazy summer sporting event that has become a summer tradition is the bathtub races held between Vancouver Island and the mainland. The first bathtub race took place during Canada's Centennial in 1967. Nowadays it includes more than a hundred competitors from all over the world.*

shucking championship. And at the Tyne Valley Oyster Festival in P.E.I., there's the Canadian Oyster-Shucking Championship! Much farther west in Canada, the Northern Pike Festival runs all summer in Nipawin, Saskatchewan. And all the way west, on Vancouver Island, there are salmon festivals at Campbell River and Port McNeill during July.

Vegetables get special attention too! In mid-July, the Potato Blossom Festival takes place in O'Leary, P.E.I., before there's anything to eat. Later, the Corn and Apple Festival takes place in Morden, Manitoba.

By late summer there are so many fresh foods in the fields that food festivals are simply called harvest festivals. Most offer heaping plates full of the food and often family activities such as crafts, raffles, games and parades.

Some festivals go to great lengths to attract visitors. For example, at the Festival du Bleuet in Mistassini, Quebec, in the Lac-Saint-Jean region, a huge blueberry pie weighing over 130 kg (286 pounds) is made every year. It feeds about a thousand people! The locals say, "It takes only three blueberries from Lac Saint-Jean to make a pie." If so, how many berries do you think go into this special pie?

# Crayfish Day

*August 8*

Do you love to eat lobster in the summer season? Every summer, Swedish-Canadians hold a traditional feast and eat crayfish (similar to lobster) on August 8. (In Toronto, the local crayfish are too expensive, so supper is flown in from California for the feast.) Swedes hang up paper lanterns outdoors for the crayfish party. Everyone uses paper tablecloths and big paper bibs, because eating crayfish is very messy! They all enjoy eating with their fingers and noisily sucking the crayfish out of their bright red shells.

## Crop predictions

*There is an old English superstition that the crop that is most abundant will tell you something about the year to come.*

*A cherry year, a merry year.*
*A pear year, a dear year.*
*A plum year, a dumb year.*

*Try adding more lines to this rhyme for other fruits or vegetables. How about "A beet year, a _____ year"? Keep going!*

## Corn husk dolls

Sure, corn's great to eat, but the leftover corn husks also make terrific dolls.

You'll need:
the husks from an ear of corn (fresh husks are easier to work with than old ones)
some cotton batting
some yarn

1. Wrap one piece of corn husk around some cotton batting as shown, and tie to make a head for your doll.
2. Roll a piece of husk into a long tube and tie the ends for hands.
3. Fold a long piece of husk over the arms as shown, and insert the head into a slit in the neck.
4. Draw on a face, and add clothes or hair as you wish.

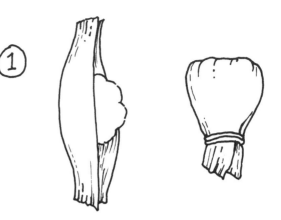

# North Buxton Homecoming

*Labour Day weekend*

North Buxton, Ontario, was originally part of the Elgin Settlement, a colony of former black slaves founded in 1849 by the Reverend William King, an Irish immigrant. In 1850 King brought 15 slaves to North Buxton from the southern United States and set them free. After the American Civil War, the Buxton community taught many more newly freed slaves how to read and write and use the freedoms granted them. Then in the 1870s more than 700 blacks educated in North Buxton returned to the southern states to settle and help lead their people.

Today North Buxton is the home of the Raleigh Township Centennial Museum, a memorial to the original Elgin Settlement and a unique record of black history. Every Labour Day weekend, about 2 500 former residents, friends and descendants travel to North Buxton to celebrate their rich heritage and attend reunion parties, church services, a dance, a parade and a baseball game. This big homecoming all started with a baseball game in 1924!

## Sweet dreams

*I wear my cotton nightie in the*
  *summer when it's hot;*
*I wear my red pajamas in the winter*
  *when it's not;*
*But sometimes in the springtime,*
*And sometimes in the fall,*
*I jump right in between the sheets*
*With nothing on at all!*

## German paper cone crafts

*German-Canadians used to fill paper cones with sweets as a traditional gift for a child on his or her first day of school. The idea was that the candies would sweeten your learning!*

# Labour Day

*The first Monday in September*

Today many of us think of Labour Day as the last long weekend before school starts. But a hundred years ago it meant something very different. Back then, life was much harder for miners, railroad builders, factory workers and other "labourers." People, particularly new immigrants to Canada, often worked under terrible conditions or were paid poorly. Workers needed unions to protect their rights. But in the 19th century, unions were not legal.

In 1872, a city-wide printers' strike in Toronto forced the federal government to give official recognition to the trade union movement in Canada. After gaining this victory, the unions decided to hold annual parades so that their political power and support for one another would not be forgotten.

In the United States, workers were also organizing, and the labour movement was growing. In 1882, 1883 and 1884 the Knights of Labor paraded in New York City on the first Mon-

day of September. In 1887 Oregon was the first state to recognize Labor Day as a holiday. It became a U.S. national holiday in 1894.

In Canada, the Trades and Labour Congress asked the federal government for a national day in 1888. Labour Day was declared a national holiday on July 23, 1894, honouring working people everywhere in Canada. Today Labour Day parades are held in most large Canadian cities. In Toronto the parade goes right into the huge Canadian National Exhibition grounds. Marchers get to stay and join the fun of the last day of the CNE.

All across the country, Labour Day signals the end of summer vacation. The day after the Labour Day parades, there are parades of a different kind — out front doors and down lanes parade children returning to school. Many children are given new clothes, shoes and school supplies to begin the school year. Once you go back to school, summer really seems to be over, doesn't it?

# FALL

Lots of things fall in the fall — just as growing things spring up in the spring! Green growth fades, changes colours and withers. The plant world is drying up and dying. Stems loosen and break, and leaves, nuts and fruits fall from the trees.

The word "fall" was first used by the early settlers in North America. They borrowed the term from some native people who spoke of the time of "the fall of the leaf." The other name for this season is autumn, which comes from the Latin word *autumnus*. It has two older roots, one meaning turning or change, and one meaning increase or harvest. In English Canada we use both English words for the season; the French use *automne*.

What do you think of as a sign of fall? The harvest? Many people do. However, fall *officially* begins well after most of the harvesting in Canada has taken place, on the autumn equinox, September 22 or 23.

The power of the sun weakens as we approach the autumn equinox. This is because the hours of daylight are steadily decreasing — a signal for wild plants and farmers' crops to mature. By the fall equinox, the hours of daylight are equal to the hours of night. From then on, the days grow shorter and shorter. Autumn means winter is on its way.

The colder air that comes with shorter days means good-bye to shorts and T-shirts. First it is jacket-and-raincoat weather outdoors, then hats-and-mittens weather, then time for warm boots, woolly scarves and snowsuits. Indoors we close windows, stop up drafts and turn on the furnace or light a fire in the hearth. Fires lit outside — for burning garden leaves or as part of fall festivals — are bright and warm too. For thousands of years, humans have lit autumn fires to fight off the cold and dark. Some fall festivals emphasize the triumph of good over evil by lighting special fires to counteract the darkness. Fall fires are also for good luck, for protection and for fun and merriment as people enter the dark and cold time of the year.

The moon is an important source of light in the fall too — perhaps because we see more of it. Several fall festivals acknowledge the importance of the moon. For example the Chinese Mid-Autumn Festival is often called the Moon Festival. It is celebrated when the harvest moon is full. Two other special days — the Jewish New Year and the Hindu Navaratri festival — are timed around the harvest moon too.

There is lots to do in the animal world as well as the human world to get ready for winter. Animals eat well while they can, putting on some extra fat to protect them from the coming cold. Some animals grow thicker fur, while others store winter food supplies in their nests and burrows. Have you ever watched a squirrel in the fall? No wonder we use the expression ''to squirrel away.''

All across Canada the darkness draws in as the nights grow longer and longer. On Ellesmere Island, near the North Pole, the sun sets on October 22 and does not appear above the horizon again until March 1. It is dark all day and all night! In southern Canada the sun can still be seen, but it grows weaker and weaker as the year dies. No wonder there is so much mention made of ghosts and the spirits of the dead at this time of the year.

Fall is a time when the year seems to be ending. Rather than waiting for new life and longer days in the spring, some cultures celebrate their New Year in the fall. Halloween, for example, was once a New Year's festival. Many modern Halloween customs have to do with the old Celtic New Year in northern Europe. Watch for the Celtic influence on other autumn celebrations too.

## The red maple leaf

No tree is more spectacular in the fall than the maple. Its leaves don't merely change colour; they blaze into stunning reds and yellows. The maple leaf has been an important symbol for Canadians for a long time. It was stamped on early coins and was the emblem of the Saint-Jean-Baptiste Society in French Canada in the 1830s. And the song "The Maple Leaf Forever," written by Alexander Muir, was like a national anthem for many years. However, the maple leaf has only been our national emblem since 1965. In 1964 special parliamentary committees considered over 2 000 possible flag designs before choosing our striking red maple leaf on a white background.

## Nuts to you

In Europe, nuts are an important part of the harvest. Long ago the Romans made offerings of nuts to their goddess Pomona at this season. In Great Britain, Halloween or some other night in late October was called Nutcrack Night or Crack-a-Nut Night. One game was to bob for nuts or coins the way we bob for apples. But because nuts and coins don't float, players got much wetter. It was worth it, though. Players who succeeded in pulling a coin or nut out of the water were guaranteed luck in money matters all the next year.

## Autumn groaner

Tim: I forgot to wear my gloves today.
Jim: Why don't you tie a string around your finger?
Tim: Because my gloves are warmer.

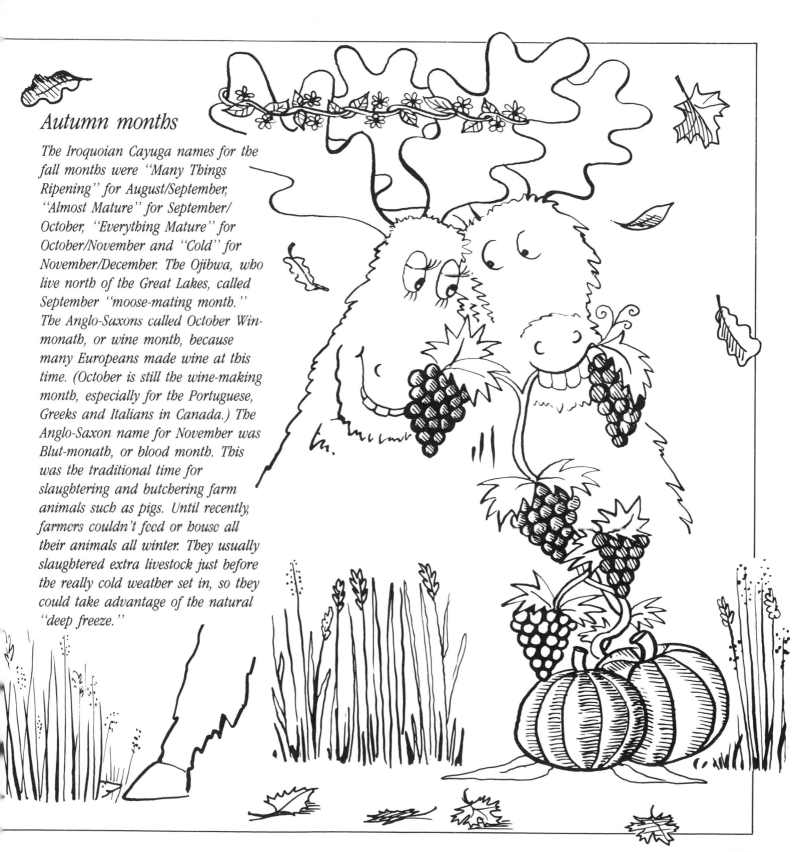

## Autumn months

The Iroquoian Cayuga names for the fall months were "Many Things Ripening" for August/September, "Almost Mature" for September/October, "Everything Mature" for October/November and "Cold" for November/December. The Ojibwa, who live north of the Great Lakes, called September "moose-mating month." The Anglo-Saxons called October Win-monath, or wine month, because many Europeans made wine at this time. (October is still the wine-making month, especially for the Portuguese, Greeks and Italians in Canada.) The Anglo-Saxon name for November was Blut-monath, or blood month. This was the traditional time for slaughtering and butchering farm animals such as pigs. Until recently, farmers couldn't feed or house all their animals all winter. They usually slaughtered extra livestock just before the really cold weather set in, so they could take advantage of the natural "deep freeze."

# Egyptian or Coptic New Year

*September 11*

Have you ever spotted the Dog Star (Sirius), the brightest star in the sky? It's called the Dog Star because it's in the constellation Canis Major, which means "big dog." Egyptians call the Dog Star Sothis. Ancient Egyptians calculated their year from the first appearance of this bright star after a period when it could not be seen. The date when Sothis reappears in the Egyptian sky, just before dawn, is September 11. About 4 000 years ago, in the time of the Pharaohs, the reappearance of Sothis was a signal that soon the Nile River would rise, its waters would flood the fertile plains area, and planting would begin. And so September 11 became the Egyptian New Year.

The Coptic Orthodox Church, to which many Egyptian-Canadians belong, celebrates its New Year on this day too. They honour their church's martyrs (people who died for their beliefs). Because the martyrs' blood was spilled, it is said that everything must be red on this day. Today, priests wear red vestments and the altar has red coverings for the special Coptic New Year service. At home, people eat red dates. The red skin of the dates is supposed to signify the blood of the martyrs, the inner white part the purity of their hearts and the unsplit pit their faith.

# Chilean Holiday

*September 18*

Every fall the Chilean community in Canada celebrates on September 18 to commemorate both the anniversary of their country's independence in 1818 and the election of Salvador Allende as president of Chile in 1970. Allende was the first Marxist to be democratically elected to head a nation in the Western hemisphere, and he launched programs of social welfare, land reform and nationalization of industries and banks. His government was overthrown by a military *junta*, or council, in 1973, and many Chileans fled the country.

For Chilean-Canadians, September 18 is a time for a *peña*, or party. They celebrate being Chilean and dance the national dance for couples, called the *cueca*. They eat *empanadas* (a kind of meat pastry with eggs and olives in the filling) and drink *chicha*, which is like cider.

## International Hispanic Festival

*Second weekend in September*

Since 1982, Spanish-speaking Canadians have attended a huge Hispanic Festival, held at the Canadian National Exhibition grounds in Toronto, to celebrate their roots. Mid-September is the time for the national holidays of Costa Rica, El Salvador, Guatemala, Honduras, Nicaragua and Mexico, so there's lots of reason to celebrate. The Festival is a *peña* on a gigantic scale. There is music, dancing and delicious regional foods from all the Hispanic countries. Plus there are *piñatas* for the children (see page 33 for how to make a *piñata*.)

# The Autumn Equinox

*September 22 or 23*

There are lots of ways to celebrate autumn in Canada, but no one seems to observe the autumn equinox itself. Remember, it and the spring equinox are the only two days in the year when the hours of daylight and darkness are exactly the same. Why not create your own festival? Perhaps you could launch your celebration with a game of Day and Night Tag.

## Day and Night Tag

1. You need a small box painted white on three sides and black on the other three. Choose a leader and divide into two teams, one called Day and one called Night.

2. The two teams face each other about two giant steps apart. Five giant steps behind each team are goal lines.

3. The leader stands between the two lines at one end and tosses the block up. If it lands with white uppermost, the Day players turn around and run towards the goal behind them, chased by the Nights. The Nights try to tag as many Days as possible before they cross their goal line. Anyone they tag joins their team. If the box lands with black uppermost, Days chase Nights towards their goal.

4. The game starts over again, with the new numbers of players on the Day and Night teams. It finishes whenever you decide you've had enough — you might want to set a number of rounds in advance. The winning side is the one that has the most players by the end.

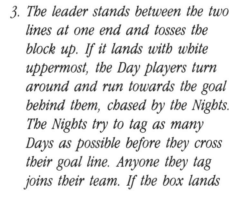

# The Iroquois Green Corn Festival

*September*

Before the beginning of the corn harvest every year, when the green corn has filled the ears but not fully ripened, the Iroquois hold a three-day thanksgiving festival. On the first day they perform the Great Feather Dance; the next day, the Skin Dance of Thanksgiving; finally they play the sacred peach-stone betting game. (See page 62.) Prayers like this one are sung as the sacred dances take place:

> We return thanks to our mother, the earth, which sustains us.
> We return thanks to the rivers, streams and lakes, which supply us with water and food.
> We return thanks to all herbs, weeds and bushes which furnish us with medicines for the cure of our diseases.
> We return thanks to the corn, and to her sisters, the beans and squashes, which give us life.
> We return thanks to the bushes and trees, which provide us with fruit.
> We return thanks to the animals which provide us with meat and skins.
> We return thanks to the wind, which, moving the air, has banished diseases.
> We return thanks to the moon and stars, which have given to us their light when the sun was gone.
> We return thanks to our grandfathers, the thunderers, that they have protected their grandchildren from witches and reptiles, and have given to us their rain.
> We return thanks to the sun, that he has looked upon the earth with a beneficent eye, and given us heat and light.
> Lastly, we return thanks to the Great Spirit, in whom is embodied all goodness, and who directs all things for the good of his children.

## Harvest moon and hunter's moon

*Before there were electric lights, imagine how important the moon must have been! The full moon that appears at or near the autumn equinox is often called the "harvest moon." The next full moon, some time in October, is the "hunter's moon." These two full moons seem especially large and beautiful. Why? The moon stays close to the horizon, where it looks larger, for a longer time in the fall. Also, trees and houses are often silhouetted against the low-lying moon; these make the moon appear larger. Long ago, people finished their winter preparations by the light of these full moons. By moonlight, they completed the harvest and even went hunting. That's how these full moons got their names.*

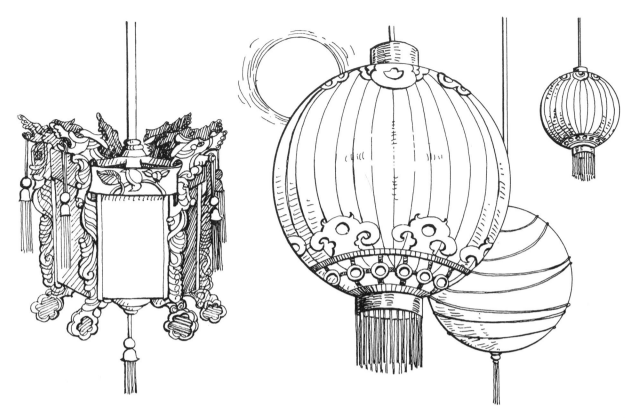

# The Chinese Mid-Autumn Festival

*September or October*

Have you ever seen paper lanterns made in the shape of fruit or birds? The Chinese are experts at making them. Chinese communities across Canada hold lantern parades during the ancient Mid-Autumn Festival. It is held on the 15th day of the eighth moon, or month, on the Chinese calendar. This falls during September. (Sometimes the festival is called the Moon Festival, because it is held on the day when the moon is at its fullest.) Traditionally this was when Chinese farmers relaxed after harvest. They worshipped the soil god, whose kindness determined the success of their crops. And so the festival is a time for rest and prayers of gratitude for the harvest, for hymns of praise and for poetry readings.

Mid-Autumn Festival is usually held outdoors. Dancing and lantern parades add to the general air of thanksgiving. All the lanterns are elaborate and colourful, made in a wide range of shapes and sizes. Some are symbolic of ancient Chinese beliefs. For example, a carp-shaped lantern was supposed to help its owner do well in his or her studies; a butterfly lantern meant you would live for a long time; a red lobster was supposed to bring you happiness and contentment. Today there may be traditional shapes and more modern ones such as automobiles and even battle-tank lanterns!

The most common lantern shape is round like the moon. To the Chinese, the moon symbolizes perfect joy and the cycle of life. It's a symbol of the family too — people think that while the moon looks down on them, it is also looking down on their relatives far away.

Chinese-Canadians have their own special ways of celebrating. In southern Ontario, many Chinese senior citizens make trips together to Niagara Falls at the time of the Mid-Autumn Festival, to enjoy the harvest moon. In Toronto an annual lantern parade starts at City Hall and moves through Chinatown early in September while the weather is still good.

## Trung-Thu

*September or October*

Vietnamese children carry lanterns in a procession on the night of the Mid-Autumn Festival too. But the name for their festival is Trung-Thu. In Vietnam, Trung-Thu is a national Children's Day. In Canada today, Vietnamese celebrations are similar to those of the Chinese. There is even a lion dance in the lantern parade. The lion symbolizes the happiness and prosperity of the community.

In Mississauga, Ontario, the 1985 Trung-Thu celebrations drew more than 1 000 adults and children. In Toronto's Parkdale area, a Vietnamese scout group organizes a children's party and makes a hundred paper lanterns shaped like diamonds, stars, fish or moons. Everyone lines up and gets a lantern with a lit candle inside, and then there is a parade. When it is over, the candles are blown out and the children take their lanterns home.

### Chusok

*Chusok is the name the Koreans give to Moon Festival Day. It was once celebrated at the same time as the Chinese festival. But then the eighth moon month became confused with the eighth month of the Western calendar, so Chusok is sometimes celebrated on August 15 instead. This date is also Korea's national holiday. It marks Korea's freedom from Japan on August 15, 1945, after 36 years of colonization. The combined national celebration and Moon Festival is something like Canadian Thanksgiving Day. Korean girls traditionally do a circle dance to the moon called Kang gang soowullai.*

## Moons, maidens and marriage

*For Malaysian-Chinese, the Mid-Autumn Festival celebrates not the harvest, but the moon's importance for maidens and marriage. Malaysian women may even spread offerings of cakes and fruit to the goddess of the moon outdoors in the moonlight.*

## Mooncakes

*At the feast for the Mid-Autumn Festival, it was once the custom for every guest to contribute food. Mooncakes are still the special treat of the day. They are available from Chinese and Vietnamese bakeries at this time of year. Mooncakes are round, the shape of the harvest moon, and have a variety of sweet fillings, such as bean paste or chestnut purée. Traditionally they were made with flour from the new grain and served with lotus tea.*

# Onam

*September*

This rice harvest festival is celebrated in Kerala in southern India. There it is customary to have threshing contests as part of Onam. Rice grows on stalks, like other grains, but rice plants grow in water. So to cut a sheaf of rice, the farmer must wade into muddy rice "paddies." When Onam threshing contests are held, contestants race into the paddies, cut the ripe grain and hurry back to a special threshing floor. Dripping with mud and sweat, they beat the heads of rice so that the grain breaks loose from the stalk and falls out of its husks. The winner is the one who threshes the most grain the quickest.

In Ontario, East Indians from Kerala have a special social and cultural evening to remember the feasting and dancing that go on in their own part of India at Onam. It is not a religious festival, so Hindus, Muslims and Christians celebrate it together.

# Native Wild Rice Harvest

*September*

The only rice that grows in Canada is wild rice, which native people harvest from shallow waters around the northern Great Lakes and in Manitoba and Saskatchewan. Gathering this special crop takes a lot of time because the rice does not grow in thick, easy-to-collect bunches. This makes it a very expensive, but delicious, specialty. Have you ever tasted wild rice? It is more nutty-flavoured than brown rice. Some Canadians serve a small amount of wild rice as part of their Thanksgiving dinner in early October.

The Algonkians, the Northern Cree and the Ojibwa hold a short thanksgiving ceremony at the beginning of the wild rice harvest. In the Kenora area, the Ojibwa hold two feasts to celebrate this special harvest. They know the rice will be ready to harvest some time after the last full moon in August. As soon as the rice grains seem "milky," the rice-pickers go to the areas that they have decided to harvest. There they get together for songs and a small feast.

When the rice grains turn hard, they are ready to harvest. Ojibwa women used to mark the areas that each family group was going to harvest by braiding rice stalks together along the borders. The entire process takes about two weeks, and the children in the rice-pickers' families get to take time off from school for that time. When the harvest finishes, a bigger feast is held for the whole community.

## Winter predictions

*Look closely at an onion in the fall and you can predict how bad the winter will be. Here's an old rhyme to use as a guide:*

*Onion skin's very thin,*
*Mild winter coming in.*
*Onion skin's thick and tough,*
*Coming winter cold and rough.*

*Long ago in Europe people thought that September 20, 21 and 22 ruled the weather for October, November and December. So record what it's like on those days and see how accurate the old prediction is:*

| Weather on... | Weather in... |
| --- | --- |
| Sept. 20 | October |
| Sept. 21 | November |
| Sept. 22 | December |

## Feast of the Exaltation of the Holy Cross

*September 14*

Some Roman Catholics and members of the Greek Orthodox Church mark this day with special church services. They celebrate the discovery of the remains of the cross on which Jesus was crucified. Empress St. Helena, the mother of Emperor Constantine the Great, is said to have found it in the spring, so there is also a May 3 holiday to celebrate its discovery (see Santa Cruzan, page 132).

In Greece, a whole congregation will watch as their priest or bishop tosses a cross into the sea from the shore. Many young men compete to dive down and find it. The victor gets to keep the cross and receives the blessing of the clergy. In Canada, it is often too cold to go swimming for the cross, but some hardy souls still continue this custom in Nova Scotia.

Lebanese Catholics traditionally hold a torchlight parade on September 14 as a sign of victory in finding the cross. Ukrainian Orthodox churchgoers celebrate the finding of the cross later in September, according to the Julian Calendar.

## International Day of Peace

*Third Tuesday in September*

The third Tuesday in September is the opening day of the United Nations General Assembly. In 1981, the General Assembly named the day the International Day of Peace. In 1986 an organization called A Peal for Peace Canada began a campaign for "one minute of silence, one moment of sound for peace" at noon on September 16. The "moment of sound" was filled with pealing church bells, honking car horns and even ringing doorbells. Peace is a simple thing, and yet it has been so difficult to achieve. All humankind yearns for it, and billions of people over the centuries have died for it.

# The Jewish High Holy Days

*September or October*

The most important festivals of the Jewish religious year are celebrated during the first ten days of the month of Tishri, which falls in September or October. The first day is called Rosh Hashanah, the Jewish New Year. It is the beginning of the High Holy Days, sometimes called the Days of Awe or the Ten Days of Repentance. From Rosh Hashanah until the last day of the High Holy Days, called Yom Kippur, Jews think about how they have lived during the past year. They are encouraged to remember wrongs they have done and ask forgiveness from God and those they have wronged. And they are supposed to extend their forgiveness to others. During this period of self-examination, Jews also consider whether they are using their own special gifts and talents fully for the improvement of their own lives and of the world around them.

# Rosh Hashanah

*September*

Rosh Hashanah, the Jewish New Year, is considered the head of the year. It is a bit like *your* head, which directs your thoughts and actions. From Rosh Hashanah flow the decisions that will mould thoughts and determine actions for the 12 months to come.

On Rosh Hashanah Jews greet each other with this wish: ''May you be inscribed in the Book of Life for a happy year!'' In synagogues everywhere a *shofar* is blown to remind those

## *Peace projects*

*Many schools think up peace projects to celebrate this special day. Here are a few ideas you could try:*

- *Paint balloons to look like the planet earth, attach envelopes filled with messages of peace and send them aloft.*
- *Use purple to represent loyalty, dignity and love of truth. Wear purple sashes or attach messages to purple badges and ribbons.*
- *Make an all-school peace chain. Each adult and child in the school makes a wish or prayer for peace then writes it on a link of a paper chain. Join the chains together, class by class. Hang the peace chain along the hallway or around the gym.*

**Blowing the shofar
in Jerusalem**

who hear it of the need to do good and to lead a God-fearing life. (A *shofar* is a ram's horn that has been hollowed out. When it is blown into, it makes an alarming, shrieking blast that can send chills down your spine.)

The Jewish New Year is a very solemn time, and yet there is also a festive New Year's family dinner after the *shofar* and the prayers in the synagogue. One tradition is eating an apple or some other fruit dipped in honey, to symbolize everyone's wish for a year filled with sweetness. The traditional Jewish *challah*, or egg bread, is baked in a circle instead of a long braid during the High Holy Days. This is to symbolize the cycle of the year and the wish for a smooth year too.

Rosh Hashanah coincides with the new moon that will be full on, or soon after, the autumn equinox. According to Jewish tradition, this day is when the first human being — Adam — was created. This happened more than 5,700 years ago. The anniversary of Adam's creation (and the beginning of the human race) seems like a good time to celebrate a new year, doesn't it?

## Yom Kippur

*September or October, ten days after Rosh Hashanah*

The final day of the Jewish High Holy Days is Yom Kippur, or the Day of Atonement. The word "atonement" means making up, reaching agreement or doing something to right a wrong you may have done. Jews believe that when you atone for your mistakes or wrongs, you can be "at one" with God. Can you see where the word "atone" came from? By Yom Kippur, Jews have made any atonements needed with their friends and family.

Yom Kippur is the most solemn of all the High Holy Days, and the most important of all the holy days on the Jewish calendar. To mark it, Jews do not work and fast from sunset to sunset. They also attend religious services. The great holy day comes to an end with a final long blast on the *shofar* at sundown.

# Michaelmas

*September 29*

Michaelmas, or St. Michael and All Angels' Day, is celebrated in Christian churches not long after the equinox. In Jewish, Christian and Islamic writings, Michael was the greatest of all God's angels — in fact, his name in Hebrew means "who is like God." The best-known story about Archangel Michael comes from the Book of Revelation in the Bible. There he is the chief fighter in a great battle in heaven. He cast the Devil — often in the guise of a dragon — out of heaven. When the Devil fell to earth, some people say, he landed in a blackberry bush! That gave rise to the superstition that blackberries are poisonous after September 29.

## Fall flowers

*Many plants die in the fall, but some late bloomers seem to like the short days and cool weather. First comes the goldenrod, often followed by wild asters and chrysanthemums. One small purple aster bears the name of St. Michael; it is called the Michaelmas daisy. Look for it along the edges of fields and roads.*

## Goose luck

*There's an old saying: "If you eat goose on Michaelmas Day, you will never want money, all the year round." In England it was once the custom to eat roast goose on this day, when many tenant farmers paid their rent. Geese were fine and fat in the fall, and farmers often paid part of their rent in produce rather than cash. Perhaps the landowners who got lots of geese for "rent" began the custom!*

## The Angel of Death

*Christians sometimes call St. Michael the Angel of Death. Do you know the song "Michael, Row the Boat Ashore"? It refers to St. Michael carrying souls to heaven.*

## Goose fun

*The Kindersley Goose Festival Days in Saskatchewan include goose-plucking, a potato-peeling contest, greased-pig contests and cow-chip-throwing. (Cow chips are what's left in the field after the cows leave.) It is an annual three-day event held on the last weekend in September, during goose-hunting season.*

St. Michael is often portrayed as a dragon-slayer, like St. George, with a dragon at his feet and a gleaming sword in his hand. He is known as the protector of all humankind, rather than the patron saint of any one group. As the days shorten and winter's darkness draws nearer, St. Michael symbolizes human courage and daring in the face of evil.

# Migration Festival

*October*

Everyone looks up when a V of Canada geese flies overhead, going south for the winter. Remember the sound of their honking as they go? You can see and hear migrating birds everywhere in Canada, but there is one very special place for this fall activity. Kingsville, Ontario, is one of Canada's southernmost towns. In 1904 Jack Miner's Bird Sanctuary was established near Kingsville. It is one of the oldest bird sanctuaries in Canada. Some time in mid-October, depending on the geese, there is an annual Migration Festival at the sanctuary to welcome the migrating geese!

To see a less common species migrating, join one of the annual nature tours run by the Saskatoon Natural History Society. In late September or early October they arrange a whooping crane tour!

Even monarch butterflies migrate south. Point Pelee, in southern Ontario (sticking out into Lake Erie), is a famous place to watch the butterflies in the fall.

# Sukkot

*September or October*

Sukkot is a joyful Jewish harvest festival that lasts nine days. It begins five days after Yom Kippur, on the day of the full moon. Sukkot has three other names, because it marks several special times in Jewish history as well as the end of the harvest:

- The Festival of Ingathering: long ago during this festival the Jews brought food they had grown to the Great Temple in Jerusalem as offerings to God. It was a great time of thanksgiving for the year's harvest, which had just been gathered in.

- The Feast of Booths or Tabernacles: a little hut or booth, called a *sukkah*, is built outdoors and decorated especially for the nine days of the festival. According to tradition, Jewish families are supposed to live as much as possible in the *sukkah* during Sukkot. This is done in remembrance of the time when the Israelites wandered in the desert for 40 years, sleeping and eating under the stars. It is often cold at this season in Canada, so Jewish families simply eat outside in their *sukkah* whenever they can. Some people have a *sukkah* in their own garden; others share one at a school or synagogue. Children enjoy decorating the little booth with harvest fruits and vegetables and autumn leaves.

- The Season of Our Rejoicing: special prayers of joy are said both in the *sukkah* and in the synagogue on certain Sukkot days. Four plants are part of these services: young palm shoots (called *lulav*), bound together with myrtle twigs and willow branches, and a citron (or *etrog*), which is a fragrant yellow fruit something like a huge lemon. These are all symbols of the ancient Palestinian harvest. Some people also believe the four foods represent different virtues or characteristics of the Jewish people. At the beginning of Sukkot the worshippers hold the palm, myrtle and willow in one hand and the citron in the other and wave them in all directions to symbolize God's presence. On the seventh day, called Hoshana Rabba, some congregations use these symbols again in a procession. Carrying the symbolic plants, they

## Sukkot and Thanksgiving

*Some scholars believe Sukkot inspired the Pilgrims in Massachusetts to hold their first Thanksgiving Day in the fall of 1621. Those early Americans had much to be thankful for — especially their first harvest in their new land. Like the early Israelites, they had been seeking religious freedom for many years.*

march around the synagogue seven times, singing *hosannas*, the prayers of salvation.

On the eighth day of Sukkot, which is called Shemini Atzeret, the congregation offers special prayers for rain, no matter what the weather. During October in Canada their prayers are likely to be answered — if it doesn't rain, it may snow!

The last day of the festival, called Simchat Torah, is also the time when the reading of the Jewish sacred books, the Torah, is completed and begun again. For Jews, the study of God's word is an unending process, and so the end and the beginning of the Torah are read on the same day as a joyful reminder of that process. Everyone is jubilant, and there is lots of music, joking and excitement — even dancing, as chanting processions circle the synagogue, carrying the Holy Scrolls of the Torah.

## Fall Fairs

All during the late summer and on into October, many towns and communities throughout North America have annual fairs. They may simply be called fall fairs or have names related to the local crops. They may also be called Harvest Festivals or Threshermen's Days (see "Old-Time Festivals," page 192). Have you heard of any of these?

- The Swan Valley Harvest Festival in Manitoba in early October includes lots of old grain-harvesting activities. There are threshing demonstrations, displays of pioneer bread-baking and flour-grinding and even a fiddling contest!
- The Eastern Townships Apple Festival in Quebec is held in late September. The special dish there is apple pancakes served with maple syrup from the spring harvest. Apple festivals are celebrated in several places in Quebec, such as Saint-Antoine-Abbé and Rougemont, both located in countryside famous for apples.

- Brighton, in eastern Ontario, holds an annual Applefest on the last weekend in September. During Applefest, there is a tractor-pulling contest as part of "Muscle Day." There are also many other competitions — baking contests, amateur talent shows and the Miss Applefest contest — plus craft displays and sales, a parade, a barbecue and a dance.
- The Fort Dauphin Museum in Dauphin, Manitoba, holds a Traders' Rendezvous in mid-September. It includes lots of voyageur games such as log-sawing, arm-wrestling and leg-wrestling, plus trapping contests, old-time music, a stage show and a flea market.
- The Niagara Grape and Wine Festival in St. Catharines, Ontario, is now more than 30 years old and lasts for ten days in late September. One special feature is the crowning of the Grape King every year. Another is the Grand Parade on the last weekend. There are also wine gardens and gourmet wine-tasting events, but the children's favourite is the Pied Piper costume parade on the first weekend. Some people cover their bodies with green or purple balloons and walk around looking like bunches of grapes; others dress up like wine bottles or even cheese and crackers.
- The Kleinburg, Ontario, Binder Twine Festival began in 1891 as a solution to a mouse problem. Every fall, a local tinsmith named Charlie Shaw was supposed to supply binder twine to the farmers who were busy with their harvest so that they could bind up their sheaves of grain. For some reason the mice liked to eat the twine, so the supplier asked all the local farmers to come to town to collect their twine on the evening of the same day it was delivered to him by train. Of course, no one hurried home from such a social gathering and soon there were annual festivities. These continued until the 1930s, when Charlie Shaw died. The festival was revived in 1967 as a Centennial project and has been flourishing ever since.

## Chestnut spiders

*Based on an idea by Loet Vos. Dutch children used to make spiders every fall with new-fallen chestnuts and straight pins. That's all you need, plus a piece of string at least 30 cm (12 inches) long.*

1. *Stick nine pins into a chestnut to make a circle, so that they stick out like the rays of the sun.*
2. *Tie the string at one end to one pin and then wrap the rest of the string around the pins any way you wish.*
3. *Hold the free end and let go. Your spider will "walk" down the string. If you change the pattern of wrapping, the walk will also change.*

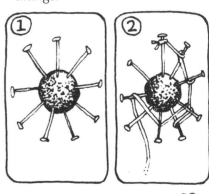

## Love and apple magic

If you want to know the name of your true love, there are many games you can play with apples to find out.

- In Dartmouth, Nova Scotia, they say you should twist an apple around until the stem breaks off, saying "A...B...C" and so on. The letter you say as the stem comes free is the initial of your boyfriend or girlfriend.
- Like Mennonite children, try to remove the entire peel of an apple in one long strip. When you are successful, throw the long strip of apple peel over your left shoulder and look at the shape it makes on the floor. It should tell you the first letter of your love's name.

## Harvest Home

If you lived two hundred years ago, you wouldn't be going to a harvest festival at a church. Back then, harvest festivals were celebrated where the harvest took place — on the farms. Harvest Home suppers were usually given by the wealthy farmers and landowners who employed everyone in the neighbourhood for the harvest period. That was the time and place for thanksgiving — and lots of merriment too!

# Oktoberfest

*During October*

Oktoberfest is a time of music and merrymaking, featuring lots of beer, sausage and sauerkraut. German Oktoberfests, a tradition from Munich and the Bavarian region of Germany, were introduced into North America in the 1960s. Originally Oktoberfest celebrated the harvest of hops, from which the Germans brew their much-loved beer. In Germany coopers, the people who make the beer barrels, perform a special 500-year-old dance every seventh Oktoberfest.

Many Oktoberfests are held across Canada now. They are usually multicultural celebrations with lots of sporting and social events. Most are held around the third Sunday in October. Some last for more than a week.

The biggest Oktoberfest is held in Kitchener-Waterloo, an area of Ontario where many people of German origin live. It attracts over 350,000 people every year! Every year on the second Monday of October a huge parade is staged. In many ways this parade is a modern version of the old Harvest Home procession, when the fieldworkers celebrated the end of their labours with decorated grain carts, feasts and toasts, and music, singing and dancing.

# The spirit of the grain

Celebrating the grain harvest may be the most universal and ancient form of thanksgiving, as old as farming itself. Many civilizations and cultures offer the first foods grown to the chief priests or to the gods. So grain farmers would offer the first ripe stalks they had cut. Others think that the end of the harvest is more important. For them, the very last sheaf is the home of the "grain spirit" — sometimes called the Corn Mother. In the days before machine harvesting, it was considered unlucky to be the person to cut the last sheaf of grain. Sometimes all the workers stood in a circle around it and threw their sickles at the same time, to avoid blame for killing the spirit of the grain.

There were many other elaborate rituals connected with cutting the grain. Often a decorated "corn doll" of some variety (human shapes, pyramids, braided straw, hanging ears of grain, and miniature sheaves were all common) was made from the last sheaf. This symbol was treated as a kind of good luck piece for the next year's harvest and hung up in homes or churches from the end of one harvest to the next.

---

# Apple schnitzing

McIntosh, Spartan, Idared, Golden Delicious, Red Delicious, Winesap, Northern Spy — there are dozens of varieties of apples ripening in Canada all through the fall season. Apples have been a favourite food of many people for centuries. In fact, 3 000 years ago they were sacred to the Celts.

Apples were a very important harvest to the early Canadian settlers. They not only ate them fresh, they also dried them to eat in the winter and pressed them for cider. Mennonite Canadians still hold schnitzing bees during the apple harvest. This is a time for lots of songs and jokes as everyone peels, cores and slices apples to make schnitz, or dried apple rings.

# Corn kissing

An old French-Canadian harvest custom, called épluchette de blé d'Inde, says that you can kiss anyone you choose if you are lucky to find an ear of corn with red, rather than yellow kernels! There's that magic colour red again....

## The main course

*For the early settlers' Thanksgiving dinners, the turkeys were not the fat farm-fed gobblers we have today. They were freshly shot wild turkeys, with stringier, less juicy meat. Goose, venison, partridge and even beaver tail were frequent main-course items, instead of turkey or alongside it.*

# Canadian Thanksgiving

*The second Monday in October*

The Sunday before Thanksgiving Monday is often marked in Christian churches by services thanking God not only for the harvest of food in the fall but for other blessings too. On Thanksgiving Day itself, many Canadian families and close friends gather together to share Thanksgiving dinner. Usually this dinner includes turkey, mashed potatoes, cranberry sauce and pumpkin pie. There may also be wild rice and maple syrup pie, two Canadian specialties.

## A borrowed custom

The Puritans, who first celebrated Thanksgiving in 1621, may have modelled their celebrations on a thanksgiving festival held in the city of Leyden in the Netherlands, where many of them stayed before sailing to North America. The citizens of Leyden celebrated their Thanksgiving on October 3 to commemorate the end of a long Spanish siege.

## Pumpkins

Pumpkins and other members of the squash family are New World plants; they did not grow in the Old World (Europe). The early European settlers had never seen pumpkins or squash. But when many of the plants they brought with them failed, the settlers were glad to learn about these huge vegetables from the native people. They even made a kind of beer out of pumpkins, parsnips and walnut-tree chips when their barley crops failed!

## Beef, barley and chokecherries

In Russell, Manitoba, Thanksgiving weekend is the date of the annual Beef and Barley Festival. Both beef and barley are very important products for this community, and Thanksgiving is a logical time to honour them.

In Lancer, Saskatchewan, the annual Chokecherry Festival is held at the same time. One important part of the festivities is the breakfast, featuring locally made chokecherry syrup.

## Thanksgiving in Canada

We usually think of Thanksgiving as being started by the Puritans. But 53 years before the Pilgrims celebrated Thanksgiving in North America, English settlers under Sir Martin Frobisher held a harvest feast in what is now Newfoundland.

## The three sisters

*Corn, beans and squash are the traditional native vegetable crops in North America. They are sometimes called "the three sisters." Corn and beans are good foods for vegetarians to eat together; in combination they provide a complete form of protein. The Iroquois seemed to know this long before modern science caught on; they call these plants "our sustenance." They have two minor religious ceremonies every year — one to pray that corn, beans and squash will grow, and one to give thanks for them. The first follows the Midwinter Festival (see page 62) and the second follows the Green Corn Festival (see page 209).*

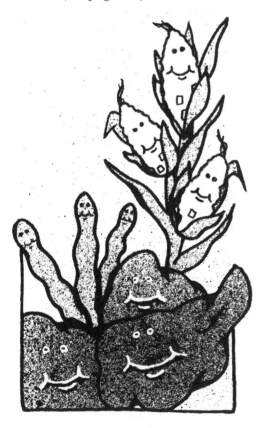

# Iroquois Harvest Ceremony

*October or November*

The Iroquois hold a one-day religious ceremony to mark the end of the period in which crops are cultivated. The actual date of the ceremony is decided by the weather. After this ceremony, the fall hunting period begins. Until recently, this change from farming to hunting was very important. Imagine how it must have felt to be a young hunter leaving the village to catch wild animals and provide for your community.

In London, Ontario, the Museum of Indian Archeology hosts an annual celebration called Native Harvest on the weekend after Thanksgiving. This event is supported by several different native groups and features native foods such as corn soup, buffalo burgers and fried bread. Many vegetables grown on the museum grounds are used. Native craftspeople and artists demonstrate their work outdoors, weather permitting. There is also storytelling and native dancing — for both watching and joining in!

# Dia de la Raza

*October 12*

Latin Americans and Hispanic-Canadians celebrate October 12 as the anniversary of Christopher Columbus's discovery of the New World. In the United States, the day is called Columbus Day; it is observed on the second Monday in October every year. The Spanish name, however, means "day of the race," and it is a time to remember how the Spanish "race" (or, more accurately, people) influenced the world. Here in Canada, Dia de la Raza is a cultural and social occasion, with a dinner-dance, parties, speeches, movies and cultural programs. In major cities such as Toronto, Vancouver and Montreal, Club Hispano organizes the annual celebrations.

# Navaratri,
# The Festival of the Nine Nights

*September or October*

In India Navaratri, which means "nine nights," is the longest Hindu festival. It starts with the new moon after the harvest moon. Navaratri ends on Dussehra (see page 228). Together these two festivals celebrate the triumph of good over evil.

Navaratri is the biggest celebration of the year in eastern India, where it is called Durga Puja (remember, *puja* means worship ceremony). Prayers to the goddess Durga call on her power of good to destroy demons. In the Hindu religion the goddess Durga has nine incarnations, so orthodox Hindus pray to her for nine days, in her nine different forms, in order to benefit from her full power.

Navaratri is also the time when much of the Indian winter wheat and rice crop is sown. Farmers ask the gods to bless their crops and help them have abundant harvests. For nine days, people do not eat grain and pray for help in overcoming difficulties.

In Nepal, bordering on northern India, special barley seeds are planted in a container in the family prayer room on the first day of Navaratri. Some sacred water is placed next to it. Prayers are said in front of the water and barley until Dussehra. On that day, children ask for blessings from their elders. To symbolize this blessing, they are given two things: a red *tika* (or dot) of coloured paste on their foreheads and a new shoot of barley. The elders say, "May the goddess grant all your wishes and help you against evil."

Here in Canada, most Hindus fast for Navaratri. They skip one or two meals before a special *puja* at night in their temples. The celebrations may last for nine days but usually are cut to three days. The three-day version starts on the seventh day of the new moon, when the story of the creation

## How to save autumn leaves

*Here are two ways to preserve the bright colours of fallen leaves.*

1. *Collect leaves that are not yet dried out from different trees. Put each leaf between sheets of waxed paper and insert the sheets between the pages of large heavy books. Wait at least a week before looking at the results — flat, dry, pretty leaves. These make good decorations for notepaper or presents.*

2. *To preserve the leaves without flattening them, dip them in wax. Melt some clear paraffin wax in a tin can set in a pot of boiling water. When the wax is melted, use a pair of tongs or old clothespins to quickly dip the leaves in and out of the hot wax. (Don't use your fingers: hot wax causes bad burns.) As soon as the wax hardens, you're a success!*

## House-visiting

*Hindu girls are often named Devi, which means "goddess." At Dussehra, one tradition is for young girls to go house-visiting. They are said to represent the innocence of a goddess and every home wants their blessing. In return, they are given money, food or gifts. This takes place by invitation in Canada.*

of Durga is broadcast in Sanskrit on CBC Radio at 4 a.m., just before dawn.

Ceremonies on the next day are meant to renew the life forces in every statue or image of a Hindu god. On the final day the statues are immersed in water as a farewell, and a communal feast is held. Everyone is supposed to hug everyone else and make sure that any quarrels that have arisen since the spring festival of Holi (page 100) are settled. As they do during Holi, people visit from house to house, eating sweets at each home. Navaratri is also the time for new clothes and charity to the poor.

# Dussehra

*October*

The tenth night after Navaratri begins is called Dussehra (which means "the tenth"). It has a number of other names, depending on which part of India you are from. No matter what it is called, it celebrates the triumph of Lord Ram over the demon Ravan. Some say that Navaratri and Dussehra last ten days because Ravan had ten heads. *Pujas* are made both to Durga, the goddess who destroys the demons that threaten our happiness, and to Sarasvati, the goddess of learning and all arts and crafts. (Sarasvati has her own *puja* day in February, but she is worshipped at Dussehra as well because, as goddess of all the arts, she has a knowledge of divinity. With this knowledge, she can tell good from evil. Hindus pray to her so that they, too, may be able to see the difference.) If you're confused about Hindu gods and goddesses, turn back to page 79.

On Dussehra, or sometimes for all the nine nights before, people gather to hear the long story of the Ramayana, one of the great Hindu epic poems. In this poem, the god Vishnu (the preserver or keeper of life) comes down to earth as a human being called Lord or Prince Ram. His job is to get rid of the terrible demon named Ravan. But Ram's lovely bride Sita is stolen by Ravan, and Ram and his brothers fight a battle against Ravan in order to win Sita back. To get the strength to kill Ravan, Ram himself has to worship Durga — the Preserver has to get energy from the Destroyer! Finally Ram wins, and Ravan, his son and his brother are all killed by burning arrows. Sita is reunited with Ram in the end, as you would expect!

Sometimes the Ramayana is performed as a play; then it is called the Ram Lila. On the final day of this festival in India, giant figures of demon gods are filled with fireworks and explosives. Then they are set alight with arrows of fire, shot from the bow of a figure dressed like Ram. Flames and fireworks shoot into the sky, people cheer wildly for Ram, and good wins out over evil once again! In Trinidad, in the West Indies, the custom is to burn a big figure of Rawan (another name for Ravan) at the end of the festival.

In Canadian Hindu temples, it is generally the custom to read the Ramayana in 24 hours. Several people take part in this marathon reading — one person taking over as soon as another is tired. Readers must fast before taking their turn. Usually the reading begins at 5 p.m. on the Saturday closest to Dussehra, finishing on Sunday about the same time. Then everyone celebrates its completion by eating sweets such as *halvah* and enjoying fireworks.

## Kathakali

*Have you ever seen the dramatic dances from southern India known as Kathakali? The dancers wear fantastic headdresses, many layers of starched skirts and elaborate makeup. Kathakali dance-dramas are traditionally performed for the nine nights before Dussehra. They, too, tell the story of Ram's fight against Ravan and other mythic episodes.*

SHRINE OF THE BAB

# Baha'i Founders' Birthdays

*October 20 and November 12*

The new religion of Baha'i was founded by Siyyid 'Ali Muhammad, who was born in Persia on October 29, 1819. He began teaching in 1844, calling himself the Bab, which means "the gate." The Bab claimed that he was the forerunner of the Great Divine Teacher, Baha'u'llah, who would appear soon after him to fulfill the promises of all the world's religions.

Baha'u'llah was born as Mirza Husayn 'Ali, the son of a wealthy merchant, on November 12, 1817, and announced his role to the followers of the Bab in 1863.

Baha'u'llah means "the glory of God" — can you see that "u'llah" is almost the same as Allah, which is the Muslim name for God? Baha'u'llah said that all people were created to carry forward an ever-advancing civilization, and he was interested in improving the lot of the entire human race. He encouraged education for everyone and the equality of the sexes; he told his people to reach out to the followers of all religions in a spirit of friendship and fellowship. Baha'is believe that in time the word of Baha'u'llah will unify all the different races, nations and religious sects.

In 1912, the Bab's son visited Canada and gained many followers. From that time Canadians have been second only to Americans in spreading the Baha'i faith. In 1937, a Montreal woman married the great-grandson of the Bab. Now her house — the Maxwell House in Montreal — is a Baha'i pilgrimage site. There is also a Baha'i National Centre in Thornhill, Ontario, and an Association for Baha'i Studies in Ottawa. On October 20 and November 12, Baha'is in Canada and around the world celebrate the birthdays of the Bab and Baha'u'llah with prayers and great joy.

# Halloween

*October 31*

Do you carve a pumpkin lantern to set on your front porch for Halloween? Or do you put on a costume to go trick-or-treating around your neighbourhood on October 31? Do you bob for apples? If so, then you are carrying on customs that are thousands of years old.

Many of today's Halloween traditions go back to the time of the Celtic people. They lived in Britain and northern Europe more than 2 000 years ago. The Celts' year began in what we call late autumn. But their calendar had only two seasons: winter, which started November 1 and lasted until April 30, and summer, which started May 1 and ended October 31. This calendar was based on the needs of their herds of sheep, goats and cows. For example, by the end of October, nights were much longer than days and the weather was cold. The animals could not be left out to graze overnight any more. That was a big change for the Celts. No wonder they thought winter had begun.

On October 31, their New Year's Eve, the Celtic herd-keepers would gather with the rest of the community and their priests, called Druids, to honour their chief god. This was Samhain (pronounced *Sa-wen*), called the Lord of the Dead. On the feast of Samhain, the Celts ate and drank, told stories of their ancestors and tried to foretell the future, as many people do when a new year begins.

The Celts believed that the spirit world became active and more alive at the time when the natural world of plants was withering and dying. And so all the spirits of people who had died in the past year were thought to be wandering outdoors, while the feasters were safe and warm indoors. No one wanted to offend them or be harmed by them. To scare off the spirits and to show them which way to go, the Celts lit

## Soulcakers and mummers

*If you could step back in time two hundred years, you would see groups of adults and children going from door to door begging for soulcakes on All Hallows' E'en, across much of Europe. Soulcakes were a bit like hot cross buns without the cross; they were a treat given out in memory of all the good spirits who were already dead. Unlike the Celtic ghosts, these spirits were supposed to be holy spirits blessed by the church. They were called "hallowed," a word that is now part of our modern name for this festival.*

*Soulcakers were also glad to receive a piece of fruit, especially apples, for a treat. Their ancestors the Celts thought apples gave immortality. So when you get an apple in your trick-or-treat bag, remember that it was originally meant to help you live longer.*

*Another European custom connected with All Souls' Day (page 235) was the performance of a mummers' play by a group of singing actors called soulers. They also begged for food, beer or money, and were regarded as good luck visitors. In Canada some of these old folk dramas, in which someone always pretends to be killed and then is brought back to life, were performed in Newfoundland, but usually around Christmastime. See pages 48-49.*

## Trick or treat?

Next Halloween try chanting this
rhyme at houses:
Trick or treat,
Smell my feet,
Give me something good to eat.
Not too big,
Not too small,
Just the size of Montreal!

hilltop bonfires and put candles in their windows. No one went out without a lantern.

We have the Irish to thank for the custom of carving pumpkins into Jack-o'-lanterns. Jack was a trickster in an Irish folk tale. He was so stingy that both St. Peter and the Devil refused to let him into heaven or hell when he died. So Jack has had to wander up and down the earth with his lantern — a turnip with a glowing coal inside — ever since. In North America the Irish used pumpkins for lanterns, instead of turnips. Pumpkins are also the source of the Halloween colour orange. The other Halloween colour, black, represents the darkness.

All over Europe, the Celtic people also thought it wise to share their feast, so at Samhain they put out little gifts of food and drink on their doorsteps. That way, the roving spirits would treat them kindly and give them good luck for the future year. When you say "Trick or treat" or "Shell out" at someone's door this year, you will be repeating this tradition. In ghost costumes and other disguises, you will be the wandering spirits to whom the householders offer gifts.

A "trick" in days gone by was not necessarily something clever, like a magic trick; it was often something mean. Not so long ago Halloween (or the night before or after) was called Mischief Night, and people often found front gates missing or windows covered with soap in the morning. Sometimes these acts of mischief were a way of paying someone back who you felt had wronged you. And sometimes they were just plain pranks. The mischief-makers felt protected from punishment by their disguises. In any case, with so many witches, ghosts and monsters abroad, anyone (or anything!) could be responsible for the "trick."

If the Celts had to go outside on the feast of Samhain, they felt it was best to go disguised, so that the spirits could not recognize them. For extra safety, people often tried to look

## Collecting money

*Soulcakers also begged for a bit of money, which the householders gave them because they thought it would bring them luck. Nowadays many Halloween visitors carry a UNICEF box and collect money to help poor children all over the world. UNICEF stands for United Nations Children's Fund. This custom was begun in 1950 by some children in the United States. Since their first contribution of $17, more than $90 million has been raised. To find out how you can participate, write to: UNICEF CANADA in Toronto.*

## Marrying pudding

*The Gaelic name for Halloween is Oidhche Samhna. On Cape Breton Gaelic people still eat a traditional dish called* fuarag, *to see who will be the first to marry. Fuarag is made of frothy beaten cream and oats or barley. It's traditional to stir a ring into it, as people do for English Christmas cake or the Greek New Year's cake called* basilopita. *If you get the ring on Oidhche Shamhna, listen for wedding bells to ring! If you really want to get married, you'll have to eat the whole bowlful!*

## Looking into the future

*Want to predict the future this Halloween? Try this:*

- *Walk out of the door backwards on Halloween Day and pick up some dust or grass. Wrap it in paper and put it under your pillow. That night you will dream of what the future holds for you.*
- *Eat a crust of dry bread and make a wish before you go to bed on Halloween. Your wish will be granted!*
- *Make a batch of Irish colcannon, a mixture of mashed potatoes and cooked spinach, cabbage or kale, with tokens hidden in it. A miniature horseshoe token means luck, a coin means wealth and a thimble or button means the finder will never marry. Put it on the table in a big dish, with a pool of melted butter in the middle. Everyone must eat together, from the outside in, dipping forkfuls into the butter. Whoever finds the tokens will know his or her fortune for the coming year. The Scots have a similar custom with plain mashed potatoes, and the Welsh mash up several different vegetables, including turnips, with hot milk for this Halloween meal.*

## Vegetable Jack-o'-lanterns

*You can make Jack-o'-lanterns from lots of vegetables, as well as pumpkins. Why not try out a huge zucchini or some strange-shaped squash or gourd this year? And don't forget that small vegetables can make wonderful decorations for your creation — try parsley for hair, red peppers for ears or a carrot for a nose. Now let's see, what could you do with some broccoli spears?*

like the ghosts and witches and monsters whom they thought were already wandering around. This idea has remained meaningful over hundreds of years and is part of the reason we still wear masks and costumes on Halloween night.

The biggest Halloween costume party in Canada is the annual Masked Masquerade in Halifax. On the evening of October 31, downtown Argyle Street is closed to traffic. Hundreds of costumed merrymakers parade through the area, enjoying the fun and stopping in bars and restaurants. But they have their seasons and customs mixed up, because lots of Nova Scotians call this "the Mardi Gras"!

# All Saints' Day and All Souls' Day

*November 1 and 2*

During the early years of Christianity, the church leaders found it was best to add their religious ideas onto earlier beliefs, rather than trying to stop old practices. Instead of trying to stop the Celtic Halloween, they first (in 837 A.D.) proclaimed November 1 to be All Saints' and All Souls' Day and later (998 A.D.) separated them, making November 2 All Souls' Day. They "borrowed" the idea of respecting the spirits at this time of year.

Today All Saints' Day is observed as a special or "red-letter" day in many Christian churches. And on the Sunday following November 1, a special service is held to remember the saints who do not have a specific day named in their honour. All Souls' Day was important in Catholic churches but not widely observed in Protestant churches until after World War I. The deaths and loss of wartime were so devastating that Protestant church leaders thought it made sense to pray for the souls of the many young men whose lives had been cut short.

Catholic Christians have a long tradition of praying for the dead, especially on these days. Filipino children in Canada may find it confusing to wear costumes and go trick-or-treating on Halloween, because in their homeland, All Saints' Day is a time to visit cemeteries and pay respects to dead relatives. November 1 is a big *fiesta* time, with lots of flowers and celebrations as well as prayers for the dead. This probably came from Spanish customs, which are similar. The Portuguese in Canada still have a feast on All Souls' Day and take flowers to family graves either after work or on the next Sunday. The Poles call All Souls' Day Dzien Zaduszny and also remember the dead by placing flowers and vigil lights on graves.

## Red-letter days

*Do you know why people sometimes call a special day a red-letter day? It has to do with the ink used by the bishops and other chief organizers of the church calendar in the Middle Ages. Because most people at that time could not read, holidays and Sundays were marked in red ink. Why red? Perhaps because it was always considered a magic colour.*

## All fall down

*There was a young fellow named*
*  Hall*
*Who fell in the spring in the fall*
*  'Twould have been a sad thing*
*  If he'd died in the spring*
*But he didn't — he died in the fall.*

## Hey guys!

*Next time you yell out "Hey, you*
*guys," think of where that expression*
*came from. "Guys" refers to Guy*
*Fawkes, and at one time calling*
*someone a guy was like calling him*
*or her a bad name.*

# Bonfire Night

*November 5*

November 5 is the time for lighting bonfires in the villages on the coast of Newfoundland. Usually the fires are simply collections of old wood, rubbish and dead leaves, but sometimes they are topped by a scarecrow-like figure called "the guy." People from British backgrounds have been burning the guy for more than 350 years. The English and the Irish preserved the custom in Newfoundland, and lots of recently emigrated West Indians from the Bahamas and Barbados know about it too. Bonfire Night is still celebrated in the West Indies, as it is in England, with special fireworks, food and fun.

Do you know who the guy represents? The story goes back to England in 1605. This was a time when the Protestant religion had become the official state religion, and many Catholics were not only angry but also persecuted for their faith. Guy Fawkes was the leader of a group of Catholic men who plotted to blow up the King and Parliament. The plotters hid 36 barrels of gunpowder under a pile of wood in the basement of the Houses of Parliament.

Fortunately Guy Fawkes was arrested and the plot failed. The thankful Parliament ordered that November 5 be observed as a public holiday. Many people "burned the guy" on their Halloween bonfires to celebrate his defeat. Unfortunately the event increased the religious strife in the country. Nowadays the old conflicts are long forgotten, and Bonfire

Night, as Guy Fawkes Day is now commonly called, has absorbed many Halloween practices, especially the big community fires and celebrations.

Children in England often go around collecting materials to burn and asking for "a penny for the guy." They usually make a figure to represent the guy from old clothes and straw and rubbish. This figure is burned at the top of the pile. Children may also chant the old rhyme as it burns:

> Remember, remember, the fifth of November,
> Gunpowder, treason and plot!
> I see no good reason why gunpowder treason
> Should ever be forgot.

In Newfoundland, people rarely talk about Guy Fawkes Day; the emphasis is on the bonfires. Even tires are jigged out of the harbour to burn — having been rolled down hillsides into the water, spinning and flaming, the previous year! Briggs and St. Mary's Bay are good places to watch the fires. Groups of young people compete to see who can make the biggest fire or the one seen from the greatest distance. Of course these fires can be dangerous, and in St. John's the city government has been trying to organize civic fires in designated parks. These are not so popular, however, and the fire department is still kept busy on Bonfire Night!

## Inuit autumn

*For the Canadian Inuit, November was the traditional time to get together for song festivals and drum dances. The fall hunting and fishing were finished, but the ice would not be thick enough to go out seal-hunting until after the end of December. Provided they had enough food stashed away for the cold days to come, this was a time of ease and enjoyment.*

*While the women sewed new fur suits for the coming winter, the men slept, told stories, played games, or danced and sang. The Inuit are very sociable, and these dark months were their most social times, until trapping and European culture changed their traditions. Here is an Inuit song about this time of year.*

*There is fear
In feeling cold
Come to the great world
And seeing the moon
— Now new moon, now full
    moon —
Follow its old footprints
In the winter night.*

## Cat's cradle to catch the sun

*A favourite Inuit pastime in the late autumn darkness was playing string games. In fact, until the early 1900s, the Inuit believed string games should only be played in the fall, when the sun no longer appeared above the horizon. In the Coronation Gulf region the taboo was based on an old legend that the sun once beheld a man playing string games and tickled him.*

*Some western Inuit believed there was a spirit of string games who made figures out of his own intestines or with an invisible cord. Some believed that certain string figures would drive this spirit away. The Inuit of Igloolik said they played string games to catch the legs of the sun. On the west coast of Hudson Bay the Inuit believed a boy should not try to make string figures because in later life his fingers might become entangled in his harpoon line.*

*Today both boys and girls like to play with strings. You can learn how to make your strings and how to play dozens of string games in Camilla Gryski's books:* Cat's Cradles, Owl's Eyes; Many Stars and More String Games; *and* Super String Games.

# Birthday of the Sikh Guru Nanak

*November*

Have you heard of a guru before? Guru is an ancient word from India that means "teacher" or "master." The Sikh religion was founded by a wise man called Guru Nanak in the early 16th century, in the northwestern part of India and what is now Pakistan. Sikhs believe in one God and in truth and honesty above all. Sikh means "disciple," and all Sikhs consider themselves disciples of Guru Nanak. Following Nanak, there were nine more wise men, also called gurus. The last guru, Gobind Singh, who lived during the late 1600s, announced that after him the Sikhs should look not to a human guru but to the holy Sikh writings for guidance. These scriptures are known as the Guru Granth Sahib or the "teacher-book," and today they are thought of as the guru of the Sikhs.

When Sikhs celebrate the birth of Guru Nanak (which occurred around November 1469), they read their scriptures from the beginning to the end. The reading takes place in Sikh temples, or *gurdwaras*, and lasts for two days and two nights. The congregation of listeners grows bigger and bigger towards the end, which falls on the day of Guru Nanak's birth. The musicians sing the hymns of Nanak, and the Guru Granth is carried at the head of a grand procession. The festival ends with a communal meal, called the *langar*. As a symbol of sharing, everyone must eat a bit of *karah parshad*, a solid sweet semolina dessert, a bit like sweet cream of wheat.

*Lakshmi*

# Divali

*October or November*

Divali (also called Diwali or Dipavali) is the most popular Hindu festival of the year. Hindus think of Divali as the beginning of winter and give it the same importance Christians give to Christmas. Traditionally it lasts for five days, and the most important celebrations take place on the night before the new moon appears, about a month after Navaratri. The word Divali means "garland of lights."

During Divali, Hindus light thousands of little oil lamps or candles in honour of Lakshmi, Vishnu's wife, the goddess of good fortune, wealth and happiness. These little lamps are called *dipas*, and they are everywhere in India — on building edges, windowsills, door frames, fences and paths! The custom in some areas is to burn mustard oil in the *dipas* to disinfect the air before shutting the doors for winter. In southern India, they burn coconut oil. In Canada, *dipas* are only lit inside homes or temples, but East Indian stores may be decorated with coloured electric lights.

All the worshippers want Lakshmi to give them a special blessing, and Hindus believe she will overlook any house that has no lights. Because *dipas* sparkle everywhere, Divali is called the Festival or Feast of Lights. The night before the festival some Hindu girls even float lighted *dipas* across rivers to see if the lamps will reach the other side still alight. If they do, it is thought their families will have good luck in the future.

Good fortune is important to everyone, so Lakshmi's picture is often the chief one at a Hindu family's altar. On the morning of Divali, Hindu families light *dipas* on their home altars and say prayers to Lakshmi. Because light takes away all darkness, Hindus respect light as a "mother" and some call Lakshmi Mother Light. Hindu temples are cleaned in honour of Lakshmi at Divali, mantras are sung and worshippers bow before her, offering fruit. People pray for prosperity and unity with one another.

Divali also celebrates Ram coming back to his kingdom with his brother and his wife, after rescuing her from the demon Ravan. (This story is celebrated at Dussehra; see page 228.) For Hindus from northern and central India, Divali is the day when Lord Ram was once again enthroned after his 14-year exile. They light *dipas* as part of the general thanksgiving for Ram's return. Hindus from Bengal worship Kali at Divali.

For many Hindus, Divali marks a new year, so it is a time when business people open new account books. Like many New Year's celebrations in other cultures, it is the custom to:
- settle all old debts. People believe they must pay all their bills to please Lakshmi.
- clean houses. In India, village houses are whitewashed, and the doorsteps decorated with patterns of rice flour to make Lakshmi want to bless them.
- dress up in your best clothes and jewels for the day.

In India, the day ends with *dipas* sparkling from private and public buildings and a final show of fireworks. In most major Canadian cities, Hindus celebrate Divali with great rejoicing, with indoor lights, greetings, entertainment and worship.

West Indian Hindus from Trinidad, Tobago or Guyana call this festival of lights Deeyah Dewali. In the West Indies, people put candles in clay pots in front of their homes, believing they stand for purity and goodness.

Jains celebrate on Divali too, but they call it Kivali or Mahavir Nirvana, in honour of Lord Mahavir, who attained salvation at this time in 527 B.C. Jains have special worship services in the morning and light lamps for Lord Mahavir at night. This holiday marks the Jain New Year and the begin-

ning of the Jain calendar. Sikhs keep the festival of Divali in memory of their sixth guru, Hargobind.

# Remembrance Day

*November 11*

Many thousands of soldiers who died in World War I were buried in graveyards in Europe, including Belgium's Flanders Fields. These are now covered with red poppies, and as a result this humble wildflower has come to be the symbol of the soldiers' sacrifice and of humanity's resolve that we shall never again let such massive death and destruction take place.

World War I came to an end at 11 o'clock on November 11, 1918 — the eleventh hour of the eleventh day of the eleventh month. The temporary peace document that was signed at the end of the war was called an armistice, which comes from Latin words meaning "arms (or weapons) stand still." A bigger peace treaty was signed somewhat later, but November 11 was known as Armistice Day for many years. Special church services have been held on this day ever since the first one in 1918; wreaths are laid at memorials to all the people who gave their lives to their country in the war; and two or three minutes of silence are observed exactly at 11 a.m., in memory of the peace. The services, the silence, the poppies and the wreaths are all meant to honour those who died.

In 1931 the Canadian Parliament changed the name of the holiday to Remembrance Day and made November 11 a legal holiday. After World War II the day became a memorial day for those who died in both wars. Veterans of World War II still march in Remembrance Day parades, but there are very few people alive now who took part in World War I.

## Holocaust Remembrance Month

*When Jews think of World War II, they remember the tragic deaths of millions of their people in Germany, Poland and other European countries. They died not because they were soldiers on one side or another, but simply because they were Jewish. Holocaust Remembrance Day is actually in the spring, but Toronto observes November as Holocaust Remembrance Month. It is a month for special lectures, talks, films and school visits, all meant to raise people's awareness of the tragedy of the Holocaust. November 9 is especially significant to many Jews. It is the anniversary of Kristallnacht in Germany, when the Nazi secret police first broke into Jewish synagogues in 1938.*

## In remembrance

*Canadians lost many brothers, fathers and husbands in World War I and II: 60,661 Canadian soldiers were killed in World War I; 42,042 were killed in World War II.*

## St. Martin's Day and Remembrance Day

*Italians in Nova Scotia celebrate San Martino Day to remember both the saint and all Italians who have died in any war. World War I came to an end on St. Martin's Day (November 11), 1918. What a coincidence that St. Martin is the patron saint of soldiers. Many soldiers probably blessed his name that day, as they heard the news of peace.*

# St. Martin's Day

*November 11*

Italians in Canada celebrate this day by sampling the first of their new wine. St. Martin's Day was once celebrated by many Europeans. In the Middle Ages it was called Martinalia and was a late autumn festival celebrating the fullness of granaries and wine vats. Martinalia itself had roots in a much older Roman festival, the Vinalia (can you see the Italian word for wine — *vino* — in this Latin word?), and in a similar Greek celebration in honour of the god of wine, Dionysus. It's not surprising that St. Martin was the patron saint of wine-makers and publicans (the people who sold wine), is it?

St. Martin was a soldier in the Roman army in the 4th century and later became Bishop of Tours, in France. He was greatly loved for his kindness. Once he met a beggar who was almost naked. Although he had no money to give, St. Martin cut his sentinel's cloak in two and gave the poor man half of it. After that, St. Martin's torn cloak was preserved in a small prayer room of a church used by the early French kings. The place where it lay came to be called a *chapelle*, from the French word *chape* (which means "cape") and the person guarding it became a *chapelain*. That's how we got the English words "chapel" and "chaplain."

November 11 was also the 12th and final day of the ancient Celtic New Year. In Celtic times, this period was special, like the Twelve Days of Christmas. The Celts believed that any ghosts who returned to their old haunts on Halloween might linger until this 12th day. So to ward off the spirits they would kill a goose or some other farm animal on this date. Then they would sprinkle its blood on the doorstep. Some Swedish-Canadians still have a Goose Feast on November 11.

# St. Catherine's Day, La Sainte-Catherine

*November 25*

Another well-known saint with a feast day in autumn is St. Catherine. Traditionally she is the patron saint of virgins and philosophers. St. Catherine lived in Alexandria in the 4th century A.D. and was martyred because she was a Christian. It is said that she was tortured on a spiked wheel, and to this day there is a kind of firework named a "Catherine wheel," which spins and throws out coloured lights.

For French-Canadians, November 25 is the day for La Tire Sainte-Catherine because a very beloved 17th-century teacher, Marguerite Bourgeoys, used to let her students pull toffee in honour of the saint. One story claims she made the toffee from molasses (and any other ingredients she could find) as a way to lure children to school.

At one time match-making balls were held on La Sainte-Catherine for all the single women who wanted to marry. The oldest woman at the ball would put a crown on St. Catherine's statue. Women who reached age 25 were thought of as too old for marriage!

# St. Andrew's Day

*November 30*

The Scots, Poles and Russians celebrate St. Andrew's Day. Andrew was the first of Christ's apostles and apparently travelled widely, preaching the Christian gospel, until he was crucified by a Roman governor in about 60 A.D. The Scots believe his body was eventually buried on the coast of Fife, where the city and cathedral of St. Andrew were later built; and the Russians say St. Andrew preached in Moscow, in the 1st century. Both Scotland and Russia claim him as a patron saint.

## Sainte-Catherine Toffee

*This pull-toffee is a traditional treat for La Sainte-Catherine.*

| | |
|---|---|
| 250 mL molasses | 1 cup |
| 250 mL white sugar | 1 cup |
| 250 mL brown sugar | 1 cup |
| 125 mL corn syrup | ½ cup |
| 15 mL margarine | 1 Tbsp |
| 15 mL vinegar | 1 Tbsp |
| 125 mL water | ½ cup |
| 5 mL baking soda | 1 tsp |

1. Grease a cookie sheet that has edges.
2. Put all the ingredients except the baking soda into a pot and boil until it reaches the soft ball stage. (You'll know that you have reached the soft ball stage when a candy thermometer reads 240°F or 115°C.)
3. Add the baking soda and stir until it is all mixed in.
4. Pour onto the greased baking tray (get an adult to help you with this).
5. As the toffee cools around the edges, start pulling and folding the outside of the toffee into the centre so that it will cool evenly.
6. When the toffee is cool enough to pick up, smear your hands with butter, twist the whole mass and p-u-l-l. Keep doing this until the toffee turns a light golden colour. Then pull and twist off small bite-sized pieces.

## Northern lights

*There is a special brilliance at night during the late autumn when the aurora borealis, or northern lights, brighten our dark skies. The Inuit say the northern lights are the spirits at play, whispering in the winter night. They say if you whistle, it will make the lights dance. At one time the Inuit believed that the lights were the souls of the dead, the good folk who have gone to heaven and now play football with a walrus skull. They thought the skull had life and showed its enjoyment of the game by chattering with its jaws.*

In Canada religious services in honour of St. Andrew take place on this day or the nearest Sunday, but Scots all across the country also have a patriotic feast on the nearest Saturday. This St. Andrew's Dinner features haggis, whiskey, bagpipes, songs from Robert Burns and a traditional dish of "singed sheep's head." The old name for this dinner was Andermas.

The Polish call November 30 Andrzejki. Their old custom for St. Andrew's night is like Celt-influenced fortune-telling at Halloween: melted wax from burning candles is poured into a bowl of water. The shapes it makes are used to foretell the future. If you try this, good luck with interpreting the meaning of your wax shapes!

## Bodhi Day

*Usually December 8*

Buddhists who follow the Mahayana school — usually Japanese Buddhists — celebrate this day as the anniversary of Buddha's enlightenment, or *bodhi*. Buddha is said to have sat for 49 days under a tree, known as the Bodhi-tree or Bo-tree, to find the answer to the riddle of life.

Some Buddhists celebrate this event on the lunar calendar, so the date moves. In Canada, many Buddhists share a common festival in the spring celebrating all three major events in the life of the Buddha — his birth, enlightenment and death, or attaining nirvana. (See pages 138-139.)

# MUSLIM SPECIAL DAYS

In 1871 there were only 13 Muslims (followers of the Islamic religion) in all of Canada. Today there are about 100,000. Muslim people from many different countries have emigrated here. Most Muslims (or Moslems) live in southern and western Asia and northern and eastern Africa.

Islam is one of the major world religions and the fastest-growing one at present. Like Christianity, Islam developed from Judaism, the religion of the Jews. Muslims believe in one God, whose Arabic name is Allah. They believe that Allah taught his prophet, Muhammad, how to worship him. Then Muhammad taught the Muslims everything Allah had taught him. The teachings of Allah are written down in the holy book of Islam, called the Qur'an, or Koran.

The word Islam comes from the Arabic word *silm*, which means peace, obedience and surrender. These ideas are important in the Muslim faith. The rules of Islam instruct Muslims to devote their lives to God and pray five times a day, stopping whatever they are doing. That isn't always easy to do in adopted homelands, such as Canada. Muslims are also

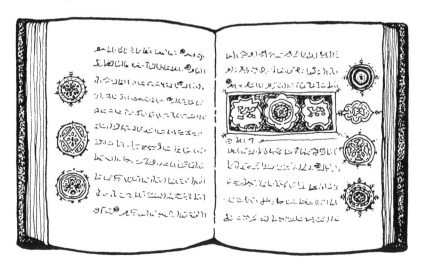

**The Koran**

supposed to fast for one month each year; to give money to the poor; and to make a pilgrimage to Mecca, the sacred city of Islam, at least once in their lifetime.

The majority of Muslims in Canada belong to the Sunni branch of Islam. They follow the Sunna, or path, of Muhammad, and accept his example as well as the guidance of the Koran. There are no clergy in the Islamic religion. The Sunnis choose their religious leaders on the basis of their learning, while Shia Muslims (another type of Muslims) believe that leaders must be descendants of Muhammad's daughter Fatima and her husband Ali. They believe these leaders, or Imams, are appointed by God. Here in Canada, most Muslims try to reduce the differences between the Shia and Sunni groups.

The Muslim year is only 354 days long, instead of 365¼. Their calendar is based on the moon. It has 12 months that are each only 29 or 30 days long. This means that Muslim holidays do not occur on the same dates every year. They happen about half a month earlier each year than in the previous year.

There are many religious holidays in the Muslim calendar, some observed by one sect, some by another. However, all Muslims celebrate the two main festivals: Eed-ul-Fitr, which marks the end of the holiest Islamic month of Ramadan, and Eed-ul-Adha, which comes two months and ten days later. After Eed-ul-Adha there is a minor festival celebrating Muhammad's ascension to heaven, the Night of Isra' and Mi'raj. Many Muslims also observe the birth of Muhammad.

# Ramadan

Ramadan is a month set aside for Muslims all over the world to pray and fast. It commemorates Muhammad's month of fasting and prayer while he waited for Allah's words about how he and his people should live. Ramadan is the equalizer, when

both rich and poor people are alike in feeling what it means to be hungry.

During Ramadan, Muslims do not eat or drink anything from dawn to dusk — not even water, unless someone is ill or travelling. (Muslims have a saying from the Koran that dawn has come when you cannot tell a black thread from a white one.) Which do you think would be easier, observing your fast when Ramadan falls in our summer or in our winter? When are there more hours of daylight?

## Eed-ul-Fitr

Eed-ul-Fitr is known as "the little festival" or the Festival of Fast-Breaking. It marks the end of Ramadan. On the eve of Eed-ul-Fitr, everyone looks for the new moon. If they see it, they can end their Ramadan fasting. If not, they must wait another 24 hours to celebrate.

After the signal that Ramadan has ended, people shout with joy and offer praise to Allah. In Islamic countries, drums are sounded and even cannons fired! Everyone prays and gathers for special sermons. Before anyone can break the fast, however, all the members of the family must give from their savings to the poor. This is called Zakat-ul-Fitr (Zakat means "purify oneself"). If a Muslim does not actually put money in the hands of a poor person, he or she must at least decide to do so. Here in Canada, most Muslims send donations back to their home countries. Then the feasting begins.

The festivities may last for three days. Many of the traditions associated with Eed-ul-Fitr are similar to New Year's customs in other cultures, or to the Christian Christmas:
- People greet each other with good holiday wishes.
- People, especially children, dress in new clothes.
- Parents give their children presents and play with them.
- Lots of cooking goes on before the holidays, and people eat

lots of sweet treats such as dates, baklava, jalabies, candies and cookies.

- Families get together, inviting as well any friends who have no family members nearby, for a special breakfast and a picnic, if the weather permits. Visits are made to friends and relatives.
- There is lots of music and street entertainment. People play different games, depending on which country they have come from originally. Some Muslims do special sword dances for this celebration.

## Good luck charm

*Islamic children often wear a golden charm on a chain, called the Hand of Fatima. Each of the five fingers of this hand-shaped charm represents one of the five leaders of Islam: Muhammad, his daughter Fatima, her husband Ali and their sons, Hassan and Hussein.*

## Mosque-building

*The first mosque in Canada was built in Edmonton in 1938. More mosques and Islamic centres were organized in the 1950s and 1970s. Two-thirds of all Canadian Muslims now live in Ontario, and there are Islamic communities in every major urban area in Canada.*

## Seeds and water

*For Eed-ul-Adha, Muslim children in Bahrain have a custom known as the "children of sacrifice," which involves a short pilgrimage to the sea. Several weeks before the holiday, they plant some barley or fenugreek seeds in a little basket woven of coarse fibres. These are hung on the wall and watered every day, so that by Eed-ul-Adha the baskets are full of young green shoots. After dinner the children feed their* hiya biya, *as the sacrificial plant is called, with some of their own food. Then they walk along the seashore, singing songs and swinging their baskets until they finally toss them into the water. Do you know of other customs in which sprouting seeds are thrown into the water?*

# Eed-ul-Adha, the Feast of Sacrifice

This was once a kind of market fair held at the time of the annual Muslim pilgrimage to Mecca. Today Eed-ul-Adha has a more religious character and is celebrated to remember both the founding of Mecca and a story that is in the Koran *and* the Bible. It is the story in which God tests Abraham's obedience. God ordered Abraham to kill one of his two sons as a sacrifice to him. Abraham was so obedient to God's will that he prepared an altar and even got his knife ready. At the last minute, God told Abraham to sacrifice a ram instead, as a reward for being so obedient. The ram was sent especially from paradise.

In Canada traditional rituals and a ceremonial dinner are held each year for Eed-ul-Adha. Devout Muslim families join together to buy a ram, kill it according to Islamic law and divide the meat among themselves and poorer Muslims. They may arrange to get their ram from an approved farm in the country (or from a Jewish kosher meat source).

The day is often a family outing, so that families can enjoy nature and God's creations.

In Mecca on this day, devout Muslims must walk around the Kaaba, the central building of the great mosque. Do you know what "mosque" means? It is the name of the Muslim place of worship.

Eed-ul-Adha and Eed-ul-Fitr have several things in common. They both begin with early-morning trips to Muslim graveyards, where family members will put flowers on the graves of their loved ones and also distribute food. Both festivals also emphasize families visiting one another, the exchange of gifts and children wearing bright new clothes.

# Meelad-al-Nabi

This holiday celebrates the birth of the prophet Muhammad. In Canada some Muslims take off work for a day to observe it. Muhammad was born in late August, 570 A.D. During the festival of his birth, stories about his life are told at home and in the mosque.

# Ras Al-Sana, New Year's Day

Ras Al-Sana means "head of the year," like the Jewish Rosh Hashanah. (The two holiday names are similar, aren't they?) It is the anniversary of Muhammad's journey from Mecca to Medina in 622 A.D. to found a religious community that grew into the world religion of Islam. Ten days later there is another anniversary: the martyrdom of Imam Hussein, the grandson of the prophet Muhammad. Sometimes a play about this martyrdom is performed to mark the date.

# Lailat-al-Isra'-wal-Mi'raj

This holiday celebrates another journey of Muhammad's — when Muhammad travelled from Mecca to Jerusalem and then to heaven. On the Night of Isra' and Mi'raj, Muslims say, the angel Gabriel — well known to Christians and Jews — brought Muhammad a shining, winged horse called Buraq, on which to fly up to heaven. This night is a special time for Muslims to talk about Muhammad's example in relation to their own lives.

# Index